THE WAR OF DESTINY

The Silent Hand Upon My Life

THE WAR OF DESTINY

The Silent Hand Upon My Life

Stephen Mathiang

Evangel
Nurturing & Equipping

A Note from the Publisher

The publisher wishes to acknowledge and thank Dr Douglas H. Johnson for his invaluable help and support for Africa World Books and its mission of preserving and promoting African cultural and literary traditions and history. Dr Johnson and fellow historians have been instrumental in ensuring that African people remain connected to their past and their identity. Africa World Books is proud to carry on this mission.

Cover design, typesetting and layout : Africa World Books

DEDICATION

First, this book is dedicated to my great grandfather whom I am named after, the indisputable hero, Mathiang Bior Deng-Ajok, known to many as Mathiang Ajoh Bior-Alak. Second, it is dedicated to all the gallant martyrs of the Republic of South Sudan who purchased our national independence with their precious blood. Third, it is dedicated to the generation that is growing up in independent South Sudan and future South Sudanese generations who have the obligation to cherish and protect the sovereignty of their nation in order for them to continue living as free people. Finally, it is dedicated to all people whose destiny is shaped against their will.

Rev. Mark Nikkel with youngsters in cattle camp, Bor, 1997

With his bull and other young men is Mabior Magot Mach in Werkok, 2006

CONTENTS

ACKNOWLEDGEMENTS

In this world, rarely does an individual make any remarkable achievement without the assistance of others. It would, therefore, be mean and ungrateful on the side of the person who has been helped not to acknowledge the assistance extended. Gentlemen and respectable ladies are always ready and willing to say "thank you" for any support they are given in one way or another. In that case, although there isn't enough space to list all who have assisted me, I feel it is imperative that I mention a few.

First and foremost, I wish to express my appreciation to my parents for the way they nurtured me and prepared me to handle the vagaries of this life.

I am grateful to my late uncle, Mabiei Mach Mayen and other esteemed elders, including my late father, for passing to me vast knowledge of our people's past.

I am grateful to the Evangel team for the effort they made to make this book worthy reading.

It would be very unfair for me not to mention my best friend and companion in life who always stands by my side as I journey through this life. Sometimes my documents get mixed up, but she painstakingly keeps them tidy and safe unless I expressly tell her to destroy them. And this is my dear wife, Elizabeth Agot Leek. She braved long periods of loneliness as I sought higher education and made other endeavours to improve myself and make others happy.

After my dear wife come our beloved children, Ajoh, Kuch, Alier, Jogaak and Areu. These always visit my study room to say, "How are you, Daddy?" And these four words have a way of giving me fresh impetus as I try to excel in life and become a role model to them. I love you all, and may our loving and gracious Lord make you even more successful in life than I am.

PREFACE

If you have been wondering how someone can be born, grow during a host of wars and yet live to excel in life, then this book is written for you. Also, if the things that you are experiencing in life differ from what you had planned, this book is for you.

Most people lack the courage to put down on paper their life's experiences for others to read. Some are scared to do so because their lives lack something to emulate. And yet some are just too lazy to allocate time to glean information pertaining to their lives and the environment in which they grew in and document it for the benefit of others. Since it is mentally demanding and time consuming, writing requires self-sacrifice and a lot of commitment.

Some people are driven by honesty, whether to themselves or to others, in sharing their life's experiences. What they perceive is exactly what they put down on paper for the successive generations. But why do they do that? This question may generate many answers, but I only have two answers.

First, some people ignore the obvious and prefer to see the unseen, to hear the unheard, and to know the unknown about other people's lives. Hence, honest writers are objective and open up their lives with brutal honesty so as to help curious guys see the unseen, hear the unheard and know the unknown about themselves as well as about their environment.

Second, unwritten words get forgotten with time, but words that are put down on paper survive, and the information they convey is hard to distort. This is what motivates writers: to ensure that information is recorded accurately and remains in that state of accuracy. Of course, I am not ignorant of the fact that some write to deliberately distort and revise history so as to conceal vital facts. But I am not in that category.

The primary purpose of this book is to show how the 'Silent Hand' of my Maker shaped and guided my destiny against my will. Between the covers of this resource, I have tried to document the little that is possible of the history of my people that is fading from the memory of the elders who are still alive. It also records my life's experiences and some key historical facts about the SPLA and SPLM (Sudan People's Liberation Army and Sudan People's Liberation Movement). Finally, it seeks to shed some light on the development and rough path of the newly born Republic of South Sudan so as to enable her people and leaders to avoid pitfalls arising from miscalculated decisions.

Other remarkable people who have shared valuable insights in this book include the retired Bishop Nathaniel Garang Anyieth of the Diocese of Bor, Paul Kon Ajith, Bior Deng, Nai Bior and my great grandfather Mathiang Ajoh Bior-Alak.

Although the book mainly explores events in the run up to 2011 and forecasts the direction the nation may take following Independence, it also acquaints the reader with key ancient events in the life our people. I encourage you to spare some of your precious time to analytically read what is shared in the pages of this book and hope that you will glean something that will be of benefit to you and your nation. The purpose of writing it was to help you. And even where you disagree with my views or interpretation of events, I will gladly want to know, since I will consider your feedback in preparing its future editions.

Stephen Mathiang

INTRODUCTION

This book documents a glimpse of the culture and history of the Jeng (Dinka), particularly the times of the author that have been characterized by many far-reaching changes in the history of South Sudan. Among other things, it explores some aspects of Anyanya One struggle, the period of interim peace in South Sudan, beginning 1972 to 1983, how the SPLA/SPLM carried out the liberation struggle from 1983 to 2005, the Christian revival in South Sudan, the poetic wisdom and the era of the Comprehensive Peace Agreement (CPA). It also touches on the events leading to the Referendum, events that followed the Referendum and the historic declaration of the independence of the Republic of South Sudan on 9 July 2011. Finally, it sets forth the remaining imperative wars to fight so as to achieve the South Sudan we want and forecasts the future.

In this book Jeng means Dinka; so the two words have been interchangeably used. Jeng is one of the Nilotic groups and traces its roots back to the ancient civilizations of the Middle East. Our people passed through the Egyptian Empire and ended in the current land of Sudan.

Because of natural and security factors, Jeng people over time continued in their migration and found themselves in their present areas in the Republic of South Sudan. I come from the Jeng of Bor and trace my genealogy back to about twenty generations, with Abuk as my great, great, great grandfather. In the absence of recorded history, I relied on traditional folklore and songs to trace my genealogy.

In Jeng culture, social roles of males and females are clearly demarcated, although they sometimes overlap. Almost all the heavy jobs are for men, whereas the light tasks are supposed to be done by women. The Jeng appreciate the physical weakness and usefulness of the women. So, as a Jeng, I usually wrestle with numerous and tiresome issues of life without seeking the help of my wife. She, too, can never blame me for being not a good cook because culturally this is not a man's domain, although I can cook if need arises.

The scars of Anyanya One civil war in Sudan are still visible and deep in the living memories of the South Sudanese people. As a teenager when the war was going on, I witnessed first hand grave violation of human rights in the hands of ruthless and merciless Khartoum Government troops. Thousands and thousands of our innocent people, including their leader William Deng Nhial, died. Others ended up incapacitated, widowed or orphaned. Many others fled and went to live in foreign lands as refugees. In the course of all this, valuable personal possessions and natural resources were destroyed or plundered by the enemy of the people.

At the end of Anyanya One war with the Khartoum Government, the vast majority of the Southerners thought durable peace had been attained at last. Successive Khartoum Governments were determined to keep our people in the den of ignorance so that they (South Sudanese) do not get to know their human rights.

The leaders of the cunning Khartoum Government were not sincere when they signed the historic Addis Ababa Agreement with the Southern leaders of Anyanya in 1972. Of course, the Northerners did not intend to enforce such an agreement because they were neither ready nor willing to see the people they had oppressed and exploited for so long gain freedom in the united Sudan. They were determined to keep the Southerners marginalized and as their slaves, politically, economically and socially.

Before the end of ten years, the Khartoum Government reneged on their undertaking in the agreement it had signed to hoodwink the international community and went back to its old ways of oppressing the Southerners. But the lull that lasted from 1973 to 1982 at least enabled me go through my primary and secondary education. It was also the time I came to know Jesus Christ as my Lord and Saviour.

The year 1983 ushered in another dirty and bloody war that affected South Sudan and other marginalised parts of the Sudan. Enthusiastically and in line with national duty, I played my part in this war of identity and emancipation as a young adult. The war claimed over two million lives. Also over four million people were displaced from their historic lands, some of them ending up as refugees in neighbouring countries. Others remained in internally displaced camps as refugees in their own land. Destruction of personal assets, wildlife and national heritage took place in the ruthless hands of the Khartoum Government. Consequently, any hope of realizing the long-awaited independence started to fade in the minds of the Southerners, and some of them withdrew their national allegiance from the SPLA/SPLM and crossed over to start collaborating with the Khartoum Government against their own helpless brothers and sisters.

But despite all that confusion and hopelessness among the children of South Sudan and other marginalised areas of the Sudan, God's sovereign plan for His people was still intact. In order to save His people from their misery and hopelessness and to give them hope and future, the omniscient, Almighty God started by ushering in spiritual revival in 1986 in Bor. Before long, this revival spread to other areas in and outside South Sudan.

Because of this divine intervention, thousands and thousands of desperate people turned to Jesus Christ as their Lord and Saviour. Some of the significant characters in this spiritual revolution are the retired Bishop Nathaniel Garang Anyieth of the Diocese of Bor and late Paul Kon Ajith who joined the church as a result of this revival. The Word of God inexplicably brought renewed hope among the SPLA/ SPLM and other war-affected people in and outside South Sudan.

I got ordained as a priest in the ECS Diocese of Bor in 1990. This was part of the evidence of the 'Silent Hand' over my life, since this is not something I had planned as I grew up. Thereafter, God used me to serve his people and accomplish some remarkable things in South Sudan.

The suffering brought about by the civil war in Sudan deeply touched the peace-loving people in other parts of the world and moved them to act in their small way. But it is the Almighty God who was touched more deeply and, accordingly, moved in a great way. When many had given up hope, the Khartoum Government and the SPLM were forced to come to the table for serious negotiations. The round of talks that followed culminated in the historic signing of the Comprehensive Peace Agreement (CPA) in 2005 in Nairobi, Kenya. The carrying out of the national census and the general elections came as a result of this agreement. In fulfilment of my national obligation, I excitedly participated in these significant events.

The year 2011 is memorable to the people of South Sudan and the international community. It is when the famous referendum took place and was crowned with the declaration of the long-awaited emancipation of the downtrodden people of the Republic of South Sudan on 9 July 2011. Within the same month, the UN officially accepted and recognised the Republic of South Sudan as its member number 193 of the community of nations. Our beloved nation also got recognition and acceptance from the AU and became member number 54 of the independent nations of Africa.

Even then, I still believe that the people of this great nation must fight at least seven more wars to benefit as a people from the national freedom. These include the war on disunity, war on corruption, war on hunger and poverty, war on illiteracy and ignorance, war on injustice, war on disease and war on insecurity. Failure to fight and win these wars will lead to a people shackled in ignorance, poverty and disease, despite living in a free nation—and this will be tantamount to tainting the highly honoured and beautiful flag of the Republic of South Sudan.

Other remarkable people who have shared valuable insights in this book include the retired Bishop Nathaniel Garang Anyieth of the Diocese of Bor, Paul Kon Ajith, Bior Deng, Nai Bior and my great grandfather, Mathiang Ajoh Bior-Alak.

Concerning the Jeng culture and the religious, socio-economic and political events in Sudan, this book is not the final authority. I wrote it sincerely intending to communicate historical facts as accurately as possible. But as an individual, there may be information that I am not privy to. As such, I hope that what I have put down will provoke other people with information that I don't have to volunteer it so that the book becomes the basis of arriving at a more accurate picture of the events that have influenced the evolution of our people as a nation.

It is also my hope and prayer that this resource will influence South Sudanese people and their leaders and friendly nations to shun what would hinder economic growth and development, taking our beloved nation back on the war path. I hope and pray that this book will influence them to embrace what unites people and enhances economic growth and development. Above all, it is my hope and prayer that what is contained in these pages will enable the reader to have a better understanding of God and His role in making people live a more peaceful and fruitful life. May this book also provoke us to value the importance of maintaining historical records!

PART ONE

Genealogy, Early Life and Anyanya One

CHAPTER ONE

Genealogy

As writing and keeping historical records were not in existence in Southern Sudan until the advent of limited modern education around the late eighteen century, vital societal information was kept and passed on from one generation to another in the oral form of legends and songs. This has, in actual fact, drastically shortened the recorded length of our genealogy. But even so this misfortune cannot prevent us from picking up on certain parts of our genealogy as far as we know.

According to our living memory, as was widely shared by our late uncle Mabiei Mach-Aguek and others, our section of the Nilotes came meandering from the north, enjoying pastures and waters from the Nile and its tributaries until our own group settled in and around Machabool. Machabool is a combination of two distinct words in Jeng language: 'Mac' means fire, and 'abool' means covering something with either soil or ashes. The name derived from the fact that during the dry season the inhabitants used to put big logs together, cover them with chaff and some soil, and set the heaps ablaze. The fire would slowly glow until the villagers returned to their homesteads during the beginning of the next rainy season. This was one of the primal modes of preserving or getting fire.

Dirich, the current lowland, which descends from the mountains of Eastern Equatoria, moving northwards and passing between Bor and Pibor, was a small ravine used by those of Machabool. When its bed gradually filled with silt and dried, people moved westwards from Machabool and settled in Baraalian, which is a historical place near the current Chuei-Kher area in Bor County.

Our great grandparents then moved northwards from Baraalian along the eastern bank of the Nile and first inhabited Tuonygeu. Tuonygeu was formerly known as Tony de Geu, meaning the swamp or the grazing land of Geu. It is a little bit north of Bor town. Later on people moved from there and lived at Pakeu. This is a traditional cattle camp where the Zion Church is currently situated. It is about 12 miles east of Bor town.

The sons of Deng Geu left the sons of Abe Geu at Pakeu and went and inhabited Wunchiir traditional cattle camp, northeast of Werkok. As time passed by, most of the sons of Deng Geu born by his wife Atong-Kaber left there and settled at Waar cattle camp, which is now part of the present Makuach Payam headquarters. Now the descendants of Abe and Deng Geu and other clans inhabited their current places in Makuach Payam. They are now collectively known as Juorkoch.

Our greatest known grandfathers came about like this: Abuk begot Deng who bore Ayuel, and Ayuel later gave birth to Geu. Geu became the father of Jooh who later begot Liet; Liet gave birth to Ngon, and Ngon bore Ariarbek who in turn gave birth to Tiok, and Tiok gave birth to Diing who later bore Luol. Luol then gave birth to Thorony, the father of Geu. Geu gave birth to Abe and Deng. Of course, these ancestors might have given birth to other children besides our own particular branch of the family tree. That is why we currently have other large groups of Juormach clans, especially in the Bor area. For instance, there are Juormach groups in Anyidi and Baidit Payams. Juormach means people who adore and worship a god that is symbolically represented by fire.

Juorkoch is part of Gok, a geographical division of Bor County. Gok consists of Juorkoch, Palek and Juorhol, which also includes Juorabiei. Administratively, they are known respectively as Makuach, Anyidi and Kolnyang Payams as of the time of this writing. These ethnic groups are quite inseparable because they are mostly genetically bonded. But how did they come to be associated with the name 'Gok'?

Before answering this question, let us remember that another geographic division of Bor County is Athooch, which consists of Baidit and Jalle Payams. Athooch begins from Makol-Chuei, along Jourkoch border, up to Jalle in the north or the border of Juet ethnic community with those of Chir Village of Twic East County. Athooch derived its name from a certain ancient famous man in that area called Athooch-Athokgorok.

The word 'Gok' is more of a geographic directional term than a genetic word. It is associated with a common tree called gok that is mostly found in Kolnyang Payam, though you can also find a lot of it in Makuach and Anyidi areas. This large and sandy area stretches southwards up to the Bor border with the people of Central and Eastern Equatoria. It is a good grazing land, especially during the wet season, unlike Athooch area which is mostly accustomed to flooding.

Traditionally, when people move with their livestock from Athooch, and even parts of Gok area, southwards in search of grazing, people say: "Wuɔr alɔ gɔɔk", meaning cattle are going to that area full of gok tree. Also, when people visit that area, they say: "Wɔ lɔ gɔɔk" – we are going to gok area. Surprisingly enough, even those of Juorkoch always say: "Wɔ lɔ gɔɔk" – we are going to gok area; "Wuɔr abɔ gɔɔk" – cattle are coming from gok area; "wɔ bɔ gɔɔk" – we are coming from gok area, etc.

Hence, as time passed by, people of Makuach, Anyidi and Kolnyang came to be known as 'Juorgok' or people of Gok. Since names are often situational and symbolic and created by people, the owners of that name also came to appreciate the name, 'Gok'. And that is how the term 'Gok' came into the societal, historical existence.

Juorkoch Community

Juorkoch Community is composed of Adumwuor, Atet, Koch, Thony and Deer. Deer community consists of Pagol, Pageer, Panaak, Panyaang, Pakuei and Adeweng. Adeweng consists of Padong, Panooi, Nhial Geu, Jok Deng, Kuel Deng and Bior Luala Deng. The writer of this book is from Adeweng.

Bior's Descendants

Bior Luala Deng married his wife Anguet and gave birth to Deng-Ajok and Ajak-Kueidit. Ajak-Kueidit became the father of Bior, Dot and Rith. Deng-Ajok married and begot Yartok, Bior, Mach-Benyder, Chamum and Anguet.

Family of Bior Deng-Ajok

Bior married Ajoh Bior-Alak as his first wife and gave birth to Mathiang, Kur-Jangdit, Agok, Mayen, Mach, Adol and Deng. He then married Yar Anyang and gave birth to Lual-Awan. His third wife Nyanroor Agoot bore Manythiei. With his fourth wife Akur Chol Tuong, Bior gave birth to Manyang. His fifth wife Awuoi Kuel gave birth to Nai-Ahok and Garang-Athokriar. And with his sixth wife Alek Akech, Bior gave birth to Keth.

A Glimpse of Bior Deng-Ajok

Bior Deng-Ajok was a man who puzzled and rendered mad those who tried to understand his unique personality. He lived sometime around the nineteenth century in his homeland of Akuoldit, predominantly known as Jakiei. It borders the present Werkok and Kapat Bomas of Makuach Payam in Bor County.

Bior's relationship with his wife Ajoh: at the time of his maturity, he officially married Ajoh Bior-Alak Chol Nyuon from Pager clan of Werkok Boma. Bior and Ajoh gave birth to their first son, Mathiang. Before they had weaned him, he sent away his wife together with the child. She decided to return to her own parents. Bior-Alak appeased Bior Deng-Ajok with a calf so as to accept his wife back, irrespective of what might have transpired between them. Then he took his calf, welcomed her back home and she soon gave birth to Kur-Jangdit. As time went on, Bior Deng-Ajok sent his wife away again and again she went back to her parents. Her father appeased him once more with a calf and he accepted her back. When she returned, their third child Agok was conceived. The same drama repeatedly occurred between Bior Deng-Ajok and his wife and Bior-Alak until four children, Mayen, Mach, Adol and Deng, were born.

But sometime in the middle of this peculiar marital arrangement, Ajang Bior-Alak wondered and asked his father why he was appeasing Bior Deng-Ajok, allowing him to take away their cows with no apparent reasons. His father replied:

> Bior Deng-Ajok did not elope with your sister but married her officially. And since he is turning her away without good reasons, I will continue to appease him so that they continue with their procreation. Ajak, my child, now do you have your own brothers? Is it not this sister of yours who is going to be your brother?

In the above quote, as Bior Deng-Ajok and Bior-Alak were living in the same village, the latter believed that the children of his daughter were to act as brothers to his son, Ajak.

When the last child, Deng was born, making a total number of seven children, five sons and two daughters, Bior sent his legal wife away with all her disgraced children. Upon their arrival to her parents, Bior-Alak, a humble and visionary man of long patience, unparalleled generosity and exemplary dignity, tried to appease Bior Deng-Ajok to see whether he would at last stop his insensitive actions. However, Ajoh, being with her unkind husband for a very long time, strongly advised her father not to do so. She said: "Father, this man will finish all your cattle, for he will not change his mind. Just leave him alone because these children of mine are enough if God is with me."

Then her parents conceded to her advice and decided to help her put up her own home nearby. After seeing that Bior-Alak had stopped his appeasement for him, Bior Deng-Ajok proudly turned a blind eye to them and went on with his life as usual. He married other wives and gave birth to many other children. He mostly lived with his wife Nyanroor Agoot, the mother of Manythiei.

Ajoh's sons as vanguards of Bior Deng-Ajok: Bior Deng-Ajok was a wealthy hard-hearted man whose motto in life was: Love those who love you, hate those who hate you and despise those who despise you. He did not know how to joke with and flatter his enemies. And this led others to label him as a man of hatred. Bior was content with his own small world. He liked and cherished what he had more than what belonged to others.

During his old age, Bior was still living in Jakiei area despite the presence of some common cattle raiders in the area. He was still neither reconciled to his wife Ajoh nor his children.

His five sons with Ajoh became adults and powerful. And so whenever Bior's cattle were taken away forcefully by raiders, they would go and fight off the attackers and bring them back to him with jubilation due to their victory. Often when people saw the cows coming back, Bior would make some scorning and jeering statements like, "You see them going, for the raiders should not return them. If they are really coming back, no one could do that only unless they were the gluttonous sons of Ajoh." Upon their receipt, without a single word of appreciation, he would just tell them to go back to their mother.

One day, a neighbouring, notorious raider called Agok and his strong sons raided Bior's area and took away his domestic animals. Then the news reached Ajoh's sons, and they took off in pursuit of the attackers. They defeated them in a fierce fight and returned the cattle to Bior. After arriving at his homestead, his powerful sons ran towards their father, uttering some war songs. Mach-Arongdit, one of his sons, said, "...I eluded the big spear of Deng Agok and the big fishing spear of his father Agok." When Bior heard that, he said: "My son, was their father Agok also in the raid? I wish I were with you to fight him." After lamenting that, he turned to his sons and ordered them to return to their mother. Did Bior Deng-Ajok not yet realize that being with your sons means unity and power in the face of the potential enemy?

Bior's jealousy towards Ajoh's family: Bior was not happy to see Ajoh and her sons flourishing in life. To show his ill intent, one day, Mayen, one of his sons, fought with him. In fact, in terms of temperament, people believe that Mayen took after his father.

This is how their fight occurred: in a particular season, Mayen used to pass near the homestead of Bior on his way to his home from their cattle camp, carrying some milk for his own family. Bior saw it as a show of fame and wealth on the side of Ajoh and her sons. Bior made some plans and agreed with his servant to waylay and attack Mayen along the road on his way home. When they saw him, they took their clubs and rushed towards him. Bior started threatening him with words. He questioned why he always passed by his homestead with milk. He asked whether Mayen, his brothers and mother wanted to show him that they were richer than him. But Mayen replied that he was only using the public path. And since he did not enter into his father's home, he wondered why they waylaid him.

Bior attacked Mayen mercilessly, aiming to hit his head with a club. Being afraid to do any physical harm to his father, Mayen was just on the defence, repelling his father's club from his head. Bior's servant was careful not to be fully involved in their family affairs, or else the whole problem would recoil on him. So instead of joining his master in the beating of Mayen, he stood by and kept telling him to watch out for his father's repeated assaults. Eventually, Mayen ran out of patience, turned his stick around quickly and beat the old man on the head. Seeing his father on the ground, he took his milk and rushed away towards his home.

With the support of others, Bior went back to his luak where a traditional expert was brought in to repair his broken skull. You can imagine how painful such a surgery is when done outside a hospital setting! But the old man endured it by focusing on his sole enemy in his mind.

Bior's revenging attitude: who was his enemy? During his recovery, Bior decided to carry out some reprisal on his enemy. Inside the luak or cowshed, especially around fireplace, people put up some wooden beds for sleeping. One of them is about eight-foot high, and the rest of them, usually two, are erected beneath it. Some people prefer to lie down just in the soft ashes by the fireplace below the tall bed.

During the heat of the day, Bior went into his luak and lay down in the upper bed while his servant decided to rest in the soft ashes below his bed. Bior used a wooden pillow. While the innocent servant was asleep, the unkind old man secretly looked and aimed at his servant's head. Then he let down his heavy wooden pillow, breaking his head. He woke up with a lot of pain from his bleeding head. Bior also woke up but with no sense of apology to his servant.

Who would have been the right expert to mend the head of the innocent servant? Whether a good or a bad traditional head surgeon, Bior took charge of mending his servant's broken head. In the process of repairing the skull, the man struggled with the severity of the pain, but Bior admonished him to keep calm. He demanded him to endure it. He questioned whether he did not know that it was painful. He told his servant to endure the surgery in the same way as he had endured his own procedure.

Bior asked his servant why he had left him alone to fight against Mayen, although they agreed to fight him together. He said Mayen managed to hit his head due to a lack of support from his servant. Bior abhorred the way in which his servant had been standing aside and kept advising Mayen to take care during the fight. He concluded by pointing out that his servant was the one who encouraged Mayen to beat him, for he did not believe that his son was going to harm him. It was not hard for the old man throughout his lifetime to find someone on whom to vent his anger.

Bior's reconciliation to Ajoh's sons: the time came for Bior Deng-Ajok to soften his heart towards his children with Ajoh. One day, Bior went to the cattle camp inhabited by the powerful sons of Ajoh and others. He requested each of his five sons to milk and gave him milk in a gourd. After drinking in turn a little bit from each of the calabashes, he blessed them by pouring the milk on their feet, saying: "Sons of Ajoh, I bless you. If you have taken my wealth by force or revenged on me because of my poor relationship with your mother, I would have cursed you." The story, however, does not inform us whether he really reconciled to his wife Ajoh in their lifetime. Up to now no one except God knows what went wrong between Bior and his wife Ajoh. Is there any good counsel for us here?

Bior's defence on the Anyar Ayool's family: during the reign of his son Mathiang Bior and Alier-Ajolnok Ngeth, Bior bravely rescued the cows of the late Anyar Ayool from the hand of Alier Ngeth. Chief Alier Ngeth falsely accused Aduot Anyar Ayool of having committed adultery with one of his wives. When this scandal reached Bior in Jakiei, he went at once and told Mathiang to go to court and defend the rights of the late Anyar Ayool. He rebuked Mathiang by saying, "This clan that you are going to live in with those of Tungkuach but without those of Arik is not going to be a clan at all.

At the time of his death, Anyar Ayool told Bior that although he was the leader of the Koch community, he did not take anything, even a small goat, from anyone during his lifetime. So he asked Bior to take care of his family. After listening to his father, Mathiang encouraged Anyar's family to go to court. Then he accompanied them and confronted Alier-Ajolnok and won the case.

As a matter of fact, Bior was very vocal when it came to the trampling of people's rights among his own community. Even at the death of Alier-Ajolnok in the hands of his own people, Bior was one of those who actually opposed in vain his humiliating death. His spirit of community protection was the reason why Juorkoch was called Konydiit de Bior de Deng or the Big Jourkoch of Bior de Deng.

Bior's reaction to Mathiang's death: the last thing to mention about Bior Deng was his reaction to the death of his son Mathiang in the war between Juorkoch and those of Baidit. While waiting restlessly in his Jakiei homestead for the unfortunate news from the battlefield, Bior saw Kuol-Ahou Aluel coming from a distance. He was in the battle and had some news to share. Kuol was good at dissemination of news, especially bad information. Before he sat down, Bior asked him whether things were okay. But he said things were not good. Then Bior asked his wife Nyaroor to bring food for Kuol to satisfy his hunger before sharing the news he had with them.

Beginning with Mathiang and his brothers down to the entire spectrum of Juorkoch community, Kuol said that Mathiang refused to leave the battlefield; so most probably he might have been killed. As Bior went on asking him, Kuol mentioned both the dead and the living. With great astonishment and grief, Bior encouraged himself and others by praising his famous clan whose many were killed and many were left. He went on and said he wished they had killed his son Mathiang but left his tongue for him so as to protect himself with. Apart from his other known characteristics, Mathiang was gifted in speech, too.

The following morning, Bior went to Pakeu cattle camp and encouraged the mourners not to cry. He said that despite the death of his son and others, Juorkoch was still very powerful. Bior Deng-Ajok was a good energizer, a man loved by many people and hated by many others.

A Glimpse of Nai Bior

Nai Bior Deng-Ajok, Nai-Ahok was a brother to Garang-Athokriar. Physically, Nai was a giant, a man of remarkable bravery whose heroism could not be tied down to specific ethnic or geographic locations. He fought many wars during his lifetime in and outside the Juorkoch region. For example, he was caught up in the Aliap area during a serious conflict, commonly known as Tong de Dhorgung, meaning the war of Dhorgung. The war took place in the 1920s between people of Jeng Aliap and colonialist troops. Without escaping, Nai-Ahok joined his tribesmen and bravely fought against the well-armed and trained soldiers and won the war before they were defeated later.

He was also among those who gallantly fought off Lou Nuer's incursion of Rem Cattle Camp in Makuach area in 1916. During his lifetime, Nai's fame travelled far and wide in and outside Bor area. Thus, an important girl from Lou Nuer heard of him. The history tells that that girl pledged to be married only to a warrior like Nai Bior, irrespective of her ethnic and geographic barriers. So she longed to be married to Nai if at all something could take him safely to Nuer area. Of course, her relatives did not want her to go to a foreign land. Hence, according to the common story, part of the mission of Nuer de Rem was to capture Nai-Ahok alive and take him to the Lou Nuer to be married to that important and brave lady. But unfortunately, the attackers ran away with their bleeding noses before the Bor warriors, left alone the notion of capturing the giant alive. I wonder whether she resorted to another local warrior, or she lived and died a virgin, waiting for Nai-Ahok.

With his own bare-hands, Nai-Ahok killed a leopard which had eaten their goats. It was while the goats were grazing that a leopard attacked and ate some of them. Those who were at the scene ran back to the camp and broke the news. People tried to arm themselves and go to fight it, but Nai prevented them. Instead, he asked people to leave it to him, for to him a leopard was just like a mongoose. To make it worse and funnier, Nai ventured to fight the beast with bare-hands, although others tried to prevent him from doing that.

He went and stoned the leopard with a piece of dry mud in order to lure it to come out from the bush. As somebody greater in its own territory and afraid of none, it jumped out of its hiding and found itself embraced by Nai. Despite its thorny claws and sharp teeth, it at once found itself lying on the ground, scratching and biting the giant above it. But without turning his attention to the surging blood and the pain, especially around his chest and abdomen, Nai held it down firmly with one hand and kept on slapping very hard on its head with the other hand. After neutralizing its strength, he pulled it towards his spears and slaughtered it. Nai almost perished of the severe wounds. He recovered slowly. These wounds and others left big scars around his chest and shoulders. I saw them with my own eyes during my childhood.

Both at the individual and community basis, Nai participated in numerous fights during his lifetime. War was his lifestyle. As an icon of war, the mention of his name used to send us, the children and particularly the naughty and disturbing ones, to mum. He married Ajith Agoot from Anyidi Payam and gave birth to five sons, Mach, Maker, Geu, Deng and Kelei. In the 1960s, Nai Bior died of a normal illness in his home area of Bairer, Deer village. I recall clearly, he died at around midday and was buried the same day according to Jeng customs.

A Glimpse of Mathiang Bior

Mathiang Bior was of medium height and average size. He lost one eye to sickness during his childhood. He was full of inborn intelligence, leadership traits, courage and bravery, kindness, determination, and hope. He was a man of quick decision, full of adventure, long patience and remarkable victories.

His intelligence: his cleverness and insightful tactics came to the surface as an adolescent. For instance, when he was still with his maternal uncle, he was resourceful to his age mates in terms of war planning when they were involved in a series of informal fights with the adolescents from other cattle camps or villages. In our culture, children are permitted to practise how to plan and execute successful fights among themselves or between them and other children from different clans. They use small sticks and other less harmful materials in such practices. Although they sometimes sustain serious injuries, it is incumbent on them to learn war tactics and how to prevent themselves from physical harm.

At this level, Mathiang greatly excelled to the extent that his group was always at the winning side. Yet it did not often perform well in his absence. This compelled his age mates from the side of his father to lobby around him and see how to win his heart to join them. As a patriarchal society, our children normally do not like to be associated very much with their mothers.

With the passing of time, and as the kids were growing up and beginning to depend upon themselves, Ajoh and her children decided to move back and live in Jakiei on their separate homestead. Bior-Alak had no big problem to see them go because all of them were in the same village of Deer.

His kindness: given the inhumane treatment they received from their dad Bior, some of Ajoh's sons grew up with a revengeful heart. For example, Mayen had wanted his brothers to join hands with him to attack Bior and take his wealth away by force. But Mathiang and others adamantly refused to do so because they did not like to repay their father for his wrong acts. To Mathiang, since God had given them good health and physical strength, they were going to find their sources of livelihood. Mathiang's kindness towards his unkind father clearly shows how caring he was, especially towards his relatives.

His hope and patience: Mathiang was a man full of endurance, expectation and perseverance, irrespective of any adverse and acute circumstances under which he found himself. As the firstborn son in their own family, he mostly shouldered their day-to-day problems with his mother. And whenever his brothers and sisters, sometimes including their mother, became somewhat hopeless, he was there to give them solid hope and patience. For example, at adolescence, Mathiang would go and hunt wild animals, then bring home the meat for his mother to cook. He encouraged her to enjoy it by saying that the food provided by a husband tastes the same as the one provided by a son.

Despite their poor early background, he dragged the whole family along the path of hope and patience without earning any bad name within their neighbourhood. He hopefully and patiently told his family to look towards God's providence without complaining because they were going to get out of that situation, and indeed, they did.

Another area where Mathiang's hope and patience were clearly portrayed was when his friend Alier-Ajolnok abducted his younger brother Deng Bior and tried to go and sell him in Mading, the current Bor town, to slave traders. The event occurred like this: Mathiang was returning home from Mading, but on the way he met Alier and his men plus their expected slaves in Menymeny cattle camp. He immediately spotted his brother in the chain and asked Alier: "Who looks like my mother's last born?" And Alier's response was: "Is he your brother? I asked him before to tell me whose son he was, but he failed to respond." "Did I not tell you that I was Mathiang's brother?" Deng questioned in the chain. But Mathiang just ignored that, took him out of the rope and went back with him. What would have happened if that were your own brother?

On the other hand, Mathiang showed his long patience and hope when Alier robbed him and other family members of their wealth. He forcefully took some cows from them. To Mathiang, he hoped that he was going to take them back from him at the right time, and that actually came to pass.

His determination: no rock of life, no matter how impenetrable it may be, was hard for Mathiang during his lifetime. For example, his solid determination permitted him, his siblings and mother to survive the adverse and unkind treatments they faced in the hands of their father. His strength of mind led to his numerous life's achievements.

His adventurism: Mathiang was an adventurous man who took his failures as important opportunities, although his successes greatly overweighed his shortcomings during his lifetime. Despite being uneducated, he was very sociable and popular among his people and ready to protect them from outsiders. Because of his adventurism, Mathiang was one of the few people who first went outside Bor area to discover how things were done in other parts of the world. For instance, his emissaries went to Tunji in Bahr el Ghazal in South Sudan to seek some help during his bitter hostility with his best friend Alier-Ajolnok.

His quick decision: in a ranking format, Mathiang was among the very few decisive people in that part of the world. He was an analytical thinker who carefully and timely weighed various options and picked the best alternative out of them as an answer to his burning problem. There was no problem before him that had no solution under the sun.

Leadership traits and diplomacy: with no formal education, Mathiang was regarded as one of the best leaders of his time with regard to his leadership traits and diplomacy. He was an inspiring and influencing leader who led from the front and protected the general aspirations and interests of his followers. For instance, in his leadership time, Mathiang mobilised and led the people of Gok in fighting against the foreigners in all court centres. This national insurrection led to the heroic death of the chief Deng-Athok and others. About his diplomatic expertise, Mathiang Ajoh was well connected in and outside Bor area.

As a renowned chief, he was even better attached to the highest government officials in Mading town. He lured Turuk Pawel to come and establish their base in Mading Bor. Turuk Pawel means the Turkiyah or Turkish Colonialists' administrative system, a portion of the Ottoman-Egyptian Administration in Pawel or Kongor in Twic East County, Jonglei State. In his war with his friend Alier-Ajolnok, Mathiang employed a lot of diplomatic tactics to overthrow him and disperse his Chamcheth Army. In a nutshell, Mathiang Ajoh was full of inborn leadership and diplomatic peculiarities.

His remarkable victories: Mathiang Ajoh received some remarkable victories where thousands of his contemporaries had failed miserably. First of all, he brought cohesion among his family members, particularly between Ajoh's children and Bior and established a lasting and remarkable fame in their family circle. He was very triumphant economically, socially, politically and culturally as well as in most of the battlefields.

His courage and bravery: if there were people of his time who were known for courage and braveness, Mathiang Ajoh was not the least among them. His courage and braveness enabled him to lead various successful battles since his childhood. He was afraid of no one under the sun. To illustrate his bravery, Mathiang Ajoh did not die peacefully of old age or sickness but decided to shed his precious blood and donate his flesh and bones to wild animals and birds of the air in a bloody battlefield.

The story took this shape. As the Juorkoch community marched into the war against those of Baidit, they asked Biong community to join the side of Angakuei in the fight, for they are one community. But Biong deceivably said that they were not ready and willing to do so. So Mathiang told his men to leave them alone if they were afraid. Then Juorkoch warriors marched ahead and immediately defeated Angakuei, chasing them towards Guetalek. But Biong came and surprisingly launched a terrible rear attack on Juorkoch. As a result, the retreating men from Angakuei stood their ground and fought back. So they sandwiched those of Juorkoch. When they saw that they were pushed to a narrow corner, the men from Juorkoch decided to withdraw from the battlefield.

When he realised that the war was not in his favour, and having lost some of his best warriors, Mathiang Ajoh refused to leave the battlefield. He said he did not want to return home to a mourning and wailing reception, especially from bereaved families.

Having killed and sat on one of the giant warriors from Angakuei, Mathiang called his own brothers and other close associates and ordered them to retreat and leave him alone. To him, the best thing was to die there than to return alive because death was better than his leadership humiliated. Although they tried to persuade him to change his mind, he adamantly refused. So they left him sitting on his dead friend, physically sound, not wounded.

However, the only person who closed up her mind and decided not to leave Mathiang alive was his beloved wife Nyalueth Ngueth Ajak. She was from the Angakuei clan. Why was she in the battlefield you might ask? It is a known fact that Juorkoch warriors were almost always triumphant in their wars with their neighbours, and hence, their brave ladies always dared to accompany them to taste the essence of the real war as well as to find loot for themselves.

While those of Baidit sought the battleground for the wounded and the dead, they suddenly and surprisingly saw Mathiang Ajoh sitting on a dead body. So they shouted the message back to others, saying, "Mathiang is here." "Is he dead?", they asked. "He is alive, defiantly sitting on the dead body", they replied. An old man said, "Please do not kill him yet, but wait for me to see whether he is the one."

Mathiang Ajoh was just patiently sitting there with his wailing wife. She cried because she knew that that was going to be the last time that she would see her husband alive. Although he had his spears and shield with him, he was not ready and willing to fight and die with more people in the process. Instead, he was just very passive, waiting at the very doorstep of death.

The old man, looked at him and immediately recognized that he was the one. He then sang this quick, decisive and scorning song to Mathiang:

We have caught up with you son of Bior Deng;
We have caught up with you Mathiang.
Mathiang Ajoh even if he were appeased, he would not accept the appeasement.
Mathiangdit could not accept the appeasement even if he were appeased.
The Blind-Mathiang will not look into somebody's luak during the next rainy season.

After listening to the song for a little while, he contemptuously responded to them by saying, "What about this big shield that I sat on, will it look into somebody's luak during the next rainy season? Would you have gotten me if it were your might? Just let me receive your spears". By saying, "Just let me receive your spears", he was saying, "Just kill me". His wife tried to save his life by throwing herself over him but in vain. Hence, the hero, a man afraid of nothing under the sun, including death itself, met his calculated death upon the top of his dead enemy at the Pool of Jooh-Kuei. Although her own people spared her life, Nyalueth Ngeth Ajak left with a broken skull. For instead of killing her also, somebody beat and broke her head.

People of Mathiang Bior

Mathiang married his first wife Nyalueth Ngeth from Angakuei community and gave birth to Alier-Kuorwel, Makuach, Mach-Jam and Ayen. Then he married his second wife Achot Leek from Atet community and gave birth to Mayen-thiei and Dhiany. Mathiang married his third wife Nyalueth Deng-Kuach-Khoor from Biong of Makol-Chuei and begot Deng-Beny, Ajoh and Maluk. With his fourth wife Yar Aboot from Angakuei community, he gave birth to Mach-Gordit and Achol. Mathiang married his fifth wife Adier Jokbolok from Atet community and gave birth to Piel, Abeny and Nyiel. He got married to his sixth wife Aluel Lual and gave birth to Lou and Nyangot. He married his seventh wife Anyieth Abuk and gave birth to one girl only.

Mathiang and his eighth wife: it is good to note here that Mathiang betrothed Akher Dot-Adem from Abiei of Chuei-Kher Boma, but he died before settling the final marital arrangements. Upon his death, his own brother Mach finished the marriage rites and inherited her. But in the course of their procreation, Mach violated the Jeng culture by naming the children after himself instead of his late brother, and that is why we have Ajak Mach rather than calling him Ajak Mathiang.

But as members of the same family, other relatives, especially those from the very family lineage of Mathiang, ignored it until Ajak himself came to realise that a mistake was committed. Hence, he tried to remedy the situation by giving his first wife Aboot Kuany to Mathiang while the rest of his wives and their children remained under the name of Mach Bior.

However, as Jeng people say the horns of an old bull cannot be twisted and shaped to the desired positions, it even became quite awkward for others and the children of Akher Dot-Adem to adopt and rename themselves after Mathiang. Yet the best thing to know is that our people have no big deal over this parental issue. We should also know that the descendants of Anyieth Awalith are the prominent members of Mathiang Bior's family.

Early Life and Cultural Norms

Alier-Kurwel Mathiang married Yar Biar Akol from Gak Boma of Kolnyang Payam and gave birth to Kuch, Nyankoor, Dit, Aret, Nyabol and Mathiang. He married his second wife, Agoot Kuorwel from Biong of Makol-Chuei and born Machar, Nyanwut, Nyanachiek and Aboi. Then Kuch married Areu Jok Kher from Atet of Makuach Payam and gave birth to Ayoor, Bech, Akon, Wuoi and myself plus four other children (Akher, Manyang, Achiek and Ateny) who passed away during their childhood.

I was born in Bairer Village of Werkok Boma during the first civil war in Sudan that lasted seventeen years, 1955 to 1972. Adol Lual, a neighbouring woman, acted as midwife during my birth. Automatically, the family named me Chol due to the death of my immediate elder sister Akher. The meaning of Chol in Jeng language refers to compensation or payback for the lost. Hence, I was considered as a compensation for her. I was also nicknamed Chol Adol Lual after the mid-wife Adol Lual who took care of my mother during her birth.

Since there were no maternal health care centres in Bor at the time, some local women specialized as traditional mid-wives, and so Adol Lual was one of them. Was it safe for women to deliver in such remote villages? Of course, it was not safe due to poor hygiene, lack of relevant medicine and medical knowledge. Sometimes women passed away with their little ones during the delivery time. Often women died at birth, leaving the little new-borns behind. Such nascent orphans were cared for locally by feeding them with cow or goat milk. And one of the common and traditional names given to such orphans is Agup, meaning pouring liquid, like milk, into the mouth. Obviously, there were no feeding bottles at the time. Also when related women gave birth at the same time or at closer intervals, and one of them happened to pass away, leaving her child behind, such an orphan could be allowed to breast feed from the living woman. They became conditional twins.

Customary Beliefs

Jeng people believe in a universal God (Nhialic), the Creator of heavens and earth and all things therein. In other words, our people, just like other African commu-nities as well as other global societies, are very devoted religious people. For they believe in the existence of the eternal God who created the entire universe. They believe that the dead is not dead per se. Instead, they consider death as a transfer of physical existence of a creature to a spiritual realm – the dead are absent in the body but present in soul or spirit.

On the other hand, Jeng people interestingly used to believe that demons are spiritual beings created by the Creator to serve him. They did not understand that Satan is a fallen angel who constantly opposes the plans of his Creator. Also what they did not quite understand by then is the incarnation of Nhialic in the person of Jesus Christ. Because of such beliefs, it was a common practice for Jeng people to worship and serve both God and Satan and his demons.

Since I was born and grew up within the African Traditional Religion (ATR), I just followed their ways of worship and beliefs. I hope that the Lord was well aware of my ignorance as well as the lack of knowledge to understand the antagonism between the Almighty God and his rebellious angel (Satan). But as for now, Jeng people, including myself, well understand the real meaning of Christianity because most of them are currently followers of Jesus Christ.

Traditional Treatments

The traditional order of taking care of the sick was that, those suffering from mea-sles were to be confined in dark places, full of burning fire and smoke. They were not permitted to bathe during their illness. People believed that those suffering from measles should not be exposed to cold or wind, and that is why they were advised to stay indoors.

As religious people, when a person got sick among the Jeng society, people sought divine intervention both from Nhialic and other gods. This always led to offering of sacrifices by slaughtering some animals to such deities. People also resorted to some kinds of herbal medicines, which were effective sometimes. Some famous magicians always attended to and took spiritual care of the sick. They offered rudimental physiotherapy by stretching muscles while uttering some rejuvenating, spiritual words to invoke the ancestral deities to save the life. Sometimes magicians spat into patients' mouths because they and common people believed that their saliva had saving power in them. Imagine a magician who chews tobacco wanting as part of his spiritual duty, to spit his dirty saliva into your month as part of a healing process, what will you do? Can you refuse and die or you accept and live? Of course, a magician's saliva was not always a life-saving guarantee.

The fact is that the Lord always works and wills in every situation, regardless of whether the people concerned believe in him or not because he cares for both Christian and non-Christian believers. Most often I would hear people lamenting over the sick, saying "*atuɔr lɔ tuɛŋ*," meaning, sickness go west. And in fact, it used to go west sometimes, particularly when the sick recovered miraculously. But what I really don't know in such a saying is why going west especially and not to the east, north or south? Is it going to the west to affect other people or just to linger there?

Measles Robbed the Family

In the absence of modern medical treatment, at the age of about four years, my late younger brother (Manyang) and I were seriously affected by measles. We were taken to Jerkuat cattle camp along the river, for it was during the dry season. That is, dry season is the time in which herds move to cattle camps along the western bank of River Nile in search of water and green pastures.

What types of treatment did we receive in such a squalid environment? Consider the sick being admitted in a cattle camp with cows lowing, goats and sheep bleating and people laughing and singing around. It is a place where animals relieve themselves here and there with no firewood except dry cow dung to maintain the fire. It is a place full of bad odour and endless smoke, emanating from the burning cow dung.

Cattle camp is the best home for the herders. In such a place the best mattresses include ashes of the cow dung, cow skin and mats made of papyrus. Undoubtedly, according to Jeng, the food contents are good in the camp because the main food consists of milk, sorghum, fish and meat sometimes. But now life in the cattle camp has somewhat improved.

We became sick when our father was absent. So we were taken care of by our mother and other relatives. As you know, in African culture it takes the entire village to bring up a child. However, this notion is now wearing away, especially in urban centres where people have foreign influences and embrace the alien spirit of individualism.

There was a missionary base in a place called Malek, situated south of Bor town along the eastern bank of River Nile. Some missionaries who came from the Church Missionary Society (CMS) in United Kingdom established it in 1905. This base had a primary school, a chapel and a clinic. Most of the well-known, educated southerners were baptised into Christianity and got their basic education from this historical and significant missionary base. The base also acted as a pivot where Christianity reached other places in South Sudan. But at the time of my writing, this famous base is overgrown with big trees, for it got destroyed during the first civil war in Sudan. And the just-ended civil war broke out before people thought of its rehabilitation. People of Bor and other interested southerners want to revitalise Malek Missionary base in due course.

At the time of our sickness, the man in charge of Malek base was Bishop Daniel Deng Atong and his wife Anai Nyieth. As our illness progressed from bad to worse with no sign of recovering despite the traditional treatment, the general decision in the camp was to seek further treatment from Malek clinic. So our mother and uncle Riak Mach-Gordit Mathiang took us to Malek. My uncle carried me while mother carried the little one.

Immediately, we were attended by a nurse in the presence of Bishop Daniel and his wife. After examining us, the bishop told my mother and uncle that it was too late for them to even try any drugs on my younger brother, let alone saving his life because his illness was at its climax. So they left him to die. As for me, they gave me some drugs. Eventually, my life was saved while mother and relatives hopelessly watched my brother dying due to ignorance and lack of modern medical facilities and knowledge in the area at the time. He died of the war of ignorance and disease. At the moment, measles is no longer an incurable disease in most parts of the world.

Although my parents and I plus other members of the family were not Christians, Nhialic was still in control. He knows why he saved my life and let my brother die. Knowing the future from the past, the Silent Hand was upon my life.

Gender Roles

Male roles: in the life of Jeng society, boys cling to males, and girls stay closer to their females. In this culture there are some distinct divisions of labour between males and females. For instance, males shoulder hard and serious tasks like looking after cattle and family and societal protection from outsiders' attacks. Their other duties include digging deep holes and water pools, chopping big woods for fire or building, cultivation (although this is a shared task), fishing and hunting, just to name a few. These and other male activities are rarely done by a woman, for if she does, it brings humiliation to the family. In the event of the absence of an adult male in a family, other males within the extended family are to take care of such tasks. In some few cases when there is no man in the family, a teenage boy is to gather the courage of manhood and take care of his family with some little help from outsiders.

Female roles: the role of women in Jeng culture incorporates house management, especially in terms of food control, kitchen affairs, fetching of water, collecting of dry twigs for fire wood. Other tasks include cultivation, milking, gathering wild fruits, cutting grass for thatching, taking care of the little ones, and plastering the floors and the mudded walls of houses within the family setting. These and other feminine activities are the primary roles of females. Only on very rare occasions are males allowed to undertake them. In the event that no female adult is available within the family to shoulder these activities, particularly food preparations, any female from the extended family is completely obliged and culturally bound to intervene in such a situation. If there is a teenage girl in the family, such a situation will force her to take care of the feminine roles with some assistance from other neighbouring ladies.

If you compare the above gender roles, you will find that male activities are quite heavier and harder than the ones of the females. For example, it is not very easy for one to herd animals in a forest mostly full of wild animals like lions, hyenas, leopards, elephants, wolves, etc. Jeng consider women valuable and physically weak to shoulder such huge tasks. Also they believe women have good managerial skills, and that is why they entrust the household management to them.

It is worth pointing out that a man has an equal duty to cultivate and look for surplus food items either from the wild or from the neighbourhoods. But the moment these food items enter into the house, his role ceases right away. This feminine role of household management is one of the factors of which cooking is believed in the Jeng culture to be the task of females. It is the responsibility of a woman to critically examine the type and quantity of food served to the members of the family at any given mealtime.

Where did I fit in the clearly defined gender roles in the family during my childhood? Your opinion is as good as mine. As I grew up, I started associating myself with my father, elder brothers and other male relatives, especially my peer group. Then I automatically participated in exercising the male tasks such as looking after goats and sheep, calves or cows. Before my initiation into adulthood, I also learned to milk cows, especially in cattle camp.

In this age of conflicting gender issues, Jeng people, like others, should carefully examine their rich culture, remove and replace what is bad with what is good from other cultures and maintain what is culturally right. They should know that all global cultures are relative – no single culture is absolutely to be the only yardstick for the rest of human cultures. The right civilization is to improve on your own culture without necessarily discarding it all and merely copying and owning someone else's culture. The only absolute culture is God's.

Life in the Village

Sometimes I used to live with my parents and other siblings in the homestead and carry out some minor male activities; I often helped my mother to accomplish her tasks. At night I had a shelter to sleep in with other members of the family. So I felt safe from marauding wild animals and adverse rains, particularly during the rainy seasons. Although my parents were there to protect me from heavy work and other dangers, I was not immune to face the harsh environments in which I took part in looking after the family's domestic animals. For instance, I wandered barefoot in the forests, herding cattle. During the wet seasons, we used to go out with my peers to fish in the nearby pools and look for other wild food items.

Imagine in the high grass, swampy grounds full of poisonous snakes, you find children moving up and down, looking for wild food or taking care of their animals. If you encountered a snake once a day, you might be lucky. Death from snakebite was a usual occurrence in the village. Sometimes when we were caught up in the tropical rain while in the bush, we had to endure the harsh condition of the rain and cold weather with our bodies being in the state of nature – totally naked without clothing. Being pricked by long, sharp thorns was considered to be a normal phenomenon. Some of these thorns have now become part of my flesh, especially in the soles of my feet.

Sometimes we were terribly beaten by angry neighbours when we failed to prevent our farm animals from intruding into and destroying crops in their small gardens. Such beating was not considered child abuse but reasonable discipline. Even your parents would not come to your rescue in such an ordeal.

Life in the Cattle Camp

Life in the homestead was even better compared to the life in the cattle camp. Let me paint here a brief picture of the nomadic way of life in Jeng society. It is a kind of nomadic life whereby people move with their animals from one place to another in search of greener pastures and fresh water. It is very unlikely for people and their animals to spend more than one month in the same camp. Most often children live with the related youngsters in the camp, very far away from their parents. Thus, being in the camp means less personal protection, especially from bullying and unnecessary beating from older youngsters. The main food here is pure milk. Cattle camp is a place for serious discipline, which others may call child abuse. This harsh environment is considered to be normal condition and the way of life for the Jeng people.

My tasks in the camp were similar to the ones in the village. But they were now very intense in that while looking after the calves, I and other age mates had to maintain high vigilance not to allow the calves to mix with the cows. This is because the calves would suck their mothers and leave people to sleep on empty stomachs had they to mix. The proportional verdict in line with this offence is severe corporal punishment, followed by being denied food.

Other serious duties for the boys to undertake in the cattle camp include tethering the animals and making sure that the calves don't suck their mothers at night. This implies that elders can wake the boys at any time in the night to tie down the animals that might have pulled out their sticks. The boys are also supposed to wake up in the night to clear the animal dung and urine for the animals to sleep well. For an unkind adult to wake a boy, he would spank or beat him.

Sometimes, the boys have lesser milk in comparison to the adults. For people believe that a boy child can survive on anything, including wild fruits. But the little children and girls are taken good care of in terms of feeding and other physical protection. The boys have no good places to sleep in the camp. Sometimes, they are pushed away by elders even from warming themselves by the fire by night.

Traditionally, during the rainy season people in the camp used to cover themselves from the rains with either animal skin or a mat. Such skins or mats were very few, and so when it rained you saw people rushing for them. Can you imagine who were left out at the mercy of the rains? Boys were mostly the victims.

The youngsters send boys here and there, even at night. To Jeng, they consider these tasks and harsh treatment as part of early child training to prepare them for the challenging life of adulthood.

Our cattle camp was in Aguarkou, a traditional camp south of Bor town on the eastern bank of the River Nile. One time, while looking after the calves, a long thorn pricked my foot deeply. My friends tried to take it out in vain for it was deep inside the foot. I went back limping to the camp for the elders to help pull it out. Using some sharp objects, they tried to open the skin around and pull it but failed because I was writhing in pain and blood was just gushing out. So it was left inside my foot with the hope that it would come out by itself when the wound formed some pus.

Although the thorn remained in my foot, I was not excused from my normal tasks as a boy. One day about two weeks later, I was sent by an elder to go to the nearby lagoon to fetch some drinking water. I limped there, bathed and returned to the camp. But on the way, it came out with some pus. The thorn which was originally white in colour had now turned brown. I took it and proceeded to the camp for others to see.

Among the peer groups one was also supposed to protect himself from others. Most often they fought amongst themselves and bullied each other like cocks. According to Jeng culture, parents and other relatives expect their child to be able to defend himself physically and verbally from any attack by his peers. As a result, they don't feel good when their child is defeated, especially verbally. Instead, they often beat and tell him to gather his courage and go back and fight his opponent. Jeng culturally prepare their children to be courageous and articulate. Like other people who went through the same ordeal during their childhoods, today I have some abiding scars on my body as evidence.

Village School

In the early 1960s, my brother Wuoi was in Grade Two in Makol-Chuei Primary School. It is about ten kilometres north of my home village of Bairer. He used to walk back home from the school, particularly during weekends to stay with the family and collect some needed food items to use in the school. We were totally impressed by the way he dressed in school uniform as well as the way he spoke both

English and Arabic languages, although we did not understand what he talked about at the time. Even thong (thoŋ) de Jeng, our own mother tongue, was learned in the school at lower levels. Imagine how such semi-literate pupils were upheld by their illiterate relatives! They were the highest elite in the village and given very high esteem by the villagers.

Mother in Opposition to My Education

Because of my intimate relationship with my brother Wuoi and the general exposure of my father to urban life, both enticed me to go to the same school. This decision was against my mother's will. The whole plan was done without her knowledge because of the fear that she did not want me, as the last child in the family, to go to school. However, she was eventually told by my father of my need to go to school. After hearing that, she protested bitterly and tried very hard to beseech me to abandon such an ignorant idea. But I vehemently refused to listen to her. She then said that her word was final; school was not going to be an option for me.

When I heard her last comment, and knowing that my mother was not an easy lady to persuade, I started screaming and uttering some foreign words: "She wants me to be a cultivator (farmer)." They were foreign because they were the words used by my father and brother to entice me to go to school. Generally, cultivation was not considered a good profession in the area. So she came, canned and chased me away from home saying, "Go away from my house; are you the one who cultivates for us?" But where would I go? So I lingered just around the compound, sobbing while allowing both mine and her temperatures to cool down before making a family reconciliation. Thankfully, I won this education war and that was the beginning of my educational journey.

Nevertheless, when you see the village life and do a kind of critical analysis you might be tempted to say that, my mother was right to prevent me from going to school. For my other two elder brothers and sister were already young adults and living by themselves in cattle camp. My father was sometimes away from home, following his chieftain work. All the family activities were, therefore, often left in her hand. Also, given the scattered settlements in the village as well as the irregular presence of my father in the house, my mother was afraid of loneliness.

Despite all these explanations, she eventually allowed me wholeheartedly to go to school. Of course, I was not also happy to leave the comfort and love of my parents. This made my days at home very joyous to me with my parents during school holidays and weekends.

Class Nought

I was put in Class Nought in Makol-Chuei Primary School, while my brother Wuoi was in class two. Life in the school was not very simple. In this unique level of education, we used to sit on the floor under trees and used our little fingers as pencils and sand as exercise books.

Imagine if these were the writing materials, was the mind the right place to store notes for future references? What would happen if it were to rain for many hours as is the case always during rainy seasons in South Sudan? Also do you expect pupils in such squalid conditions to maintain a high standard of hygiene? These are some of the soul-searching questions whose answers sum up the quality of class nought in those days.

Almost all of our current leaders in South Sudan are products of this historical zero class of basic education. I believe the present pre-primary schools resemble our old class nought.

After one year of Class Nought we were promoted to Class One; it was a luxurious one at that time. And one was no longer termed as 'a nought boy'. In this class, pupils used pencils, exercise and textbooks plus other writing materials and sat on benches made of mud by the pupils themselves. Now it was our time to bully those of Class Nought. They did respect us, but the ones of Class Two were still our bosses.

Tough School Discipline

High discipline was administered among the pupils by the school management. Corporal punishment was one of the disciplinary actions employed by the school administration to maintain law and order in the school. In our school there were and still are some old tamarind trees as I write. In those days, some notorious teachers used to carry any one of the rebellious pupils and asked him to embrace and hold on to the stem of such a huge tree and cling there while being beaten by a teacher. If he were to loose his grip, he would fall down and injure himself.

You see, the stem of the tree is big in comparison with the little, short arms of a child. So when the child is placed there, he looks like a big lizard. Did I hang on any of these huge disciplinary trees one day while there? Maybe, but I cannot really recall such an important experience. All in all, child discipline used to be a normal occurrence in the life of Jeng society, including the school.

Preparation of Meals

Pupils were responsible for preparing their meals on daily basis. This entailed the collection of fire wood from the nearby forests, fetching water from nearby pools, grinding the grains and cooking the food itself, among others. Without shoes, the pupils used to go and collect the fire wood in such very wild forests, full of dangerous snakes and scorpions. It was seen as normal when one was pricked by thorns. The pupils stayed in small, manageable groups to care for themselves. Sometimes the food was not cooked well, for some of the children were too young to know how to prepare food in the right way. Cooking utensils and cooking grounds were not well kept in terms of cleanliness. Mostly, the food was also not very nutritious, and this was the cause of some common sicknesses like diarrhoea among the pupils. Hence, poor feeding in the schools was one of the main reasons why Jeng refused to allow their children to have access to modern education.

School and Accommodation Facilities

In terms of accommodation and teaching facilities, both classrooms and residential quarters were made of local materials – mud walls and grass-thatched roofs. They were frequently destroyed by termites and renewed by the local communities. Dormitories were just big halls where pupils spread their own local mats side by side. Some children shared their few mosquito-nets, especially during the rainy seasons. It was a typical poor accommodation in comparison with anything you can see at the moment, even in the present African rural areas.

CHAPTER TWO

❧❦❧❦❧❦

The Plight of the War

The war between Anyanya and Khartoum Government intensified and forced almost all the schools in rural areas of Southern Sudan to close in compliance with the government order. Our school was affected by this order and was closed indefinitely. The students who had their relatives in urban centres went there and continued with their education. But those who had no such connections returned to their respective villages and endured the ugly stigma of the war with their parents and other relatives.

My brother and I returned to the village and continued with our traditional activities. We went back to herding our family livestock and doing other mundane jobs. Our mother was happy to receive us back in the family. With our father, since it was an act of nature, as the villagers called it, there was nothing for him to do but just to welcome us back home happily.

The beautiful days of primary education were now a thing of the past. As for me, the little knowledge from books began to fade, giving way to cultural norms and familiarity. Within a few years, I remained with nothing in terms of modern education but just some alphabets and a few terms that I used to verbalise to threaten and bully some young illiterate villagers. But in the eyes of educated people, I was merely as illiterate as any child in the village who had not been to school. For the few words and alphabets that I knew made little difference. Education was now beyond my reach and the farming vocation was no longer a choice but a necessity for me.

The Intensity of the War

The war between Anyanya and the army of the Khartoum Government intensified with some unbearable consequences falling on the innocent villagers. Those who were in the government controlled areas, especially urban centres, were considered as government collaborators by the Southern guerrillas. Thus, they were subjected to mistreatment, leading to death in some cases. Likewise, those who chose to remain in the villages were treated as pro Anyanya by the government army and were consequently entitled to brutal treatment.

In comparison, the government army was very superior in terms of weaponry and other aspects. This is because Anyanya troops were very ill equipped militarily, were not well trained and lacked good clothing and proper feeding. But despite their inferiority, they had sufficient will to fight and endure the bush hardships. On the other hand, the government soldiers, because of their superiority, were constantly on the roads, looking for Anyanya in and around villages. Sometimes when they failed to find them, they turned their unmerciful weapons on the innocent villagers. That is, they tortured, raped, killed and burned down their squalid buildings with all their meagre belongings inside. The only way to survive in such a difficult situation was for one to remain vigilant always and run whenever such hostile troops were spotted nearby.

It is said that country community is like water, and the guerrilla like the fish. But sometimes when the hospitality of the community is abused by the guerrilla, the tying relationship between the two parties greatly suffers. Hence, the relationship between Southerners in rural areas and Anyanya was not often very smooth due to the harassment inflicted on the poor communities by brutal armed men. The frequent acquisition by coercion of food items from the local civilians by these armed forces was received rarely with a smiling face. But all in all, there was no way the fish would have survived without the impatient communities that acted as the needed water.

This terrible life forced some weak villagers to become government informers merely for the sake of survival. Unfortunately, some of them met dehumanising deaths either in the hands of the government or Anyanya troops. Such informers have now left bad names behind in total disgrace to their family members.

Relationships During War

Relationships may do harm more than good during wartime. One of my distant relatives named Mareer was serving in Anyanya. His work was to carve and sell ivory on behalf of the guerrillas. Because of his connection with them, the government soldiers in Bor town heard about him and looked for any possible opportunity to catch and kill him. One day, Mareer returned from Equatoria with some guerrillas to Bor rural area. While there, he attended a feast in our home. By night, right after the feast, some government troops moved from Makuach Court Centre to our home in search of him. They came and surrounded our compound and vehemently asked for him.

It is suspected that a certain person who happened to be around during the feast was the one who informed the troops about the man in question. He might have been the one who arranged and directed the government soldiers to our home because they did not know it before.

My sister and brother were sleeping in the big hut; mother was in another hut, while father was in the cowshed or luak. Mother put her head out of her hut and told them in Jeng language that Mareer had gone to Uganda a very long time ago. Hearing that, one of the soldiers responded terribly to her with nothing but a fierce kick in the face. Fortunately, she dodged his merciless leg and quickly moved back inside the darkness of her room. Father was completely asleep. Since it was too dark to see, it was difficult for them to search the buildings. Also as trained soldiers, it was unwise for them to enter into such dark houses in enemy territory.

No one can tell for sure why these troops were moving by night without even a single matchbox or torch. Maybe, the Lord concealed their remembrance to save the lives of my innocent parents and siblings. Luckily, one of the soldiers asked for fire, and immediately my mother seized that opportunity by pointing them to a neighbouring homestead. To confirm that it was absolutely God's protection, they all went there instead of sending one or few of them.

After seeing them off, my mother rushed and angrily but quietly woke her husband. She rebuked him for being a sound sleeper. Then he dashed out and took off with all suspicious documents and hid among nearby bushes. As the deputy chief, he had some letters from those of Anyanya. Hence, they would have killed him, harmed other family members and burned the buildings if he was caught with such documents.

The troops returned with fire and thoroughly searched the buildings. They entered into the big hut and woke my brother and sister, threatening them and calling the name of Mareer. Having not completely awoken and not knowing what was happening, my brother told the soldiers of his whereabouts. But after a little while, the boy completely got the message and tried to withdraw his word but in vain. The soldiers adamantly and forcefully demanded to be taken to Mareer's home.

To end the ordeal and save the family, my sister who was around 12-years-old at the time, came out bravely. She told the soldiers that what her brother meant was the original home of Mareer but not Mareer himself. For he had long, long time ago gone to Uganda. This is what others term a 'white lie.' Then they pushed her in front to go and show them that old homestead. To the family and other relatives, the crisis was not over, for the fate of this little girl was unknown.

During those days, people cultivated and harvested second crops, commonly known as 'aŋul' in the beginning of dry season. Usually, they were guarded at night by the farmers from wild animals. Also the villagers knew Anyanya soldiers for their constant movements by night.

While approaching Mareer's homestead, my sister and government troops came across one man in his farm. The man thought that they were guerrillas, and so he greeted them friendly in Jeng language. But to his deep surprise, the assumed friendly soldiers turned out to be the enemy troops, the government soldiers. They instantly approached and asked him to show them Mareer's home. He nervously agreed; so they left my sister to return. She then hurriedly and happily went back and told our parents and others what had occurred on the way. My people were enshrouded with some gratitude but totally mixed with trembling and fear.

The man took the soldiers to the home of Mareer. And for sure you don't expect a man on the run to have spent the night there. The denial there was the same – that this man had gone a very long time ago to Uganda. But why did people refer to Uganda? This is because Anyanya was mostly associated with Uganda and Zaire where they sometimes got their training and armaments. Also some Southerners took refuge in those nations.

Mareer's brother bravely accepted the family tie but vigorously denied having seen him lately. The soldiers tied him and took him to Makuach where he was eventually released after a long, concerted investigation. His return to the village boosted the joy of the entire community, especially my parents, because his arrest was somewhat connected with my sister who first took the soldiers there. The man who eventually took them to Mareer's home was also thankful for his release.

My Father Joins Anyanya

The above event was not the only incidence in which my father narrowly escaped death from the unkind government soldiers, for there were other occasions where he also missed death. Now he had to decide wisely about what to do. Should he cross over to the government's side and collaborate with them to fight against his own people in Southern Sudan or take the bull by the horns by joining Anyanya and face this merciless regime? He chose the latter and left his home for bush life. He became one of the experienced, para-legal judges to deal with some relevant legal issues.

But what did that mean for the welfare of our family as it was seen from the government's perspective? As far as my father was concerned, his fate was now final. He was an absolute opponent of the Khartoum Government. In other words, he became a rebel and a real enemy who would deserve nothing better than death in the hands of government troops if he were to be caught. And he was ready to do the same to any government agents if conditions allowed him. Thus, our family was considered pro Anyanya. This drastically increased our fear because the government was now allegedly justified to inflict suffering on any member of the family due to his rebellious or revolutionary status. Nevertheless, so far so good, God took complete care of us, and none of us was affected in one way or the other by the end of that war in 1972.

Brother Wuoi in Juba

My brother Wuoi grew up and attained the age of cultural initiation from boyhood to manhood, around the age of 14. After passing through this significant passage of rite, he joined his age mates and did the typical things men in society generally do at that age. Between the late 1960s and early 1970s, he went to Juba in search of employment and to look for possible opportunities to continue with his studies. But his early primary education was not good enough to get him an appropriate salary-earning job. He found some casual work to make his ends meet. Meanwhile, he enrolled in an adult education school there with the aim of pursuing his education. As time went on, he joined the police force and continued with his studies after finishing his training course. Because of his determination and teachable spirit, Wuoi finished his high school level and took some other significant courses right after the war of Anyanya.

Transition to Manhood

Back home, I went on with village life but still under the constant fear of government attacks and some harassment by the guerrillas. Sometimes I stayed in the cattle camp with my older brothers and sister and left our mother and other relatives to stay in the village. I often lived with her so as to help her with cultivation and to look after the remaining livestock in the homestead.

My family did not expect me to return to school, for things were messed up by the civil war. I had also grown up beyond the reasonable age for primary school studies. After all, the war situation was a convincing reason for me not to resume school. So it was justifiable to remain uneducated as my parents were if I were not to pursue it further in future. Our primary concern as Southern Sudanese people at that time was how to bring the destructive war to an end because we were tired of it.

The time came for me to be initiated, and this was a joyous moment for me and others. I was overwhelmed with intense excitement because it was an admirable moment for me to cross the cultural bridge from childhood to adulthood. To be called a man is very important in the life of Jeng because it earns you respect, freedom, responsibility and authority. It shows one's disconnection from female and childish activities. During the initiation, my father gave me a stick (locally known as 'Thieech') and a spear. As a man, these were meant for defence. I was now associated mostly with men, especially my peers. The initiation gave me the right to fight and die anywhere in the defence of our people and the land as well as in defence of my own self-worth.

A Youngster after Cattle

One day, our livestock were in one of our traditional cattle camps known as Palabach. It was at the onset of the dry season, with the grass burned, and new vegetation growing. Yet grass and water were very scarce. So the herders were to take the animals to places with some green pastures and clean waters. To make the matters worse, that area was full of lions. Therefore, looking after livestock was risky business. Four men had to be on duty looking after the herds every day.

A day before my turn came, some young men were in charge of the cattle, but unfortunately, the lions attacked the herds and killed two cows. When the information reached the cattle camp, people were not happy and blamed the shepherds for not being vigilant enough.

The following day was my turn with three other guys to go herding. I armed myself with two sharp spears and a big club. My colleagues were also armed with traditional weapons. We vowed to make our time joyous by taking the animals to where there was greener pastures and clean waters and to protect them from wild animals, particularly lions. We moved with them until we reached where lions had attacked them the previous day. Upon sighting the carcases of the cows that had been killed by animals, our determination to protect the herd was radically boosted.

As they looked for grass, the animals kept wandering, thus outstretching us. To keep off the lions, we kept shouting and singing some meaningless songs. One of us was an adult, while the rest of us were teenagers.

Three strong men went ahead of the herds, while I followed with the rest, especially the young and the weak ones. After a long march, the herd reached a pool where our animals quenched their thirst. Thereafter, the cows took a different direction, moving eastwards.

Shortly after the cattle left the pool, they ran away from a certain thick bush. One large group ran towards the northern part while the smaller herd ran towards the southern part. In order to know what provoked them to run, the men went near the bush and tried to look for the footmarks of whatever might have been there. Right away they identified the foot prints of lions. The cows might have stampeded upon sensing the presence of the lions. Then one old man, plus another young man, decided to run after the large group and told the other to pursue the smaller herd. I immediately followed them and saw them going in different directions to round up the cattle together so that they can be in one central position where they can be closely monitored.

Because I didn't know what had happened, I just decided to stand in the shade of some bushes, waiting for the two groups of fellow herders to join me there. There were some high dry grass between where I sat and the small group of cattle that had been rounded up by the young man. The tip of the blade of one of my spears was somewhat bent, and I didn't know what had caused this. While trying to straighten it, I heard some terrible sound coming from one of the herds. Immediately I rushed in that direction with my spear ready. This was the best weapon I had.

I knew beyond a shadow of doubt that the fierce attackers were lions. But had I ever seen how a lion looked like? No, although I could easily know it, based on earlier stories by people, including my parents, describing how it looks like, its behaviour, big hairy head, wide chest, big and strong arms, narrow hips, etc. Before this particular incident, I had heard lions roaring and moving around by night. For sure, the beast doesn't openly show itself during the day, although it may do so in places where people are rarely found.

This was a real test on my tender manhood. As I rushed towards the struggling animals, the escaping livestock swiftly bypassed me, and I eventually found myself facing the giants face-to-face for the first time in my life. What I saw directly confirmed the mental picture that these were the real lions. The lioness had killed a small bull, and the other lion was on a big cow. I rushed before any of them had any chance to even lick blood from their victims. Actually, I didn't see the lioness, for the prominent lion immediately caught my whole attention. Like any naughty, brave youngster, I dashed towards it, holding my sharp spear up in the air to attack it. The big cat firmly pushed down the struggling cow with three legs and fiercely aimed at me with the remaining forearm. But before my spear left my thin palm, it roared and leaped up and down. The innocent cow was badly injured with a broken shoulder and some deep wounds pierced by the big cat's claws. It was at this time that I saw the lioness leaping away from its victim. After reaching a short distance, they turned their heads and looked at me; then they continued moving away. Immediately, I felt good, like a real man not afraid of lions!

The bull was dead, but the cow was still alive. Shortly after the rescue mission was done, the other three men came, beating their chests. They beat their chests because they knew it was our turn to be blamed by the campers for having not vigilantly looked after the livestock.

The decision was now taken to skin and take the meat of the bull and try to drag the wounded cow along with the herds back to the cattle camp. But unfortunately, it appeared that the injuries sustained by the cow were too serious for it to move. The only option was to slaughter it for meat.

Obviously, the beasts hadn't run far away. And chances were that they could come back for the meat of their victims or go and attack and kill the other cows. So the old man and another youngster remained to guard the meat and the injured cow from the lions, while two of us chased the rest of the herd back to the cattle camp.

Upon our arrival there, we narrated our experience. On hearing our story, a few of the young men decided to run off following our trail back to the spot where the killing had happened. They slaughtered the injured cow, roasted and ate some meat and returned with the remainder to the camp. This was one of the very rare occasions whereby people of Jeng could taste meat, for their livestock was mostly kept for milk, marriage and prestige. As such it was a joyous day for those whose cows were not attacked but a gloomy one for the ones affected. Protecting domestic animals from beasts was and still is one of the usual rural wars waged by brave villagers.

The End of the Civil War

As life moved from bad to worse, especially in the rural areas, it was very hard for us to imagine how this terrible war was going to end. People were dying all over Southern Sudan from the sword and war-related causes. Some families were divided up by the war with some members living in urban centres and others living under the control of Anyanya. With the death of William Deng Nhial in the hands of merciless government troops in 1968, things turned for the worse for the Southerners in general. Deng was a renowned Southern politician. The government also engineered unnecessary tribal conflicts among the Southerners. This led to the bloody conflict between Jeng Bor and Bari speaking tribes in the late 1960s.

But as it is biblically written that there is time for everything under the sun, God had a definite time in store to bring this destructive war to an end. As peace negotiations were going on in Addis Ababa, Ethiopia, some of us, especially the majority of the rural community, were unaware of this significant event. Nevertheless, life was gradually returning to normality with some eager people crossing over to any side of the dividing line of the two warring parties. Yet some of us, me included, were hesitant to venture into Bor town because of the previous known brutality of the government soldiers and their informers on the civil population.

As the security situation got better and better, the door to the movements began to open wider and wider with some people even going from Southern to Northern Sudan and vice versa. Shortly after the signing of the Addis Ababa Agreement between the Khartoum Government and Anyanya, and the subsequent cessation of hostilities between them, we came to understand that the war had been brought to an end. The ugly page of war was at last turned and a fresh page of peace and development was opened.

For the villagers, especially in Southern Sudan, 1972 was a joyous historical moment because of two main reasons. Firstly, government troops were no longer to attack or harass the villagers and loot their meagre belongings by force. Secondly,

Anyanya would no longer demand the villagers to contribute resources towards the purpose of war.

The autonomous government of Southern Sudan was now in position to protect the civil population from any unnecessary violation of their rights by anybody. This vital event was marked all over the nation, particularly in Southern Sudan, with some traditional and national dances and other festivals. It was time now to heal some deep, national wounds between the south and the north of the country. But was this agreement inclusive and guaranteed to last longer? Only the future held the right answer to this question.

PART TWO

くぞんぐんそんぐぶ

Urban Life and the Signs of Sudan's Second War, 1970s – 1983

Peter Wuoi Kuch in Juba, 1970s

From Left to Right: *Stephen Mathiang Kuch & Malual Yartok Deng in Juba, 1970s*

CHAPTER THREE

Urban Life

Now after the war, people were free to move as they liked, especially those looking for greener pastures in big towns. My brother Wuoi was now working and attending an adult school in Juba. Promotion of adult literacy particularly in urban centres was a general policy of the autonomous government of Southern Sudan to bridge the wide educational gap created by the seventeen-year civil war. The government made it financially free for all interested citizens to learn.

Since my other three siblings were taking care of the family herds and other activities, I was lured by my peers who had been to urban centres before to pay a visit with them to Juba to see my brother. They told me how good he was doing in Juba. They talked impressively about huge hills and mountains around Juba, especially Jabel Lado. There are no rocks, let alone hills and mountains, in Bor. For it is a very plain and flat, muddy land, which is acclimatized to flooding during the wet seasons.

Thus, my curiosity increased when they mentioned such elegant hills and mountains. Also they spoke fondly about the importance of travelling along the river by a streamer or boat. Although I had seen many streamers moving along the river south and north of Bor since my childhood, it was a golden opportunity to board one of these vessels for the first time in my life. So I was excited.

I tremblingly went to my father and mother and told them of my dream to pay a visit to Juba. I was afraid that they were going to say no. So I told them that my sole purpose was to visit my brother and bring back news about him.

Since it was my first time to go there, their first question was whether there were some reliable persons to go with me. In those days it was not easy to go from Bor to Juba and vice versa, although it is a short distance of about 127 miles.

This is simply because people were not used to venturing out from their comfort zones. After sharing with them my decision and the names of the guys who were going with me, their answer was unequivocal yes. My father then gave me a little money for the journey. They wished me journey mercies but asked me to come back quickly, for they didn't want to see me disappearing into an unknown world like other people.

I was anxious to break the good news to my peers. We then prepared for the journey and went to Bor town to wait for the streamer going to Juba from Kosti. It normally used to arrive in Bor on a Friday night. Upon its arrival, we boarded it excitedly and sailed along the river towards Juba, a journey of about two days.

Although the streamers were somewhat old and not very clean, on my part, the movement of the streamer along the river was very exciting. As for my guiding friends, they were constantly looking for any possible opportunity to spot Jabel Lado and direct my ignorant attention to it. It was one of the greatest wonders of my little world to see. When I saw it, it became quite difficult for me to shift my tiring eyes away from its beautiful scenery. It looked like a huge, distant and dark cloud.

I was overwhelmed and experienced culture shock when we arrived in Juba – by the hugeness of the town itself and many other things like the surrounding hills and mountains. But like any kind of culture shock, what had greatly impressed me soon melted away in to thin air. In fact, I came to understand in time that Juba was not so huge as such, unless one compared it to my little town of Bor.

It was good for my brother Wuoi and I to meet again after quite a long time of separation. I spent that particular dry season with him, helping him with what he was doing. I also spent my leisure times with my peers, attending some traditional dances and spending some good times with girls coming from the surrounding cattle camps. It was better to spend the time there than to do it in the village, for town life is busy and exciting compared to daily life in the cattle camp.

Shortly after the beginning of the rainy season, I returned to Bor with some little, hard-earned money and bought a goat (Thaakuach). My people were greatly happy to see me returning home with something valuable for the first time in my young adulthood. For it signified my seriousness with life. Their sincere appreciation in turn boosted my morale. So thereafter, I managed to acquire a few livestock for the family. To me, urban life became more productive than the life in the cattle camp. But for those who failed to take absolute care of themselves, it was somehow disastrous.

Conversion to Christianity

Despite being introduced to urban life, I was still deeply immersed in our African Traditional Religion in which people believed in the one and only Creator of the whole universe plus other less-deities. Even when people did some sacrifices to any of our ancestral gods in my absence, it was their sole duty to remember before such a deity their relatives who could not be around at the time.

My brother Wuoi made a personal decision to become a Christian and got baptised and was given the name Peter. According to conservative Anglicanism in my country, one is to choose a biblical name during his baptismal time. Although his choice did not necessarily influence me, I began to properly consider what Christianity was all about and started to shift my spiritual allegiance from ATR to Christianity. I got some biblical literatures plus a Bible and studied them critically to inform myself about Christianity.

Eventually, I made up my mind and discarded the ATR and replaced it with Christianity. Nevertheless, I refused to attend church services and shunned baptism. I failed to join church services because I was not baptised, and I was not baptised simply because I was not ready to accept a biblical name, which was mandatory for me to choose during baptism.

But why did I refuse to choose such a name? It means a lot in Jeng culture to give a child a family name. The child is expected to uphold and cherish such a name and try to conform to the societal, acceptable and good moral values associated with the owner of the name. Otherwise, if he turns out to behave contrary to the acceptable norms and behaviour within the society, people will denounce and often rebuke him openly for not respecting the family name.

In my lifetime, I came across people with Christian names who would misbehave in public. Some were terrible drunkards; others were thieves and robbers; still some were adulterers, just to name a few. Were they respecting such important names and living to the very standard of the ancient owners of the names? By no means! Connecting the Jeng cultural naming and Christian naming enshrined in the Anglican doctrine, I became deeply disturbed by the deliberate misuse of such sacred, Christian names by their bearers. To me, if one is utterly uncertain of upholding his Christian name, the best thing is for him to be baptised with his own family name.

Hence, since I was not very sure of my future as a Christian and being afraid of misusing such a name, I declined to take a name. Yet the church was not willing to baptise me with my family name. Some of my best friends and other church people

instead tried in vain to persuade me to change my mind and choose any Christian name. I did not change my mind, for they failed to convince me reasonably and logically.

This standoff did not, however, affect my personal relationship with God. Because I wholeheartedly took Jesus Christ as my Lord and Saviour, although what was missing was to be baptised into the family of God. I went on for some years living my new Christian life in seclusion without attending church services and other Christian fellowships.

One of the best Christian literature books I had at the time was a small booklet of Acts of the Apostles. I thoroughly read it several times. It was in this book that I came to know the life story of the first Christian martyr, Stephen. I was and am still deeply touched by his faith. One day, sometime in December 1976, I just had a change of heart. I said, "Why don't I just choose a name as others do, get baptised, and leave the rest with God?" Can you imagine which name I chose?

After having read the life's story of Stephen and knowing what he went through, I wholeheartedly chose to be named after him. After making this golden choice, I joyfully attended the Christmas Celebration of 1976 in Juba and had my baptism in January 1977. Since then, I have been growing steadily with my God, with no regrets at having chosen this vital name. It is my earnest prayer that the Lord will assist me to live the remaining part of life in accordance with His will, upholding and cherishing this noble name. This was another 'Silent Hand' upon my life.

Back to School

Now with the help of my brother, I opened a small kiosk near the government premises. I mainly sold cigars, matchboxes, pens and pencils, sweets and biscuits. It did not give me good returns but it was a nice, mundane job that I loved. Its time of operation was in line with the government official working hours. So my working hours would begin at around 7am through to 4pm.

St. Joseph Adult School

Mr. Simon Ateny Jok Malou was one of my best friends, and he was working for the Senior Guest House, Juba in the 1970s. He was one of the people who tried to persuade me in vain to take any Christian name and be baptised. One day, Ateny came and told me of some adult school classes being opened in Merkes Chabab (Youth Centre) and other places in Juba. He asked me whether I could be ready to attend such evening classes with him because there was nothing for us to do. These were late afternoon classes.

The idea was good, but where were we going to begin? Of course, my basic educational knowledge of the 1960s was really a thing of the past. So if I were to return to school, I would start afresh from the zero level. Ateny had no basic education, and it did not matter to him at which level he begun. We went there and embarked on our serious educational journey in 1973. Others joined us in their pursuit of education. The subjects taught were only Basic English and arithmetic.

It was not an easy task for us to accomplish. This is because youngsters always have some conflicting emotions warring over the same juvenile desires. For us, our deep primary desires ranged from befriending young beautiful girls, attending cultural dances, and having leisure times to hang around and chat with our peers. Returning home and reconnecting with the ageless village life was still very real in our life. I would go back to the village at least once per year.

But before long, most of us left the school in sequence, with some leaving without even finishing learning the alphabet. One of the unique things about me is that once I make a decision, I adhere to it. This spirit gave me an indisputable zeal to hang on to my education in spite of losing some of my best friends to the world of youth.

Since the Youth Centre was farther away from where we lived, we moved and joined evening adult education classes at St. Joseph Primary School, Juba. Although the government covered the school financially, we contributed a little money to support our teachers. They were part of the teaching staff of this primary school. I worked very hard with the hope of changing myself from adult school to the real primary school. Upon my completion of Class One, I skipped Class Two and joined Grade Three.

Because of my frequent return to the village, I missed twice the opportunity to join the primary school at St. Joseph. This is because I would return to Juba from the village after the opening of schools and the admission of new pupils. Seeing that it was late for me to do so, I went on with my studies in the adult school. Also, one of our teachers informed me that it would be easy for me to join intermediate school if I were to finish my adult education successfully.

I fruitfully completed my Grade Three and skipped to Grade Five, although we were still learning only two subjects. I successfully completed my Grade Six sometime in December 1976. With adult school complete, I looked forward to joining intermediate school in 1977.

To my disappointment, I was awarded a nice but discouraging adult school certificate by the Ministry of Education, Southern Sudan. The certificate was simply and clearly worded as follows: "He knows how to read and write English." The immediate question I asked myself and others was: "Would this certificate enable me join any of the public intermediate schools?" My next questions were: "Now what do I do? Is this the end of my educational journey?" These and other relevant questions flooded my eager mind and inquisitive heart. However, there was no easy answer because my single will was to pursue education despite my age and other difficulties.

Experimental Exams

I went to my teacher, showed him the certificate and sought his opinion as to whether this kind of certificate would help me join any intermediate school. His direct answer was no, for it lacked some necessary subjects done in formal primary schools. Instead, he advised me to be patient and wait for the next academic year in which he would assist me to join primary six at St. Joseph Primary School. But I refused his advice and told him instead to help me sit in the same school with grade six pupils that were scheduled to sit for their national exams in January 1977.

This was quite a hard request for him to agree to simply because my school was not inclusive in that I did only two basic subjects: English and mathematics while the ones covered in formal primary school included, apart from the above subjects: biology, Christian religion, and geography. My explanation to him was to let me try, and if I failed, I would then remain and enrol in the same school. After a long, endless and fruitless discussion with him, he decided to take me to the headmaster, a catholic priest, of St. Joseph Primary School to see whether he could allow me to sit with their grade six candidates.

His first question to me was to inform him about the background of my education and capability to tackle the hard national exams. Learning that I was merely one of the adult education students, he immediately rejected my request. He justified his decision by pointing out that it would be too difficult for me to sit and pass the required subjects (biology, geography, Christian education plus the actual English and mathematics) which I had not done.

But was this headmaster capable of persuading me to change my mind and drop my single determination to become educated? Absolutely not, this man failed to do so, and he was totally frustrated with my strong will. In the end, his response was: "I don't want many failures in this school." What he meant was that by allowing me to sit the exams as one of his pupils, I would, to him, definitely fail, and thus increase the number of his pupils who were likely to fail the exams.

Instead, he told me to go to the Ministry of Education and make a request for them to register me as an outside candidate in his school. This was a nice, possible solution for me because my primary concern was not to be just a part of the school system but to properly contest the exams.

I went to the Ministry of Education immediately and made my request. I thought that they were not going to give many, hard questions to me before registration. Instead, the two girls I met in the office inquired about my educational background. After learning that I was in adult school, they told me that I was not qualified to sit for such difficult exams. Nevertheless, I insisted to be registered, irrespective of their sincere judgemental opinion.

At the end of a long discussion, they cautioned me not to claim back the registration fee of 180 Sudanese piasters in the event of my obvious failure. I responded sarcastically by saying: "What about those who play the lottery, do they claim their money when they are defeated?" They laughed, took my money and registered me to my full happiness. They told me that my index number would appear against my name in the school during the exams.

Getting the registration is one thing but preparing for exams is quite another. I was quite naively determined to master them despite my shallow educational background. I was not afraid, for I was driven by my heart and mind. Since I did not know even where to begin in relation to preparation for the exams, particularly concerning the subjects which were foreign to me, I relaxed and went on with my usual life as I waited for the big day.

But other children who knew what was happening were very busy with the preparations. Joseph Garang Tiel Malual, one of my relatives, was also preparing to sit the same national exams. However, I was from the English pattern, and he was from the Arabic pattern. As a result, he was of little help to me when it came to the exchange of class notes. He, however, gave me his extra school uniform to wear during the exam period. He also advised me to take the required examination materials which included a pen, pencil and ruler.

The day to start exams was getting closer day by day. My intense excitement was not only to sit the exams but also to quickly finish them and pay a visit to my people back home. On the first day I went there, saw my index number and stood lonely in the school compound, while waiting anxiously for the bell to ring. During the exams, my sole aim was to do what I knew, try the rest, and leave what I totally didn't know.

The sitting pupils knew each other. Thus, they were on and off consulting their class notes and sharing their viewpoints among themselves. But I was a real loner with no notes to glance at as well as no single friend to turn to for any assistance. As a result, I completely switched off my mind and refused to consult any teacher when I was confronted with unclear questions in the examination hall. In spite of all difficulties, I finished them gratefully. For there was no one to blame apart from my own strong will if at all there was any sense of who to blame for the hard exams. I successfully did my part, and it was now for the examiners to mark and give me what I deserved.

Right after the exams, I went to my home village to reconnect with my relatives and the village life. When the school results were out, I returned to Juba and rushed to the Ministry of Education to see mine. Do you know what I obtained? I completely proved wrong all the people who advised me to think otherwise because I successfully passed the exams, with my lowest mark being in biology. The educational door was now wide open before me.

Strong will is always the key to an unknown future and a brighter torch to shed light along the darkest unknown path. This was the beginning of my victory over the war on education and ignorance. But deep inside my innermost being I sensed the 'Silent Hand' upon my life, opening the door of education before me.

Buluk Intermediate School

Now it was time for me to make some hard decisions, for I was not going to be able to manage both my small kiosk and do my school studies at the same time. For me, the best decision was to pursue my education at the expense of my business because my interest in life was beyond immediate financial benefits. But to maintain myself while in school, and not wanting to become a big burden to my family financially, I mobilised my meagre resources, acquired a piece of land in the market, and built a small semi-permanent kiosk. I then rented it out to a certain trader. The rent was enough to take care of all my school and other expenses.

In 1977, I was officially admitted into the famous Buluk Intermediate School, English section. In the beginning of my studies there, I was still a lone wolf because almost all my schoolmates knew each other, for they came as groups from some primary schools in and around Juba. Due to the limited school facilities in Southern Sudan by then because of the just ended seventeen-year civil war, and because of the huge number of school children, students were packed in small classrooms like sardines in a can. For instance, our first year class accommodated about 150 students. You can imagine, about three classes combined in one!

I was elected as a class monitor to take charge of such a huge class. Of course, you cannot fail to find some naughty students in such a big sea of youngsters. Yet it was not my first time to shoulder this kind of responsibility, for I had done that several times during my adult school. Some of my classmates were Isaac Mamur, Nixon Lure, Aluel Mading Garang, Elizabeth Kenyikwe, Agnes Dudu, Diu Dau and Hussein Yokwe.

My culture shock in this school, as a respected class monitor, occurred during the first algebra lesson in the first year. The maths that we did in adult school excluded algebra and other complicated parts of mathematics. But they were covered in the formal primary schools. And so my colleagues were well versed with them. During morning classes, a maths teacher came and gave us a friendly greeting, and we responded likewise. He turned to the chalkboard and taught us some common algebraic methodologies. For others it was somewhat a revision of the primary school maths, but unfortunately for me it was the beginning of a real journey.

I took my writing items and tried keenly to follow the teacher. Obviously, he was not aware of having such a naïve student in his classroom. So he went with the pace of the majority students who were just saying, "yes", "yes", "yes", when he said, "Is it correct?" By the way I must say here that, this is what is wrong with 'democracy', the principle of 'majority rules', for the right of the 'minority' is not taken care of, even when they have the absolute right.

Shortly thereafter, the teacher gave us some questions as class work and asked me to collect and take the exercise books to him for marking. I thought I had followed the teacher keenly. As I tried the first question, other students were already flooding my desk with their exercise books in readiness for collection. Then I struggled quickly, finished my neat work, took all the exercise books and gave them to the teacher.

He marked them hurriedly and asked me to return them. I breathlessly opened my exercise book and closed it within the twinkling of an eye. I saw what my own eyes had never seen before in the entire life of my simple educational background. A very high-opinionated class monitor had just received a big zero in algebra!

I was utterly annoyed and made sure that none of my subjects got a peek at it, just for the fear of being mocked. The fact of the matter is that no one likes to be associated with mediocrity. Who wants to be a tail and not the head?

After a lot of soul-searching, I said to myself in consolation, "Yes, this is a real sign of being in formal school. If I don't work hard, then I am in the wrong place." That was my first and last zero, not only in the intermediate school but in my whole school life. In the first term school exams, I achieved position 24 out of about 150 students.

When my closest friend Nixon Lure saw what I had obtained, he congratulated me for the effort. Unfortunately, I sincerely told him that it was not my rightful position. Why? He asked me surprisingly. But I told him that my logical place was still somewhere at the top of the echelon. Then I honestly shared with him about my poor, early educational background. He was deeply impressed about my earnest attempts. In the end term exams, I reached position 4 in the class and eventually settled for position 2 when my colleague Elizabeth Kenyikwe stood like an invincible rock before me.

If I were to wallow in the valley of despair due to my underprivileged educational background without exerting some concerted efforts in the field of studies, the majority of people would have agreed with me. Alas, I came to discover that some of my age mates were also in the same school standard with me. So it was just a matter of doubling one's attempts to reach the limitless goal of education. Precious stones like diamond and gold are always there deeply imbedded in the ground waiting for the hard and determined diggers to unearth them. Yet the 'Silent Hand' gave me such a strong educational zeal to walk along the rough path of education.

Career Choice

Early choice of a career is important in life because wrong career choices can ruin one's future. What did I want to be in the future? During our time, people did not necessarily go for the so-called marketable careers. And particularly in the Jeng ethnic group, the best careers included being a lawyer, a medical doctor, an army officer and a teacher. Even now, Jeng people encourage their educational pursuers to choose law-related careers to work in the legal system.

Hence, in order to follow the logical pattern of my people, and also because of my own inborn traits, I decided wholeheartedly to pursue a law career. By then it was mandatory for law students to know Arabic as it was one of the primary criteria for one to join the faculty of law in Khartoum University.

Among our good teachers at Buluk were Mabil Gideon Duot, Adhuong Kuch Adhuong and Wilson Deng Kuoirot. These gentlemen took teaching jobs while waiting to pursue their further education at the tertiary level. At the time of my writing they are serving the nation in different, important capacities.

In 1980, the time came for us to choose the high schools to go to after the three-year studies at intermediate school. My wish was to go only to one of the best academic schools in Southern Sudan, especially the one in which Arabic language was taught.

I was admitted into a newly established secondary school at Palataka, but it is located deep in the heart of the Equatoria region where people were somewhat cynical to learn Arabic language. So I was advised by some of my relatives and friends to go to Malek Secondary School in Bor, though the school was also newly established. I eventually ended up at Rumbek Secondary School with the hope of learning Arabic language therein. In fact, I passed special Arabic in my intermediate school certificate, but my worry here was to see how to upgrade it.

Rumbek Secondary School

Admission: in August 1980, I joined the famous Rumbek Secondary School with great enthusiasm. Unlike in the intermediate school where I joined with a half-baked educational background, this time I had good educational credentials. The school facilities were very attractive, and being associated with this prestigious, historical school meant a lot to us. Our heads were held high. We had a lot of respect for the headmaster, Mr. Matthew Allahjabu, an experienced teacher.

For the first time in my school life, I found myself in a noisy boarding facility. Teachers were not enough, with no good library, and the laboratory was ill equipped. Getting the right textbooks, especially for Sudanese history, was very difficult. On top of that, although Arabic language was on the school timetable, the class had no teacher. My hope to boost my Arabic language in pursuit of my judicial career was now coming to naught. This greatly frustrated me, although there was no possible option.

In the first year, I was elected as a class monitor, and I happily accepted it. I continued with my steady academic work with ease. In the subsequent year, I successfully finished my first year, and the school closed for the long three-month vacation. Then I went to Juba and proceeded to Bor to see my relatives. They received me happily. I went back to Juba to spend part of the holiday with my brother and others.

Nightmare Journey to and from the School: according to the school calendar in Sudan in those days, schools closed for long vacation during dry season and opened at some stage in wet season. For example, secondary schools opened in August, and this is the time when there are heavy rains in the south of the country. The roads leading to Rumbek either from Juba or Wau were in a bad shape. And the only reliable means of transport were commercial lorries on which poor students were loaded like pieces of wood. They would stand on nothing but the hard iron body of the vehicle. Serious injuries and even death among the helpless students was a common happening.

Because of the terrible roads, students often appeared and looked like armies of ants, especially when they pulled the stuck vehicles out of the mud. The distance between Juba and Rumbek, for example, was very long and tiresome. Most often, students ran out of food and damaged their own meagre belongings in the process because both students and luggage were packed into the same vehicles. Such journeys began with anxiety and ended with relief. Good roads are one of the surest backbones of a nation; they are some of the formidable pillars of national development.

Distorted class notes: one of the main problems we encountered at Rumbek Secondary School was the lack of most of the recommended textbooks, and especially the ones for Sudanese history. Our teachers were powerless as things were beyond their control. Officials in the Ministry of Education in Southern Sudan used to try to get some necessary textbooks in line with the recommended syllabuses from the Ministry of Education at the national level but with little success. One really wonders! How could the national government expect students in the south of the country to sit for and pass exams for which they have not learned the syllabus? And how could such students learn the syllabuses without laying their hands on the required textbooks?

Another funny scenario worth mentioning here is that sometimes national school syllabuses were not brought in time from Khartoum to Juba. This made it quite awkward for our poor head teachers to know where to begin the learning process. To us, this was a clear discrimination among the sons and daughters within the same nation. It was deviously planned and executed by the unworthy government to marginalise one part of the country.

As you will see later, these were some of the reasons which led most of the youngsters in Southern Sudan to take up arms and wage a protracted war against the Khartoum regime. The obvious lesson is that leaders should always weigh the dire and far-reaching consequences of their decisions.

Without some possible, visible remedies at our disposal, we were left to behave like a drowning person who grasps anything floating within his reach. There were some old class notes of Sudanese history that were consistently booked and copied by the arts students in our school. I also booked and copied the same notes. As the notes passed from one hand to another with some varied judgemental viewpoints, they got distorted. And what remained of them in the end was a kind of imaginary, polluted Sudan history.

It often puzzles me when I see some blessed children who have favourable learning environments fail to excel highly in their educational endeavours. Yet one of the apparent reasons is that the more you have, the more you become passive, inattentive and lazy.

Shorten my studies: as Arabic language was no longer taught in Rumbek Secondary School, and because I was able academically to do well in the Sudan School Certificate exams, I decided to shorten my high school studies. I thought it a waste of time to chronologically finish my studies in three years. The education system in Sudan was that academic school takes three years, while commercial school takes four years. Rumbek was an academic school.

After consulting with some of my colleagues and examining my intellectual strength, I decided to skip Senior Two and head on straight for Senior Three in order to sit for the national exams in the following year, 1982. As this was my normal hobby since primary school level, I took the decision with ease, knowing that I was going to excel.

After the school vacation, I went and negotiated with the school authorities on my idea to skip to Senior Three. The school management accepted my request. So I was thrilled and worked very hard to make my decision count.

In March 1982, we finally sat for the national exams for the Sudan School Certificate. Despite all the difficulties we had encountered during the learning process, we managed well. I got an overall average mark of 71.2%. Although to me this was not an excellent mark to smile at, it was good, given the nature of our learning environment.

Quest for Educational Studies Outside Sudan

Now my law career hit a hard rock, for without having passed Arabic language, the prospects of going to Khartoum University were not there. Although my results would have warranted me to join any other faculty in the same school, I refused to take on another career. I was determined to pursue legal studies whether in or outside Sudan. To carry on with my studies outside Sudan, I decided to modify my career by choosing international relations instead. I gathered some addresses and applied to some foreign universities.

While waiting for replies and possible admissions into any of these foreign institutions of higher learning, I prepared myself at home and re-sat the Sudan School Certificate exams in 1983 at Malek Secondary School. I got another good certificate. Since I was still not ready to sit Arabic, my aim was not to qualify again for the faculty of law in University of Khartoum but just to maintain the continuity of my educational studies.

CHAPTER FOUR

The Signs of Looming Second Civil War in Sudan

Socio-Political and Economic Demonstrations

The infant Addis Ababa Agreement was not given sufficient rest by the Khartoum Government. Even the late Mr. Jaffer Mohammed Nimari, former President of Sudan, once said that this agreement was neither the Koran nor Bible. He meant that it could be abrogated at anytime. In order to undermine the agreement and to fulfil his sarcastic statement, his regime took several unfavourable measures against the Southern government and its people. Such measures were taken in the interests of Northern Sudan despite the opposing strong viewpoints from the government of Southern Sudan. These measures include the digging of the Jonglei Canal, a re-demarcation of the north-south boundaries, the division of Southern Sudan into three regions and the annexing of some areas from Southern Sudan to Northern Sudan. Some valuable natural resources were discovered in such areas.

As an angry youth, I participated in almost all these desperate students' demonstrations against the illegal policies. But for the Khartoum Government, these demonstrations and other bitter sentiments from the Southern masses were ignored like very distant thunderstorms. And instead, these doomed policies were implemented to the letter. These and other causes were the deepest wounds that later left Sudan bleeding for 21 years.

Korkoro (division)

Applying the famous policy of divide and rule, the architects of defunct Sudanese policies did not hesitate to annihilate the vital Addis Ababa Agreement by dividing the semi-autonomous Southern Sudan into three regions: Equatoria, Upper Nile and

Bahr el Ghazal. This was done against the wishes of the majority of sound-minded Southerners. 1983 was the culmination of this divisive policy, which was very much characterized by the so-called Korkoro. It unfortunately led to the loss of many innocent lives, particularly in Juba where Southerners killed each other in the name of Korkoro. For example, people from Equatoria Region began to chase away non-Equatorians to their respective regions.

One of the foreign universities that I had previously applied to was the United States International University (USIU), in Nairobi Kenya. The school sent me a letter indicating that my application had been sent to the university headquarters in San Diego, California, USA for further processing, and so I had to wait for the September quarter. The Ministry of Education, South Sudan, was the body to sponsor my further studies.

Korkoro brought in some problems that directly affected me. Since Mr. Isaac Wiel Lual, the Director General for Education is from Upper Nile, he was redirected automatically to go to Malakal, the capital city of the Upper Nile Region. As I also came from Upper Nile Region, Isaac Wiel advised me to take my school admission letter to Malakal for final approval. Of course, because of such a divisive policy, those of Equatoria in Juba were not going to take care of my scholarship.

My brother Peter Wuoi also went to Malakal. Although I remained in Juba to wait for my final admission letter from the University, life was hard. And I had to limit my movements in town, especially by avoiding some suspicious areas and night walks due to the high politicised Korkoro fever.

Southern Army Mutiny

Due to the high level of frustration among most of the Southerners because of the wrong policies of the Khartoum Government, there were rumours of imminent feuds between the South and the North. These rumours were at fever pitch, and this showed that the revolutionary atmosphere was highly ripe and volatile. To quench the thirst for such rumours, many people, especially youngsters from Jeng ethnic community used the famous, so-called 'Standing Club' in Juba as their pool of reactionary waters. The club was merely an open air venue with no seats.

On May 16, 1983, the ugly launch of the bloody civil war started in Bor, the capital city of the then Jonglei Province. Bor is now the Jonglei State capital. This Battalion 105 which mutinied was under the direct control of the late Major Kerubino

Kwanyin Bol. Shortly after, it was followed by the mutiny of Battalion 104 in Ayod under the leadership of the late Major William Nyuon Bany.

After inflicting heavy losses on the government side in terms of human and material resources, the dissatisfied army troops and their loyal civilians moved to the bushes in the countryside and waged a type of guerrilla warfare. Planning behind these officers and men was the late Col. Dr. John Garang Mabior who later became the focal point person and leader of the SPLA/M.

In order for them to get sufficient manpower and armaments and achieve proper leadership organization, among others, they walked to Bilpam in Ethiopia. There they trained, organized and took a complete rest before the launching of the protracted and bloody war. Sooner or later, thousands and thousands of angry Sudanese joined them. The disgraced, discontented students formed the bulk of the Southern rebels. The Khartoum Government put its own house to the torch by being blinded to the fact that it is very simple and easy to set fire to the house but difficult to extinguish it; it is also simple and easy to start a war but difficult to bring it to an end.

The aftermath of the Southern rebellion was not pleasant for the remaining Southern masses, especially the Jeng people because the government supporters considered them as national enemies. As a result, some people lost their precious lives and property in the hands of merciless government soldiers. The government even instigated some ethnic communities in Southern Sudan to attack and take away valuable resources from those of Bor. Being from or associated with Jeng Bor was at the time something to shun with much trembling, for they were connected with the rebellion. But was it correct for one to deny his ethnicity because of such a situation of phobia? As time went by with people from other ethnic communities pouring into the rank and file of the SPLA/M, the persecution of the general civil Southern population by the Khartoum Government was no longer limited to those of Bor, though they were still seen as the worst national enemies.

What I completely abhorred was the strict search of travellers' baggage by security guards, especially at Juba Bridge and Pakuaw in Bor. Passengers were told to stand with legs apart at gunpoint by rude soldiers while their luggage were recklessly searched for any suspicious items. Everything, regardless of its importance, was thrown on dirty ground. And if the owner tried to protest against such unlawful rudeness and a blatant violation of total human rights, the unkind soldiers would descend upon him and ruthlessly clobber him. Imagine the reaction of the youths towards such unwarranted mistreatment with the government roughing up its own innocent civilians who had actually refused to follow the rebels! Those who refused to submit to such unwarranted security checks ended up with physical injuries, or they were thrown in prison or worse still, killed.

I believe one of the primary reasons that forced most of the students to join the early rank and file of the SPLA/M was these kind of barbaric, racial and merciless treatments inflicted upon them by the government agencies. The government thought that it was doing justice by carrying out these policies. But instead, it was inflating their already bursting bag of anger and helping them join the rebels. You don't win by increasing your enemies but rather by minimizing them and even turning some of them into friends.

Choosing the Right Path

Now the war condition in Southern Sudan forced me to make a hard, decisive decision. There were two paths before me. One path was for me to succumb to this unkind government and endure its ruthless mistreatment, while pursuing with the fragile Southern Government to approve funds for my further studies abroad. The other path was to abandon my education pursuit and join the popular people's movement sacrificially.

As iron sharpens iron, 'Standing Club' was one of the places where people sharpened each other and crystallised their revolutionary ideas. Here I met two gentlemen who were my best brothers and friends, the late Kon Bion and Gai Manyang Dot sometime in July 1983. In the course of our discussion, they asked me to leave Juba immediately with them for Ethiopia to join the movement. Although such viewpoints were not shared openly, especially with non-trustworthy people, for the fear of falling into unkind hands of government informers, they were comfortable to talk with me in confidence. But this was the wrong time for me to advance my personal opinion to them because I was still wrestling with the choice of the right path. A unique part of my personality is, I always do a critical analysis of anything, even building friendships with others, before I wholeheartedly place my allegiance because I don't like jumping in and jumping out of something quickly. Therefore, I told them to go ahead, with the expectation that I would follow them in due course.

The university wrote and asked me to be prepared for September quarter classes, for I was already late for the June quarter of 1983. Nevertheless, such an admission letter was completely overshadowed by the fierce revolutionary circumstances in our part of the nation. To fight the Khartoum Government and set our people free from the bondage of backwardness and discrimination was the daily slogan sung by the destitute Southerners, especially the angry youths.

In July 1983, I made up my mind to forsake my educational pursuit and the little things that I had and trek with my colleagues to the unknown land, Ethiopia. I gave away some belongings and took my books and other items to Bor from Juba. It was difficult for me to take them to my parents in the village, for moving such materials from town to the countryside was an appropriate ground for being suspected as a rebels' collaborator by the watchful government security personnel. As a result, I put my best books into a large metallic box and left them in the house of Nathaniel Garang Anyieth who was a rural dean in charge of ECS church in Bor at the time.

In the middle of August 1983, I wrote a letter and sent it to my brother Peter Wuoi in Malakal. In the letter I told him that I had decided to remain in Bor instead of joining him as we had agreed before. I concealed in the content of the letter my going to Ethiopia, for it would cause him trouble if it was to be intercepted by the government agents. I gave it to my friend Jok Reng who I regrettably heard was later murdered in cold blood in Malakal by some government agents.

From Left to Right: *Stephen Mathiang Kuch & Achiek Mach Aluong in Juba, 1970s*

From Left to Right: *Stephen Mathiang Kuch & Joseph Garang Tiel in Juba, 1980s*

PART THREE

My Guerrilla Life, 1983–1990

CHAPTER FIVE

Among Unarmed Young Guerrillas

The First Sign of My Guerrilla Life

It was simple to make a personal decision to join the movement but it was quite another to exit the fortified government towns. All the main routes leading to Bor town were fully manned by rude and merciless government troops. The town itself was full of roaming and marauding, plain clothes security guards who moved like hunting dogs looking for something to devour. Hence, people were keen about who they associated with, what to carry and how to sneak out of town. Other towns in Southern Sudan faced the same security measures.

I did proper networking with those who were going with me to Ethiopia, and our rallying point was Baidit, a distance of about 16 miles north of Bor town. Some of my group members came to Bor from Juba and other places. It was now time for us to eventually leave there separately for the countryside en route to Bilpam. The closest relatives who left the town with me were Gai Aret Manyang and Malual Mabiei Mach-Aguek. We sneaked out at broad daylight via the Malou area. Then we joined Gakyuom road, a little bit beyond Langbaar Military Garrison. Like a wanted criminal escaping from a remand prison, we reached the main road after some hardship and accelerated heartbeats. Even the few personal items we took with us were a heavy burden by the time we reached the assembly point.

On arrival along the main road, I said, "If the small forest we crossed between town and this junction gave us these difficulties, then what will it look like for us to roam and live in the entire jungle of the Southern Sudan?" Guerrilla life is not an easy thing to choose without a self-sacrificial attitude. Even the worst type of the nomadic life is far better than the typical guerrilla life, for the former is in constant movement in the search of greener pastures, clean water and food, while the latter is being hunted down and chased like a rat fleeing from a cruel cat and fighting for its own survival.

From there we proceeded and spent a night in Wunchuei cattle camp. As usual, it was covered with animal dung, urine and irritating smoke emitted by the burning dung and logs. Here I joyfully met my two brothers and other relatives. They were happy to see us but worried that we had joined the movement and were going to Ethiopia, a foreign land.

The following morning, we hurriedly walked to the village, shared with our parents about our plans, kissed them goodbye and dashed back to the cattle camp on the way to Baidit to join our group of youngsters. My parents reluctantly permitted me to join the movement, for the choice was just a matter of life or death. They poured their blessings upon me and saw me off, hoping to see me again in good health. I also wished them good luck and left with a heavy heart and already feeling homesick. This was my first time to go on a very long, uncertain trip. But this is what manhood is all about. We left everything entirely in God's hands.

The youngsters in the cattle camp escorted us on our way to Baidit, wished us journey mercies and returned after a long distance. But before we left each other, my brother Ayoor Goigoi said, "The way things are going on now will force these young men in the cattle camps to follow you in search of firearms so as to protect themselves, their possessions and the land from their various enemies." His prediction came to pass immediately in the following dry season when thousands of angry youths left Bor for Bilpam, Ethiopia. This was the last time I saw my beloved brother Ayoor Goigoi alive.

The Beginning of a Long Wild March

The year 1983 saw many parts of Southern Sudan experienced very heavy rains and floods. As a result, the roads between Bor and Ethiopia were full of water. The road users had no option but to wade in the deep waters. What do you think happened to our shoes? Of course, we carried them; hence, they increased our load. Can you carry your personal food items on such a long journey? Absolutely not, but we managed to take with us some money and small cans of pastes of peanut and others. The money was meant for the purchase of some food items and hiring of some people to show us the right way leading to Ethiopia. Unfortunately, some guiding folks were not reliable. The size and heaviness of a bag one could carry on the journey was determined by some particular factors like the strength of the person, the weight of an item in the bag, etc. The heaviest bag one had to carry weighed ten kilograms.

On 22 August 1983, we left Baidit and trekked northwards to join the road going to Akobo, a Southern Sudanese town right along the Sudan-Ethiopia border. Although the movement was officially formed and named as the Sudan People's Liberation Army and Sudan People's Liberation Movement (SPLA/M), and its office bearers were nominated and elected in Bilpam, the information did not reach us by the time we left Bor. So whatever had happened there during its official organization was not yet communicated to us and others, especially those living deep inside Sudan. The mode of communication was very remote in those days in the area.

Wading in the water full of harmful snakes, swimming fish, open-mouthed floating snails and hovering mosquitoes, we passed via Jalle, Maar, Paliau, Wangelei, Pawel, Wernyol, Poktap, Duk Payuel and Panyang. The journey took us about two weeks. Between Duk Payuel and Panyang we began to meet the retreating young-sters who had been tortured and looted of everything they had by Southern armed groups commonly known as Anyanya 2 or Committee. Most of the Committee sol-diers were Nuers. Why did they do that to their own people? They were not happy with Col. Dr. John Garang's group. Because, according to them, he had hijacked their movement by making himself the head of the SPLA/M instead of Akuot Atem and Samuel Gai Tut. So they considered as their potential enemies those, especially people from Jeng, who wanted to cross over to Garang's side.

Some of our members were persuaded by some of their relatives and friends among the withdrawing guys to go back to their respective villages. But others and I continued the journey until we reached Panyang, a small court centre along Jeng of Nyarweng – Lou Nuer border. Here we met again youngsters who had been attacked, tortured and left at the mercy of hunger, nakedness and bloodthirsty mos-quitoes. They were on the way back to Bor. They gave us some vital information concerning the division that had occurred within the SPLA/M. Some of our mem-bers were convinced of the danger ahead and returned to Bor with these frustrated guys.

Despite this discouraging news, my colleagues and I restrained ourselves and decided to give this tiresome journey another try. I was not ready to go back to Bor before I personally experienced the fact of the matter, for had I to return home, I would not had gone back to the movement, no matter what. Instead, I gave my radio, shoes and some clothes to my friend Abraham Ajak Mayen to give to my parents. As a reliable person, he took them safely to them.

Three-Month Hostage

Over one hundred diehards stuck with me. Among these young people, besides those who went with me from Bor town, included the late Stephen Kut Bol Leek, the late Jok Ngong Mabiei, the late Herjok-abuchok, the late Ayuen Jongkuch, the late Alier Athoch, the late Malual Mabiei Mach-Aguek, James Gai Aret Manyang, Mach Alier Mach-Aguek, Rok Anyieth, Bior Yuang, Gar Yuang, James Juach Akuen, Mabil Yom Alier, Magot Jok-Guelhok, the late Mayen Akuak, the late Maluk Diing (Abuajer), the late Agoot Achol, the late Malual Piel Malual, the late Deng Piel Malual and Leek Ajak. I wish I had enough space to name all of them. Most of them are not alive now, for they have shed their precious blood for the historic national cause. I love them all.

Like an innocent animal dashing into a snare, we moved to Payai to meet the breakaway SPLA/M group who included Akuot Atem Mayen, Samuel Gai Tut, Abdullah Chuol, Diig Aluong (Makurdit), Abdul Patah, Gabriel Gany and other prominent figures. Some notable politicians and other outstanding people from Bahr el Ghazal including Lual Diing Wuol, Dr. Amon Mon Wantok, the late Bol Ayuolnhom and Daniel Ayuel Makoi also joined us in our journey.

The rebels told us to go with them to Pabuor where Akuot and Gai were. With respected politicians with us, our interest now was to go, meet those leaders, hear their concerns and try to convince them to return to Ethiopia with us and commence peace talks with Col. Dr. John Garang. We were not happy at all, for this disunity within the members of the SPLA/M would not meet the collective aspirations of the Southern Sudanese people rather it would benefit the Khartoum Government. The more Southerners divide, the more the Khartoum Government smiled broadly.

Upon our arrival there, a big rally was conducted in which we were informed of what had led to the split within the SPLA/M. In other words, Akuot and Gai told the rally that during the formation of the SPLA/M in Bilpam, Akuot was elected as Chairman, Gai as Minister of Defence and Dr. John as Chief of Staff, among others. But according to them, Dr. John defiantly took over the leadership of the movement by force with the help of the Ethiopian Government. As a result, they were not happy with such a militant decision. So they dashed out with their followers and returned to Sudan to avoid being captured by the Ethiopian government troops. Their return also was to enable them go and organise themselves and see the best possible way forward.

Hence, Akuot, Gai and their followers considered Garang's decision to be an organized coup d'état within the movement. Asked about their agenda and the way forward, Samuel Gai Tut responded clearly by saying, "Our first agenda is to destroy Nyagatism (that is, armed groups of Anyanya 2 or Committee), then move to the border in the forthcoming dry season and commence peace talks with Dr. John's group." Although in the words of Abdullah Chuol, there was no one capable to reconcile a chairman (Akuot) and a chief of staff (Dr. John Garang). This was in direct response to the reconciliatory suggestion put forward by our group. Instead, he saw the solution could come only through the barrel of a merciless gun. But was it easy and possible to achieve that?

In order to execute his leadership plans, Gai took the valiant armed men, about twenty three, from those of Bahr el Ghazal to his headquarters and moved around with them as he carried out his strategic military plan of disarming and/or absorbing the locally armed groups (Nyagats) into his army. Meanwhile, the Bahr el Ghazalian politicians and other civilians were left in Pabuor with those of Akuot. Also after the rally, we the students from Bor, were grouped into smaller, manageable platoons of about fifty people each. The arrangement was to take each of our three platoons into a separate village so as to have easy access to some food items from the host villagers.

But being from Bor, we took advantage and sought an audience with uncle Akuot Atem, and so he arranged a meeting with us. I was one of the people selected to see him. As one of the elders from Bor, we hoped that he was going to sympathise with our situation, give us exact information as per what had taken place between his group and those of Dr. John Garang and eventually advise us of what to do.

Thus, we happily went and met with him in his luak, a sort of presidential palace. In the meeting were Diing Aluong and Abdul Patah. He briefly shared with us of what had led to the split in the SPLA/M and the way forward. He entertained and responded to some of our questions. But as we attempted to dig further into the problem and tried to urge him to reconsider his group's position for the sake of the unity of the Southerners, he hastily and tactically squared up the talks and brought the meeting to an abrupt conclusion. He politely but unintentionally promised to meet us again whenever necessary.

Did we come out of our meeting with uncle Akuot with something remark-able? For our own benefit, the answer was no, but for his own personal and political aspiration, the response was yes because his aim was to convince us to stay with his forces, get some military training and receive some local armaments. Of course, one of his challenges, as the chairman of the breakaway group, was lack of manpower from his Jeng tribe, for almost all of the fighting forces were from Nuer tribe. So he hoped that our staying with them was going to strengthen his leadership position. Still his viewpoint was a kind of wishful thinking, for our primary aim was to go to Ethiopia and join the main SPLA/M. Or else, the secondary option was to return home if the road to Ethiopia was totally blocked.

Our Stay in Liaiwut

I was put in charge of one platoon that was taken to Liaiwut village. Those who helped me in my leadership role were Joshua Juach, Mabil Yom-Ardolo, Jok Ngong Mabiei and Herjok-Abuchok. We stayed there for about two months before returning to Pabuor.

Although the poor communities tried their level best to take care of us, life became quite unbearable in terms of accommodation and feeding. There was no building large enough to shelter us, particularly at night because the animal-shed (luak) was meant for cattle. Hence, we alternated with the domestic animals that used it at night while we occupied it during daytime. However, sometimes the rains forced us to mingle with them at night because our mosquito nets could not protect us. Despite all the difficulties we encountered, the villagers in Liaiwut were like water, and we were like fish. Our survival totally depended on them.

Imminent Fears of the Dry Season

The dry season was just around the corner, and the prospect of Akuot's group going to Ethiopia to meet Dr. John's group was uncertain. There were quite a lot of reasons why we feared the advent of the dry season at that time. Firstly, in those days, villagers used to leave their homesteads in search of drinking water and animal pastures during dry seasons. So our hosts were preparing to leave their villages. As a result, like fish and water, it was not good for us to remain in the villages alone without the villagers. Secondly, roads were passable in dry seasons. And that was the right time in which the government troops hotly pursued the rebels in the countryside. Above all, since we were not militarily trained and equipped, we were afraid to remain there and be associated with the rebels. Or else, we would become vulnerable to any possible attacks from the government army and other hostile groups.

Due to the scarcity of food and other problems, our platoon returned to the headquarters in Pabuor. While there, we tried once more to see Akuot but in vain, most probably, because he might have heard that we were planning to leave his group if they were not ready to go to Ethiopia and meet and reconcile with those of Dr. John Garang. His refusal to see us might have also been influenced by his lack of convincing arguments to put before us, given the fact that we, as the revolutionary youths, were not easy to persuade and rally behind.

In fact, the purpose of our trying to meet him was to make a request of him to issue us with an official written departure order to give us a safe passage on our return journey. We knew very well that without an authentic document with us, looming danger was waiting for us along the way; even mere villagers would consider us as real escapists, potential enemies for that matter.

In order to avoid such a likely and anticipated danger, we decided to meet Samuel Gai Tut and ask him to give us an official departure order. Our request was for him to allow us to return to Bor and wait there until the dispute between their forces and those of Dr. John was amicably resolved and all dangers removed along the road to Ethiopia. He did not give us any document but instead told us to leave saying that nothing bad was going to occur to us on the way.

So since all doors of dialogue and possible windows of assistance were closed in our eyes, we bravely decided to put everything to God in prayer and leave. To tell the truth, our concealed focus was not to return to Bor per se but to see how to manoeuvre our way out to Ethiopia via Akobo area. I believe that, as wise elders and political veterans, Akuot and Gai clearly read our minds and knew our hidden motive of why we were leaving them. That is why they refused to supply us with an authentic departure order.

From a Trap to Bondage

Tiresome Walk: we secretly planned and mapped out our possible routes from Pabuor up to Akobo where we would finally cross the river over to Ethiopia. Before we left there on the following day, Magot Jok-Guelhok and other young men, about twenty-one in number, were restless. So they took advantage of the darkness and left at night ahead of us with the hope that they were going to make it out safely.

After having said goodbye both to Akuot and Bahr el Ghazal group, we left Pabuor at around 9am, on 21 November 1983. We trekked southward towards Waat territory. The reason why we left the headquarters in broad daylight was to let people, especially the soldiers and the surrounding communities, know that we were free to leave.

The weather pattern in Southern Sudan is normally hot and humid. Within the last quarter of the year, the grass is above normal human height, almost sandwiching completely the paths in the countryside. So with such humidity and towering grass, we found it quite unbearable to trek along the path during daytime. But in spite of the tiresomeness of the journey, we tightened our belts and travelled the whole day and quenched our frequent thirst here and there with some dirty, stagnating water. Having something to eat was somewhat beyond our imagination because it was difficult to get food along such a hasty and threatening trip. We were like Israelites fleeing from the Egyptian realm of bondage to the Promised Land but unfortunately, ended up facing further suffering in the wilderness. The Israelites, however, suffered immensely because of their disobedience to the Lord who had led them out from Egypt. Unlike the rebelling Jews, we fled from a trap and entered into a short-term and frightening bondage of tribalism.

The following morning, we hurriedly moved towards Kaikuin area and hoped to cross the wilderness of Duochan by night to Akobo region. As we joyfully dragged on along the narrow path, despite a lack of sleep and hunger, we were happy because it appeared that the real enemy was now behind us.

Two young brave men, Ngong Malueth and another, heroically moved with us despite their serious sickness. We had even proposed early to leave them behind in Pabuor with Akuot's group to recover and follow us later, but they adamantly refused and moved with us. They simply refused to remain there because of the unfriendly environment.

Falling into merciless hands: at around 8am, on 22 November 1983, we suddenly and surprisingly met some armed soldiers along the way. Our hope was smashed into pieces again because we knew very well that these soldiers were part of Abdullah Chuol's troops. For one to fall into his merciless hands was very frightening. They asked us where we were coming from and going to. We told them falsely that we had come from Pabuor and were going to join their forces under the leadership of Abdullah Chuol. They nodded and commanded us to go with them.

The soldiers moved with us, some leading the way while others followed us with guns. Comrade Chuol was resting under a tree behind his office (luak) with some of his senior officers. Upon our arrival there, we were told to sit down under a big tree while soldiers stood guard around us. Then their leader went to Chuol, stamped his foot heavily on the ground and made his report about us. Then our leader, Stephen Kut was summoned to appear before the commander. I did not sit down but just stood with my small bag slung on my left shoulder to see what was unfolding. Within no time at all, I saw Kut lying on the ground on his stomach while receiving five severe lashes from a fat soldier obeying harsh orders from Chuol. To execute such corporal punishment on their subjects, they used a leather whip made of dried hippopotamus skin. The whip is very strong and hard to break. I told the others about Kut's beating.

One of us was carrying an automatic, empty pistol in his bag while other had a grenade. Thus, I told them to hide them inside some of the deep cracks in the ground, and they did that quickly without being seen by the standing guards. Being one of the leaders of the group, the soldier came back and asked for me: who is C.K? Kut passed on my name to them in the process of investigation. Like Jesus Christ during his humiliating arrest, I immediately presented myself to him and went right before Commander Chuol. I knew clearly that the dreadful flogging element was waiting in the merciless hand of the executing soldier to warm and discipline my innocent buttocks.

Chuol's question was very simple and authoritative. "Are you C.K?" He asked. "Yes I am", I responded. "Do you have an official letter, the departure order from the headquarters in Pabuor?" He asked. I said no and tried to expand about that, but he blared at me: "duai ye", meaning beat him. And within the twinkling of an eye, I found myself facing down at the mercy of this merciless soldier.

I neither knew for sure how my colleagues received their five terrible lashes nor did the executing man understood the severity of his beating. Yet I saw them trying to sustain their manhood on the ground in front of the shameless people. But my own wounded body and my soul have this to say: the painfulness of the first stroke is noticed during the receipt of the second stroke and so on. In fact, the severity of this corporal punishment was later seen on our scarred buttocks. After receiving my lashes, they took away my coat, some money, a small New Testament Bible in my possession, among other items.

At this time, we discovered that some of our men who left Pabuor just some hours before our departure were caught and held by Chuol's troops. Their leader Magot Jok received the same corporal punishment. We the leaders were then escorted to the prison (luak). Then three armed men mounted a very strict guard at the entrance of the prison under the unbearable heat of the sun. Our colleagues outside did not know the treatment we had inside the prison nor did we know what happened to them.

While in the prison, I said it would be good if Chuol and his men could just kill us the leaders and spare the lives of our innocent colleagues. At the same time, I pitied the guards at the entrance of the prison because they were just sitting in the sun. The implication is that our suffering was their suffering. But all in all, we surrendered the entire situation to the Almighty God. Because of our long and tiresome trek, my prison-mates and I fell asleep and took a good afternoon nap.

As we came to know later, Commander Chuol and some of his senior men went and rudely addressed the youngsters. He hated the way we had joined and stayed friendly with them, ate what they had and then tried to cheat our way out to join those of Dr. John. He knew our joining Dr. John meant us getting military training and returning to fight against them. His conclusion was that instead of leaving us to go to Ethiopia or return to Bor to be harassed and killed by the Arabs, it would be good for him to kill us all. He told them that they were going to hear his final word very soon. So my colleagues were fully aware that we were to die in the hands of this unkind man.

Shortly after his address, Mr. Gabriel Gany, the former commissioner of Bor, Jonglei Province, went and gave word to these demoralised young men. When they saw him, their strength was somewhat energised because, being the former government leader in Bor, they hoped that he was going to intervene and plea with commander Chuol to change his death sentence on us. But unfortunately, to them, his words were sharper and painful like a two-edged sword. For instance, Mr. Gany squarely put all the worst blames that had led to the sufferings of the Southerners on the shoulders of the Bor people. He blamed the government of Mr. Abel Alier for some malpractices that had led dissatisfied people in the south of the country to rebel and went to the bush. Mr. Gany also blamed the recent split within the members of the SPLM/A on some Bor people like Dr. John. His concluding remarks were:

> You heard that the Commander Chuol had sentenced all of you to death. He is the top authority here, and no one can change his word. Thus, my coming here is merely to inform you about the mistakes of your people, and so when you die, you don't blame anybody but yourselves.

Then he left, leaving grumbling youngsters to make good use of their desperate words. Apart from the heavenward intervention, all doors of influence seemed to be closed at this time.

While sitting under the tree under maximum guard, good showers of rain descended on the hostages. At around 2pm, some of Chuol's men did a rather crazy thing in that they called some of our men to go and collect some grains of sorghum for our feeding. The collection of this food brought a bit of relief because the hostages thought that the next thing was for them to be shown where to go and cook some meal for themselves.

What made it a crazy idea is that after collecting the grains, we were brought out of the prison and joined our colleagues who were parading in front of Commander Chuol and his men. We saw a platoon of well-armed men standing in parade next to us. It was under the command of a second lieutenant. Then Commander Chuol stood up to address us. He told us that he had changed his death sentence upon us because of some humane advice from some of his junior officers. He went on by saying that each of us was going to receive 50 strokes. Some of his soldiers were standing by ready with leather whips to carry out this order. He ordered us to return to Bor and not to come back again using the same route because, according to him, the road was closed indefinitely for those going to Ethiopia. He sternly instructed us to tell our people not to use the same route, or otherwise, they would meet their death at his hands.

While talking, one of us, Mr. Mawut Kon Mabil coughed and tried to clear his dried throat. Unfortunately, Mr. Chuol's anger flared, and hence, he ordered him to march to the front of the parade to receive some severe strokes. This made it hard, especially for the sick people among us, to try not cough. Nevertheless, I asked them to return my belongings that they had previously taken from me before being put into the prison. My money was actually returned to me.

Chuol turned to his platoon and gave them stern orders in Nuer language. He ordered them to chase us without rest and without entertaining any complaints from anyone along the road. The mission was to travel a distance from Kaikuin to Panyang, a court centre inside Jeng area, along Nuer – Jeng of Nyarweng border, a distance of about 70 miles. He also ordered them to shoot anyone complaining, trying to sit down, running away, etc. Chuol kept saying the word 'yot ye' while addressing his men. 'Yot ye', means 'shoot him'. These orders particularly sent an alarming bell ringing in the minds of our sick brothers, for the choice was to run – or they would die.

Then Commander Chuol ordered his men to carry out right away corporal punishment on all of us. But one of his senior officers beseeched him to leave us alone. He did so because he feared that some of us were going to succumb to death in the course of beating due to our general weakness.

The rescue we obtained from this Nuer officer is a direct proof of my non-stereotyping behaviour. If one Jeng is morally wrong, it doesn't mean that all people of Jeng are the same; or if a Nuer guy falls short of some admirable moral values, it doesn't mean that all Nuers are the same. We should avoid ethnocentric viewpoints and consider people on their personal merits, for all human beings have both advantages and disadvantages as part of their moral components, irrespective of their geographic, ethnic and religious backgrounds. After being convinced by his officer, Commander Chuol picked up a stick and chased us away from his headquarters, hence ushering in the start of the terrible chase.

Chase to Rob But Run to Live

We were told to move with the three tins of grains that were given to us, and so I saw Mr. Joshua Juach struggling with one tin. I don't think we were in need of those grains because our hunger immediately left us at the mercy of the danger of being killed at gunpoint. Our movement from Pabuor headquarters to Kaikuin was better by far than our harsh and rushed departure from Chuol's headquarters because the pursuing platoon started looting us of our meagre resources right within the eyesight of Mr. Chuol. Since none of us exactly knew the route from Kaikuin to Panyang, the order of the march was: some soldiers led the way, leaving some of their colleagues to follow behind while others flanked us on both sides. Although most of the pursuing soldiers apparently knew no foreign language apart from their own mother tongue, the commanding language was: 'Harwil', referring to the word 'hurry'. It was my first time hearing this new linguistic jargon, which I assumed is normally used to chase animals rather than human beings.

Without a single sign of personal satisfaction and humanity, and like hungry wolves devouring their prey, the platoon looted us of everything as we ran. Whenever they had enough of their loot, they hid goods with their known villagers or even in the bushes to collect later after accomplishing the mission. The villagers along the route were greatly bewildered at what was happening and continued to ask: "My children, what happened?" And the response was: "these are Jeng children trying to escape to Ethiopia to join those of Dr. John." Most of them were concerned with our situation, but what could they do?

About 7pm the same day, the escorting troops ordered us to sit down in rows. They circled us, and their leader said any money, wristwatch, good clothes or bag, etc. belonged to the government. He demanded us that we voluntarily surrender all our belongings before them; otherwise, they would use unlimited force to collect them.

There was complete silence among us, for besides refusing to surrender our meagre resources it was a chance for us to rest. Some of the soldiers begun to search us. I was the first to be singled out because they knew what was returned to me by those of Chuol's office. They told me to stand up and give them the money that I had. I tried not to comply with their demand. Instead, I said the money was not there, for what they had seen before had been intended for others, and thus I had given the cash out. But they insisted, and some of my friends told me to surrender all the money to them. Otherwise, they would torture or kill me. I reluctantly did as they asked and told them not to disturb me again because there was nothing else left with me.

They collected whatever they could lay their greedy hands on, including some dry food items like peanut paste. Yet some angry students hurled their precious items such as wristwatches into the bushes so that they would benefit no one. Stephen Kut was taking care of our collective funds. For safety's sake, he put them inside his socks. In the end, they took all their spoils and hid them in the surrounding bushes and took off with us again.

The soldiers chased us again like wild animals, and one could hear here and there the sounds of their sticks falling on any part of the helpless youngsters. As a result, some of us sustained serious injuries in the process. What do you think of the two sick young men? As a matter of life or death, they also ran with us. Some of us started bravely pouring out our disgust and called out insults fearlessly against our enemies. The pattern was the same as before; they chased us while looting any remaining items from us.

After some hours, we reached another high ground (panom) where they commanded us to sit down in rows. They took further loot from us and hid them in the surrounding bushes. The grains were no longer there because they had poured out during the chase. Most of us were completely plundered and left naked or half naked.

We took another long march towards Pannyang with our pursuing soldiers. Their unsatisfied eyes restlessly moved in our midst, looking for any possible remains. It was not easy for them to loot all items from such a huge number of running, cunning and energetic people in a short period of time, especially by night, although there was light from the full moon. For example, my small bag was still with me with a few clothes and books inside. I gave my small folder, full of vital documents such as school certificates, to Maluk-Abuajer to carry because all his belongings were already taken away by the soldiers. The soldiers maintained the same order and nature of march, beating and insulting people as they wanted.

At around 1am, they ordered us to sit down as before. The platoon commander gave an order of search based on 'ramkel', 'ramkel', which means one person, one person. Now it was too hard for us to dodge them with our little remains. I was sitting next to my friend Kut, and he told me: "C.K, let's go to be searched by them and relieved." Those of us whose belongings were taken by the soldiers were freed and in a better state, for the soldiers were not very severe on them again.

So I took my bag and moved forward and waited for the soldier to search me. Before me, a soldier was searching one of my colleagues. Upon taking the bag and opening it, he rummaged through personal effects, spreading clothing items and sorting what he supposed beneficial to him with the help of the moon light, while throwing back into the bag whatever was not good. Upon being released, the young man stealthily went behind the soldier and picked up his undergarments. This reminded me the fact that those who cheat others will go on cheating and being cheated by others, too.

It was now my turn for the search, and I gave him my bag. We both put our hands inside the bag and got hold of one large book, 'Rise Up and Walk' by Bishop Abel Muzorewa. He threw it down because his interest was not in the books. We did the same again and came out with batteries and body lotion, which he took and put behind him. After picking up another book inside the bag, he asked me whether I was a student, and my answer was yes. Then he told me to go with my bag. I nervously proceeded and sat down on the bag. The search was very meticulous; pockets were checked and desirable shoes, socks, clothes, including undergarments, wristwatches, etc. were removed and taken by the soldiers. One soldier took nice pairs of safari shoes from Mawut Kon Mabil. And being a humane man, he gave his torn pairs of shoes to Mawut in return to use on the journey, but Mawut asked him to take them all.

Enough was now enough, for if it meant beating and torturing, enough damage had already been done on the youngsters, and in terms of looting, almost all the meagre resources had been taken by the hungry soldiers from us. Commander Chuol was too far away to know whether we had reached Panyang or not as per his orders. Above all, the soldiers were exhausted and eager to hurry back and lay hands on their hidden loot before daybreak.

After giving a long, boring speech to us, the platoon leader showed us the way to Panyang without informing us whether that was the end of their journey. We thought that they remained behind to hide their final loot. But after covering a short distance without the usual chase by the pursuing soldiers, we began to wonder whether the soldiers were still with us or not. But none of them was around.

We were happy that we had at least been left alone to nurse our wounds and find our way out from Nuer area to Bor. We came to discover amazingly that Mr. Kut pounded our money into a sort of inedible flour inside his socks during the harsh march. Also it is quite interesting to know that Mr. Kut had also broken off the chain of his Seiko 5 wristwatch and hid it inside his month during the last search. While the watch was in his mouth, communication with others, especially the soldiers became very remote, and so his other belongings were taken without saying a single word.

Now that we were alone, sleep, tiredness, hunger, thirst, you name them, overwhelmed us. Following the right path by night also became a big problem because all of us, as foreigners, were not acquainted with that particular environment of Waat area. Total exhaustion returned upon the two sick youngsters. And they slowed us down. Nevertheless, I and other members of the group decided to slow down our speed to take care of the weak ones. The issue of being robbed of some belongings was no longer a threat since we had lost almost everything to the looting soldiers.

The Extension of an Olive Branch

The sun harshly rose behind us. It was almost the third day of our inescapable fasting. But our focus was to take advantage of the cold morning hours to trek along the road in pursuit of our colleagues before looking for anything to eat. We met two soldiers on our way going towards the opposite direction. They just bypassed us without a word. At around 10am, we rested in the shade of some large trees by a big pool. There we saw the same two soldiers heading for our direction, and a lot of questions began ringing in our minds as to what they were coming to do. They came and greeted us politely, told us about themselves and why they came to see us.

The prominent figure at the time in Lou Nuer area was Mr. Simon Gatwich Dual, the former paramount chief of Lou Nuer. He was a military commander of some armed groups in that area. His forces were neither part of those of Akuot Atem and Gai nor of those of Dr. John. The two soldiers mentioned above belonged to him.

After meeting us on the way, these soldiers went and reported us to their Commander Simon. They told him that we might have been looted and beaten by Chuol's forces and left with no food and clothing. Then he sent them back to find more information of what had occurred to us. According to these two soldiers, Gatwich was not happy with what had happened to us under the leadership of Chuol. Hence, he authorised them verbally to persuade us to join his forces and be ready to go with them to Ethiopia sometime in December 1983. But as for those of us who would have wanted to return to Bor, he gave them freedom to do so.

After hearing from them, we told these soldiers to give our appreciation to Commander Simon for his concern and invitation. However, since most of our people were already ahead of us going to Panyang, we told them to inform him that our final decision was going to go out after meeting all members of our group. But they asked me to put it in writing; so I wrote a letter and gave it to them for him. I mentioned in the letter all that was said by Chuol as well as what had taken place. Then I asked him to Give us a guarantee that the same forces would not come and attack us again if we were to go and stay with him.

Upon our arrival in Panyang, we found that some of our members had already left there for their respective places in Bor area. I immediately called a meeting to share with them about Simon's invitation. Some people were not even willing to entertain sitting in such a meeting to discuss an invitation from a Nuer guy.

In the end, few of us were left in Panyang, waiting a reply to our letter from Simon. The same two soldiers brought back a reply from Commander Simon. In his letter, he tried to answer all our concerns. He even went ahead and promised that those who dared to kill us would have to kill him first. After examining his letter keenly, we decided to honour his invitation and return to him. We went back and joined his forces, and they highly received us. We remained there happily while waiting to go with them to Ethiopia to fulfil our national obligation.

Colonel Majur's SPLA Platoon in Poktap

At the time we were in Pabuor, a gallant SPLA platoon under the leadership of Col. Majur Nhial Makol came from Ethiopia, attacked and captured Poktap. Poktap was the operational base of the Jonglei Canal Project. His forces remained there for some weeks. Although it was a short-lived lie, Akuot and Gai even alleged that their marauding forces had carried out this attack and captured Poktap. The fact of the matter is that reliable means of communication in the bush were very scarce during those days. That is why it was very hard to verify the information in a timely fashion.

Some of our colleagues went and tried to join Majur's platoon in readiness to move back to Ethiopia with them. But he told them to go and wait in their villages as he did not want the responsibility of feeding them. This gave some of them a bigger chance to proceed to Bor South to see their relatives and friends once more and to replenish their meagre belongings for the next trip to Ethiopia.

The Final March to Ethiopia

The leadership of the SPLA/M ordered Majur to move with his platoon and recruits back to Ethiopia. Bior Ajang Duot took advantage of this and closed his intermediate school in Pawel and joined Majur's forces. Most of his students and other civilians did the same. Almost all of those early recruits came from Bor area.

We closely monitored their movement because we decided to join his forces and move with them ahead of Gatwich's troops. It was unwise for anyone, especially recruits to lag behind on such an awful journey.

In the course of time, his forces found us somewhere near Waat. We were thrilled to meet them in their beautiful and enticing military uniforms and automatic rifles. One day, some of my colleagues and I went and met Majur and his men under a big tree. As we interacted, we keenly and with much interest listened to their inflated tales. To us, their uniforms and guns were very impressive. Thus, our aspiration was to cross quickly to Ethiopia and get some military training to enhance our esteem like those soldiers.

As we chatted at the time, comrade Majur told us without the slightest shame that SPLA/M was going to celebrate the forthcoming Christmas occasion in Juba. He added that we the recruits were not going to fight after obtaining military train-ing. On the contrary, we were just going to safeguard the revolutionary government from any possible reactionaries and foreign attacks. We were greatly bewildered as he proceeded with his unwelcoming talks, with his men supported his arguments. This was sometime within the second week of December 1983, and we were left with about ten days to celebrate the significant birth of Jesus Christ. To me, this was the biggest lie that I had ever heard in my lifetime.

After ending his talk, I immediately asked him whether the movement had enough manpower and equipment to capture the fortified town of Juba before the Christmas celebration of that year. Although his answer was a strong, concerted yes, I was still not convinced. Nevertheless, some of my naïve colleagues lamented bitterly and regrettably that they would not be able to fire their bullets on their common enemy after their training. I looked at them and with a smile told them just to hold their breath with the hope that they would shoot and shoot at their enemy until they could shoot no more.

But in the course of time, I came to realise that for one to become a real comrade in the SPLA/M he needed to be an expert liar, for lying is an essential element of any military propaganda. The Bible says, 'Then you will know the truth, and the truth will set you free' (Jn.8:31b-32), but the government system or any revolutionary ideology, for that matter, says, 'tell a lie, and the lie will set you free'. Of course, the SPLA/M did not celebrate the Christmas ceremony in Juba in 1983 until 25 December 2005.

We got military training, vigorously fought the Khartoum Government and its allies and unfortunately, some of my colleagues perished in the war. In a nutshell, Majur Nhial was not a known liar but as a loyal member of the SPLA/M, he had no option but to tell the big lie.

Now with a combined formidable force as our vanguard, we left Waat for Ethiopia via Akobo. Despite some difficulties on the way, we arrived safely and crossed the river to Tirgol, a small Ethiopian town along the Sudan-Ethiopia border. At last, our revolutionary feet touched the Ethiopian soil. Now we seemed to have left the danger behind us in Sudan. Here we celebrated our Christmas ceremony joyfully in an open air, and our preacher was none other than Col. Majur Nhial.

On 26 December 1983, Dr. John Garang and others came by a military helicopter to warmly receive us, and we welcomed him with a lot of joyous songs and dances. After giving his revolutionary speech, we were told that there was room in the helicopter to take some of us, with the promise that it was going to return to ferry the rest to Itang. My friend Stephen Kut and I plus others took this early advantage and went to Itang by plane. To confirm a revolutionary lie, the helicopter did not return to Tirgol for the rest. So they trekked again from there to Itang, taking more than a week on the way.

The Misfortune of the Nine Men

Though our reception in Itang was very warm, the period of our staying there was very short. For it was time for Jamus (Buffalo) Battalion to graduate from Bonga Training Centre and new recruits to replace it. What later came to be known as Tiger and Timsa (crocodile) battalions were organized in Itang and kept ready to go to Bonga. Upon our arrival in Itang, we were taken and organised into those new battalions and alerted to be ready to move to Bonga.

Nine Men's One Day in Zinc

On 31 December 1983, some soldiers went from Itang town to our military base, situated in the outskirt of the town. And they selected nine men who had at least reached the level of Sudan Secondary School Certificate. I was one of them. Also among the number were my friends Ardolo Mabil and Stephen Kut. We were hurriedly told to pick our baggage and dash on foot to Itang. Neither did we know where we were going nor what we were going to do. We were just following military orders.

But before long, some recruits came complaining as to why they were left out, though they had the required levels of education. The complainers might have known more than us in terms of what was happening that is why they complained. Yet we were not told about it. To show some fairness, we were told to sit some written and oral tests that were organised by Chol Deng Alaak. When the results came out, I was still among the number besides Stephen Kut, Ardolo Mabil, Ayom Simon Ngong, Jok Ngong Mabiei, Maker Biar Angeth, Jervasto Geng Dut and two other men. Since the authorities maintained the confidentiality of the information, we did not bother ourselves to know it. We were told to wait for further information.

Some military helicopters were very busy, landing and taking off from the small airstrip of Itang. After some time, we were told to board one of them. It took off, and within fifteen minutes it landed at a place we were not familiar with. We disembarked and jumped onto a military truck which was properly covered with a green canvas. It dashed out from there, passing through a small town as we could see through transparent, small windows. After a little while, we found ourselves in a tiny military base, hedged by some towering trees. Here we recognized some familiar faces smiling broadly at us as they rushed to shake our hands. As we embraced each other, they said, "Welcome to Zinc." Among the people we met were Paul Topich Liet, Chagai Atem Biar, Kon Bion, Gai Manyang Dot, Alfred Akuoch, Majok Mach Aluong and Elijah Hon Top.

But before we socialised enough with them, we were snatched away and found ourselves in a classroom with some equipment placed on desks. In front of us was a young, authoritative man who gave us some sheets of paper and instructed us to keenly copy some notes. Apart from that instruction, there was no introduction to the subject or the course in question. He then went out and left a young instructor in charge of the class. It seemed that our role as new military trainees was just to trust and obey our bosses. So we went ahead and quickly copied the notes, an assortment of writings of English alphabet mixed with dots and dashes.

As confused students, we examined the notes and equipment before us, murmuring and looking with amazement at each other. We were afraid to say anything that might fuel the situation. Nevertheless, Mr. Ardolo Mabil spontaneously gathered courage and asked the instructor a simple, intellectual question, saying: "Is this the course that we came here to do?" Mostly, to the majority of people, this type of question seeks just some clarifications, and the obvious, clever answer is generally and always in the affirmative, perhaps with no further investigative comments. But unfortunately, this simple, sincere question ended up in very rough philosophical debate, which shed unclear light on the futurity of the nine men within the rank and file of the SPLA/M.

The young instructor responded calmly to the question by saying yes. "It is a signal course," he said. This is a kind of communication system that uses some particular keys and words to pass on secret information between a sender and receiver. I am not an authority in this area; so you are entirely free to find your own proper definition somewhere else.

Thereafter, he sneaked out and came back with comrade Gier Chuang, the one in charge of this unit, to diagnose the question. By that time, he was an officer in the SPLA with the rank of second lieutenant. Gier tried to find out whether we were informed about the course at the time of our interview or not, and our response was simply no. To him, this came as a great surprise as to why we were not told about it. Instead, he asked us whether we did not like the course, for if so, there were other courses available within the movement for any of us to take. He went on and said that people were not forced to do something against their will.

Before any of us managed to speak, Stephen Kut wisely caught this cunning question in the air and neutralised it by saying that the essence of the question was just to gain some clarifications about the course rather than to discontinue it. He further mentioned that we the nine men were ready to carry out any course that was valued by the movement. As Kut talked in response to Gier's question, most of us went on nodding in affirmation to his wise words, for our primary aim of joining the movement was to take up arms and fight for the cause of our marginalised people.

Gier then encouraged us to go ahead with our course. He, however, warned us not to share our notes with other members of the movement who were involved in other courses there in Zinc. Then he dismissed the class with the hope of seeing us again in the next session. We got some relief like a bird escaping from a snare. We thought that the problem was now totally behind us.

Since we had little time to wash our clothes from the time we had entered Ethiopia from Sudan, we rushed to the nearby river and washed them. We then brought them back to the base and hanged them out in the sun to dry. Thereafter, we went back to socialise with our relatives and friends because some of them were on standby to follow Jamus Battalion and other forces which were already inside Sudan. It was a time of real jubilation and reunion because some of us had been away from each other for a long time. Also it was a very good moment to tell tales and exchange some viewpoints.

Stephen Kut, Kon Bion, Gai Manyang and I graduated from Rumbek Second-ary School in Southern Sudan, and so we were colleagues and friends with many things in common. Because of these intimate connections, they invited Kut and I to spend the night with them in their hut by sharing their two beds with us. We had a lot to tell them, and they had the same to share with us.

Nine Men Before a Panel

At around 8pm, as we were buried in the depth of our intimate conversations, we heard someone asking from outside as to whether some of the nine men were inside the hut, and the response was yes. He said we were urgently needed outside. We told him to wait for a minute. Then Kon and Gai asked: "Big guys, what have you done to be called at night?", and we responded with naught. As we dressed ourselves, they kept questioning us and wondering about the reason we were sum-moned by a security man. We were also trying to recall any possible thing we had done to warrant such an unusual summon. But we failed to get anything tangible except Mabil's question. After learning that we did ask a question in the class upon our arrival in Zinc, they nodded and said people were not free to question anything they liked without being misunderstood. Then they gave us a word of encourage-ment to go and know why we had been called. But since we were innocent before man and God, we did not worry. So we just went out and followed him into a hall where we were shown where to sit.

Prominent in the hall were Chagai Atem, Elijah Hon, Alfred Akuoch, Paul Topich and Thon Agot. Gier Chuang was also there. Immediately we believed that it was the same hard-dying question that was still haunting us down like known criminals.

We sat down calmly and waited to hear why we were called. One of the elders explained to us what Gier told them. And what came out clearly in his explanations was our refusal to take the course because it was below our educational standards. According to Gier, we had said that some of us were government officials, while others were university students, and hence, the course was sub-standard to us. Then we were given the chance to respond. We clearly repeated what took place in the class, to us, we thought that the misunderstanding was entirely solved and thrown into a trash can, not shelved away for some future reference.

After hearing our responses, Gier got very annoyed and said, "As men, you must not deny but repeat what you had said before. No problem, what happened had already happened whether you denied it or not. You will hear the outcome very soon." We also tried to strongly state our version of the whole issue, but the panel intervened and requested for us to leave the hall while they remained with Gier to see how to address this critical problem. So we unhappily went out with some lingering questions in our minds but with some hope that having said the truth, it was going to set us free. But we knew very well that we were in the realm where lies set people free.

We went back to our respective places to spend the remaining part of the night. Our friends were waiting to hear from us about the whole issue. After hearing from us, they made a few comments before all of us slept.

Nine Men Heading for Bonga

After we appeared before the panel to answer charges brought against us by Gier, the information infiltrated the entire atmosphere of Zinc and caused some shock to the people, for most of them knew us quite well as good people. At daybreak, our sympathisers poured in to find out from us what had occurred, and we repeated our story. As Gier and others cooked the problem, no one gave us a hint of what was happening. We were totally kept in the dark; even some of our real comforters did not know the actual trend of the event. Because of frustration or the like, the panel members did not bother to call us again and tell us about the outcome of their meeting with Gier. Generally, our well-wishers, because of their knowledge of how things were magnified and done in the movement, were very nervous and suspicious about the outcomes of such implications in terms of our fate. But were we afraid of the unforeseen consequences of our sincere question? The answer was a big no; why? Our conscience was very clear and innocent.

At around lunchtime, the information leaked out that the unfinished decision was to discontinue the course and take us to Bonga for infantry training. Assuming that this was the final decision, we were very glad. This is because our collective aim, as revolutionary fighters, was to get infantry training. Many people came and shook hands with us, wishing us all the best in our training.

On 1 January 1984, we left Zinc for Bonga by a military truck. Upon our arrival there, we were taken to Crocodile Battalion. Many people rushed surprisingly to meet us, for they did not know why our course was discontinued. We told them about the whole event and got on with our life.

Nine Men in Crocodile (Timsa) Battalion

Almost all of us were absorbed into one company and given charge over platoons. We came at the right time before the actual training started. We vigorously went on with our training with the high anticipation that after finishing there, we would go to Sudan to join the few SPLA/M gallant forces to fiercely engage the enemy.

In the course of our training, Comrade Salva Kiir Mayardit arrived in Bonga from Sudan, and we welcomed him gladly. Bior Ajang Duot, still a recruit, came with him to catch up with the training. Salva Kiir, one of the senior officers of the SPLA/M, was now coming to take care of the leadership of Bonga Training Centre, and he chose to put his headquarters in our battalion. The next battalion under training was Tiger. We went on with our training as normal.

Nine Men Expelled from SPLA/M

One late afternoon, our battalion returned from the field after doing some rehearsals and noisily stood in parade. In the course of singing revolutionary songs, coupled with ululations, we saw comrade Salva Kiir gently coming towards the parade, accompanied by his bodyguards, and took his position. Following the receipt of reports, he took charge of the battalion and talked at length, sharing with us some news concerning the movement and the enemy. His speech was punctuated with cheerful ululations, applauds and singing.

As he neared the conclusion of his lengthy speech, he mentioned something about nine men, and our ears stood still to tune to the right information, while we gulped sufficient air to enhance our physiological circulation. Did he mention this odd and chronic name for good or for bad? Surely, it was for bad. He went on by saying that there were nine men among us who were selected and sent by the movement to do a signal course in Zinc. But they went and turned it down, saying that it was below their educational merits, for some of them were government officials and university students in Sudan. He added that in order to resolve this issue, the top leadership of the SPLA/M sat and came out with the decision that these men were reactionaries, and so they were not fit to be in the movement; hence, they were expelled from both SPLA and SPLM. He further mentioned that the nine men were free to return to Itang and stay as refugees or return to Sudan and join the Khartoum government if they wished. Eventually, he called our names, and we marched out of the battalion one by one and paraded ourselves before him. We discovered that the same order in which our names were written in Zinc was the same order he read them out.

Right there we sought an audience with him, and he accepted it. Without missing a single word, we thoughtfully narrated the order of the whole event until that particular day he called us out. Above all, we requested him to give us a proportional punishment there in Bonga if we were wrong and allow us to continue with our training instead of sending us to Itang. We implored him earnestly to change this verdict and permit us to achieve our patriotic, national aspiration for the common good of our people.

In the course of our heartfelt talks, Salva Kiir keenly listened to all of us and asked us some investigative questions, which we responded to clearly. In the end, he said if the issue was within his leadership domain, he would have retained us there, and launched out rapid and thorough investigations before passing out his final decision. But unfortunately, to him, the issue was above his sphere of influence. This implied that it was at the highest echelon of the leadership of the movement. Instead, he commanded us to go to Itang and seek an audience with Dr. John Garang, if we dared to do so, as he was the right person to address the issue.

Now the only road clearly opened before us was the one leading to Itang. At that moment, about the midst of January 1984, the nine men were no longer members of the SPLA/M, for their sincere patriotic volunteerism was despised and rejected. Our relatives, friends and closest associates, including some of our trainers gave us a good farewell and well wishes.

Nine Men Back in Itang

The following day, we boarded a military vehicle and went to Itang where we were received with some warm handshakes. Akobo Mayen Lual was one of the people in charge of Itang administration. Mayen came and jokingly greeted us and said: "Big men, we are told to escort you to Mangok area en route to Sudan. What have you done?" We told him nothing apart from that chronic event that took place in Zinc and followed us up to Bonga. He said though they were ordered to escort us on the way to Sudan, we were going to remain there in Itang and sort our problem out with the chairman, Dr. John Garang upon his arrival there.

Why Escort Nine Men Back to Sudan?

We trekked to Ethiopia alone despite the hardships that confronted us along the way. We were very well familiar with that route. If we had intended to return to Sudan after being reviled and disrespectfully rejected by our own folks, we would have done so without the slightest need of guidance. But surprisingly, without seeking our own opinion first to know whether we did know the road back to Sudan or not, the movement advised its own well-known people to escort us.

If we had become potential enemies to the movement, what logic did the SPLA/M have to escort us, its worst enemies, back to Sudan? Can any genuine, hungry predator escort its attractive prey to its final destination without harming it on the way?

What I know is that in a typical warfare situation, when well-armed soldiers escort their helpless enemies, the latter end up in the forest for animals and birds to feast on. The former are not held accountable to any human authority because only God and non-human beings are the real witnesses of such concealed events. But they will surely account to the Almighty, the omniscient God in the end. However, we were happy that our own deceived brothers did not escort us back to Sudan; otherwise, these memoirs would not have been written.

Paradoxically enough, SPLA/M seemed to love its real enemies and hate its genuine friends; that is, it loves those who hate it and hates those who love it. Although we consistently ignored the magnitude and far reaching consequences of our simple, sincere question, its true colours were now quite obvious and very destructive. But we kept on searching our minds for any possible hidden, grave shortcomings that we might have ignorantly done to individuals concerned or to our beloved movement but totally in vain, for we were absolutely innocent before man and God.

Although we were victims of unknown but premeditated circumstances or ulterior motives, we still maintained our innocence and an unwavering allegiance to the SPLA/M. This is because we strongly believed that the movement was ours, and no one had an absolute right to chase us away deceitfully from it. Hence, going back to Khartoum Government to be levelled as people's traitors was far beyond our wise and patriotic thinking at the time.

Nine Men Under Strict Security Surveillance

Due to a lack of accommodation in Itang, we were told just to occupy one of empty luaks or cowsheds, look for some cooking utensils and take care of ourselves. The movement kept very tight security surveillance over us. For instance, one security man, heavily armed, was assigned to spend nights with us in our residence. We were, nevertheless, not concerned with such suspicious security arrangements simply because we neither had somewhere to go nor did we have any illicit plans against our own people, especially the SPLA/M. Instead, we proceeded with our normal life, interacting and socialising with other people with no single hint of fear. We even sympathised with that security guard assigned to closely monitor all our movements, for he was busily keeping relentless watch on innocent people, wasting vital and sufficient national resources, which might have been better placed in alternative schemes.

We wrote our appeal and submitted to the office of Dr. John there in Itang. We were told to wait for him. Some of the prominent people in his headquarters included the then Sergeant Major Isaac Tut, Sergeant Oyai Deng and Sergeant James Hoth.

Nine Men's Case Before Major Arok Thon

Major Arok Thon Arok defected from the Khartoum Government army to SPLA/M while we were in Itang. After meeting the leadership of the movement, he came to Itang with Dr. John, and our case was referred to him. He summoned us right away to appear before him, and we happily turned up.

He sat under a big tamarind tree with those of Chagai Atem Biar standing behind him. We went and sat on the ground before him and calmly waited for his judicial questions. His question was for us to explain what had happened, and one of us did that precisely. Then he asked us whether we would be willing and ready to attend the same signal course, infantry training, or any of the other courses valued by and useful to the movement, if we were asked by the SPLA/M leadership. And our answer was yes, indicating that we did not refuse either signal course or infantry training but were rather sent away because of having asked a simple question to Gier's assistant.

Comrade Arok then amazingly looked around and said, "These young men have no problem." And Comrade Chagai jumped in and said that the issue was simple but made very complicated by the manner in which Gier bypassed them and took it up with General Mesafint, one of President Mengistu Haile Mariam's generals. According to Chagai, General Mesafint then passed his verdict and told Dr. John that we were reactionaries and hence, not fit to be in the movement. Then Comrade Arok declared us innocent and freed us of any charges. He went on to say that since it was late to return to Bonga and finish our infantry training, we were to remain there in Itang to attend any of the forthcoming revolutionary courses.

Now we came to know how the whole issue got entangled in the political relationship between SPLA/M and the Ethiopian Communist Government. In the early days of our movement, any advice given to it (SPLA/M) by any member of the Derg Regime or Military Junta was considered highly valuable by our leadership for the sake of the revolutionary survival of the young SPLA/M.

Although the nine men became victims of such an unhealthy, inhumane and suspicious relationship, we cannot completely, however, deny the hospitality and enormous assistance accorded to SPLA/M by this communist regime. Through its assistance SPLA/M grew and became a potential revolutionary force, which eventually brought the Khartoum Government to submission to truth as shown by the signing of the historical accord, the Comprehensive Peace Agreement (CPA). As I edited this part of the writing, SPLA/M did not only give birth to the CPA but to the Successful Referendum that cemented the Independence of the Republic of South Sudan.

Nine Men Not Yet Free

Given the trend of our misfortune, we wondered whether we were completely out of the revolutionary noose. In regard to our problem being seen by Major Arok, the likely member of the SPLA/M Military High Command, many people believed that it was done once and for all. So we were considered to be absolutely out of the concerted snare. We were, nonetheless, still nervous and became doubtful like the Thomas in the Bible because we were told that some important people in the movement were experts in not forgiving and forgetting.

The speed of wildfire is dependent upon the weather and the type of vegetation. When the wind is fierce and the vegetation is dry, the wildfire gains greater momentum. But as soon as the wind dies down, and the fire reaches greenish and soft vegetation, the wildfire tends to lie low, although it is not completely dead. That is why the flames in a burning forest always appear and disappear.

Like prairie fire burning out of control, the case of the nine men seemed to take the strange nature of wildfire, dying and reviving seemingly. For instance, while in Itang, SPLM invited interested candidates to turn up for an interview for the second batch of the political course in Zinc. Since Major Arok had finished our case and declared us free of all alleged charges, we were free to contest in this course with other members of the movement. So we sat for it and knew that most, if not all, of us were going to make it through. Unfortunately, when the results came out, nine men were proven fools, and so their names did not appear on the list of the best candidates.

We earnestly tried to find out why all of us failed, but none, even our best friends, took courage to leak out the secretive information. Were we still culprits in the eyes of the movement? To us, we did not fail the course. On the contrary, we believed that the movement did not welcome the verdict passed by Major Arok, declaring us innocent. Yet the authority was still wrong because it failed to advise him properly so as to dance according to its ways instead of examining the case fairly.

In order to prove our sudden stupidity that led us to fail the course, and also to find out whether our enemies were still dogging us, we turned up and contested the next course, an information course. Although we were politely permitted by the movement to take exams, the outcome portrayed once more our foolishness, for all nine men failed again. We were totally mum, not knowing what to do and how the whole issue was going to end.

In our earnest quest for truth, one of the key security guards in Dr. John's office confined to us that in the information course, nine men highly passed and took number one through to number eight and surfaced again in number ten but were turned down by the SPLA/M leadership during the final analysis. The leadership said we were not yet very trustworthy to take such an important course. Thus, we were not real fools but wise men made fools by the cunning men. Although our own people despised and shunned our unequivocal loyalty, we maintained our firm allegiance to the movement, and decided to wait and see whether the movement would still turn us away from the next infantry training.

Nine Men Help Organized Khoriom (Locust) Batch

Although despised by a few in the SPLA/M, the nine men were highly valued within the rank and file of the movement. They knew our historical roots, and we were not easily swayed by unhealthy winds of intimidation and jealousy. For others to justify our patriotic loyalty and volunteerism, we happily accepted an offer extended to us by Comrade Francis Ngor who was in charge of Itang Base. He told us to organise the huge numbers of recruits into formal military forces, ranging from squad, platoon, company and battalion. Organising the whole division of Khoriom by writing by hand the exact particulars of the recruits, including their ethnicity, religious and geographic backgrounds, was not an easy job. This and other administrative tasks in the camp took us several weeks to accomplish, and we excelled in that. We joyfully did our work, not under any slightest compulsion, for we loved the movement, though it hated us.

Further Humiliation of the Nine Men

To show that some of the higher ranking SPLA/M officers did not know the magnitude of our problem, one day Comrade Francis Ngor sent an urgent order to us to turn up with our belongings at his residence. As this was a military order, we hurriedly took our things, deserted our luak and surrendered ourselves to him timely. He told us to be ready to go somewhere for a course of the artillery unit. Did the movement sincerely accept our loyalty at that point and was, hence, willing to allow us to take that course? Or was Francis Ngor ignorant of our chronic sickness, which was still under a laboratory test? Either way, we anxiously waited to see if our known security surveillance was going to agree with him.

Comrade Francis Ngor, despite his high-ranking military and political position in the SPLA/M, was proven wrong by the security guards. And so we were humiliated and disgracefully signalled out, especially in the very eyes of some of the recruits whom we militarily organised. Out of such dehumanising frustration, we bravely protested against that sort of dogmatic, childish behaviour. For if they knew we were not needed to attend such a course, why had they called and ashamed us before others? But as usual, we swallowed the bitter pill, took our luggage and went back to our luak where our bewildered residents welcomed us back. Francis Ngor was also annoyed because he did not know the depth, length and width of the nine men's problem. But what was he to do about it? Nothing, because, like Comrade Salva Kiir, our problem was beyond his reach, and the only thing he told us was the word, 'sorry'.

We even became nervous that our chances of returning to Bonga were becoming minimal. Our fear was based on the way we were continuously treated and humiliated by our own people among our own brothers and sisters. As our case got complicated, some of our relatives, friends and closest associates began to rethink and distant themselves from us for the fear of being implicated and entangled in the same snare by the best loyalists and protectors of the movement. Yet by taking their safeguarding move, deep inside our sincere hearts, we sympathised with them because we did not want them to be like us. We were capable of bearing our own cross. Due to this high level of suspicion and frustration in the movement, one of the nine men, a Nuer guy, sneaked out and returned to Sudan sometime within the first quarter of 1984. Since then, I have never met him and do not know whether he is still alive or not.

Nine Men Seek Elders' Counsel

One day, we met the late uncle Martin Majer Gai Ayuel, a distinguished lawyer and veteran politician, in Itang and shared our misfortune with him. After keenly listening to us, he took a cautious, silent approach and told us to follow it up with the concerned authorities and wait for the outcome. As an experienced elder and lawyer, he knew more than us about the jungle life and how things were done in the movement. Above all, he might not have known the gist or the essence of our problem.

Again on another day, my colleagues sent me to go and share our problem with uncle Elijah Malok Aleng, a veteran politician. During our talks, he bluntly, as part of his known character, told me that he had heard our problem and the final decision arrived at by the movement was for us not to attend any course apart from returning to Bonga for the next infantry training with Khoriom Division. He advised me to tell my colleagues to wait to go to Bonga with the new recruits, rather than seeking and contesting for any other courses. My colleagues and I were extremely happy to hear that, for he told us nothing but the truth, though he was one of the new recruits coming from Sudan. He had the actual information on his fingertip because he, as a respected elder, was closely associated with the top leadership of the movement. Then we proceeded with our normal routines within the division while waiting joyfully to return to Bonga.

CHAPTER SIX

The Start of the Darkest Period in the SPLA/SPLM

Akuot and Gai's Group Honour their Promise

In the course of our staying in Itang, Akuot Atem and Gai Tut's group adhered to the promise they had made earlier before those of Lual Diing and us in September 1983 in Pabuor. They did promise to destroy Nyagatism and move to Ethiopia during the dry season to talk peace with the group of Dr. John Garang to unite SPLA/M. So they trekked from Sudan right to Itang and put up in an area known as Luakat in the outskirt, west of Itang. They expected to meet Dr. John and his group. While there, they mingled with their Sudanese fellows by exchanging friendly visits with those living in Itang. Unfortunately, I did not visit their Luakat because I knew none of them intimately.

As Dr. John and his colleagues in the top leadership were away from Itang at that time, Akuot and his followers waited patiently for them. But in the course of time, unconfirmed but unhealthy rumours filled the tense, political and tribal atmosphere in Itang and beyond. The rumours indicated that some heavily armed soldiers of the movement, backed by fortified Ethiopian troops, were coming to capture Akuot and his men. We did not know for sure whether the rumours were emanating from some reliable sources, and so we took them slightly. Nevertheless, Akuot and his men took them seriously, and without warning, they took off strategically and returned towards the Sudan border.

On their way to Sudan, Akuot and his colleagues bypassed some recruits who were going to Itang. They did nothing bad to them, though they knew very well that they were going to get some military training from those of Dr. John. I heard that Abdullah Chuol tried to prevent a group of recruits under the leadership of late Makhor Lual from proceeding to Itang, but Gai Tut commanded him not to do so. And so most of those recruits came to Itang, praising Gai as a real patriotic leader but denouncing Abdullah Chuol for being unfriendly and non-nationalistic.

Having stayed with them for those few months in Pabuor, we discovered that Gai Tut had the common interests and aspirations of the Southern Sudanese people deep inside his heart. And that is why he disputed with Abdullah Chuol for preventing the recruits from joining the group of John Garang. Gai knew very well that these recruits were going to get proper training and some armaments and become their potential enemies. To Gai, the window of opportunity to peace and unity among the sons and daughters of Southern Sudan was not completely locked, though Dr. John and his followers did not turn up to meet them in Itang.

Gai Tut's Death Marks the Darkest Period

As Akuot and Gai continued with their followers back to Sudan, they reached a small army garrison of SPLA at Thiaijak and decided to attack it so as to replenish their armaments. In the course of fighting, Gai Tut unfortunately lost his life. To SPLA/M and its alliance, his death might have been seen as a clear victory. They hoped that Gai's death plus other factors were going to either force Akuot's group to surrender to the main SPLA/M or starve it to natural death. But as history tells, they were completely wrong.

SPLA/M and its alliances failed to know the outstanding truth that war between relatives is always the fiercest and long lasting than war between aliens. With aliens, if one defeats the other, it is fine because they are not going to live together anyway to constantly remind themselves of the consequences of their war. Unlike the war between aliens, relatives who have the same geographic, socio-economic and political roots, tend to nurse the consequences of their war, especially those defeated, forever. Sometimes, the winning party tries to impose itself on the losing partner so as to perpetually maintain its social status. But the losing side constantly tries to change the historical equation physically, even if it means siding with its potential enemy to help him revenge on his own brother.

As people with a lot of similarities and common pride, there is always no winning aspect in a war between relatives. Let me assure you, you cannot definitely defeat your own brother, no matter how strong you are, because such a war will never end, only unless if one of you migrates to a far distant land so as to avoid seeing each other frequently. It is a known fact that pressure begets resistance. Hence, it is always wise for brothers and sisters to relentlessly maintain their peaceful atmosphere and consciously avoid any possible chance of igniting unnecessary feuds among themselves, which will spill over to the next generation. In a nutshell, the scars of war between relatives are more deeply rooted than the ones between foreigners.

SPLA/M and its alliances also failed to understand or totally and ignorantly underestimated the historical, political principle of divide and rule in that their minor difference with Akuot's group was the greatest opportunity for the Khartoum Government to side with the defeated, helpless party and turn them against their own brothers and sisters in Southern Sudan. In order to meet their political and racial aspirations, the Khartoum Government immediately jumped in and tribalised the difference between the leadership of the SPLA/M and Akuot's group as something between Nuer and Jeng. And it eventually engulfed almost all the ethnic groups in Southern Sudan.

Disunity among Southerners was their worst weakness, but on the contrary, it was the best strength of the Khartoum Government. For it enabled it to prolong its divisive policies of socio-economic, political and religious oppression and marginalisation, especially in the south of the country. In fact, the worst enemy of Southern Sudanese people was their destructive disunity rather than the Khartoum Government. It is high time for South Sudanese people to learn how to appreciate their God-given diversities and live together as brothers and sisters. They must understand that their nationalism is very paramount and above their unique spirit of tribalism. Unity in diversity should be the glue that binds them together for their common welfare.

The death of Gai Tut marked the beginning of heavy bloodshed and the darkest period, particularly in the history of Southern Sudan. Unfortunately, his death turned those minor, personal leadership differences between Dr. John Garang, Akot Atem, and Gai Tut, among others, into a tribal domain, first of all between Jeng and Nuer and later on among other varying ethnic communities in Southern Sudan. And because it favoured the Khartoum Government, it came and armed those whom it lured and turned them against their own brothers and sisters in Southern Sudan. It is humiliating and shameful to admit that the numbers of those who perished and suffered in the ignorant hands of their own brothers and sisters in the south of the country are more than those killed and suffered in the very hands of the potential enemy, the Khartoum Government.

Had both rebelling parties swallowed their degrading pride, made sacrificial peace, joined hands and fought their common enemy, the war between Khartoum Government and marginalised areas would have ended shortly with less bloodshed and minimal physical destruction. But the Holy Bible puts it wisely that "Pride goes before destruction, a haughty spirit before a fall" (Proverbs 16:18); because of the pride of the two warring parties, irrespective of their ethnic, political, economic and geographic similarities, the war, unfortunately, painfully took a long time with the loss of millions of precious lives, displacements of millions of innocent and vulnerable people, destruction and displacements of huge beautiful and varied wildlife, immeasurable destruction of homesteads and general physical infrastructure, especially in the south of the country. Now do the survivors of this destructive war take wise counsel of the miseries brought upon the land by their selfish and myopic pride? History is the good judge to answer this question and more.

A Farewell to Bonga

After the graduation of Crocodile and Tiger Battalions from Bonga Military Training Centre, the Khoriom (locust) batch joyfully poured into Bonga around May 1984. Some of the nine men and I were given some leadership responsibilities in Rad (lightning) Battalion. Kut Bol, Jok Ngong and Geng Dut were in charge of the first, third and fourth platoons respectively, while I took care of the second platoon.

How did our battalion get its name, Rad? One day, one of our men was struck dead by lightning in the nearby forest while we were carrying out our normal military routines. So when the time came for the SPLA/M leadership to give significant names to all the battalions, ours was named Rad, commemorating the death of that man as well as to show how this battalion, like lightning, would bring severity on government forces in battle fields. Yes, as with other battalions of Khoriom, Rad lived to its name and expectations in fighting against the enemy.

The Fate of Illness

Having vigorously and speedily started the training, our only hope was to get done with it, get our weapons and join our fellow fighters in the fields to wage the common cause. My workload, as a platoon leader, was big and required a lot of managerial skills and knowledge. But given my inborn leadership capability and physical strength, I was successful.

One day, I begun to feel unwell. I suspected I had malaria but hoped that it was quickly passing. I went on with my work and visited our local clinic where I was given some tablets to take. However, I continued to lose appetite and physical strength with each passing day. In spite of the sickness, I kept dragging myself to lead and attend daily lessons and practices with further hope that the sickness was not going to stay with me very long. It was also a norm in Bonga that sick trainees were not permitted to rest only unless the severity of such sickness was very obvious and life threatening.

On a particular occasion, there was a joint demonstration whereby all the battalions climbed on a huge mountain east of the centre. I took courage and went with my colleagues. But while on the mountain, the severity of the sickness reached its peak in that I lost any sense of attention and was unable to sit upright. Hence, I laid on the rock and waited for the lesson to finish. The illness eventually defeated my faint hope. And that occasion was the last time I put my heroic feet on that famous Ethiopian mountain and oversaw the towering hills and mountains, which sandwiched this historical training centre, Bonga.

The sun was already behind the horizon when the formidable combined forces of Khoriom were dismissed for the day. I politely told some of my closest associates who had tried to walk with me to go ahead, insisting that I was out of danger. Do you know what happened? They dashed down to the foot of the mountain like troops of locust, shouting here and there with their loud voices being echoed by the surrounding hills and mountains.

I had been on this particular mountain on several occasions and rejoiced with others to descend and ascend on it. But now it was just a matter of tightening my belt of hope and descend on it slowly or despairing and wait patiently for the wild beasts to feast on me. I chose the former and dragged myself to the seemingly bottomless foot of the mountain, while pausing here and there to gather some precious breaths. As I moved along in the darkness, I felt like I was dreaming and seeing visions. Eventually, I reached the camp and fell headlong on my bedding. Then I was rushed to our ill-equipped and poorly stocked primary health care unit. There I was looked after by some of our substandard medical personnel who frequently saw precious souls passing on without some dignified medical remedies. Of course, one could not expect some modern health services in such a ruddy place where people are taught how to kill and defend themselves. Despite being overwhelmed with the huge number of in-and-out patients, the few health workers tirelessly tried whatever they could to take care of their sick comrades.

I thought I was going to recover quickly and resume my training, but my admission there was another step out of Bonga Military Training Centre. The magnitude of my illness kept increasing with the passing of time to the extent that others and

I came to believe that my bones were going to remain, like others, there. My good friends and associates ceaselessly kept praying for and visiting me on my sickbed.

I clearly remember that on a certain day, sometime in the afternoon, the trainees were out in the field, and I was lying on my sickbed when I suddenly became somewhat insane. I don't know where I got physical strength. I uttered some words and tried to stand up and leave the ward, but people came and tried to calm me down. One of those people was the late Manyok Ayii Jok. This event took less than half an hour before I gained sanity.

Because of the worsening of my health situation, in July 1984, I was eventually referred to Itang for further medical treatment. My best friend Stephen Kut and others escorted me on foot up to the Ethiopian Military Garrison where we were put on a military truck and left Bonga for Itang via Zinc. Unfortunately, my friend Stephen Kut and I saw each other for the last time at that moment.

On the way before reaching Zinc, I saw something flashing like a strong lightning. From that point up to Zinc, I neither recognised what happened to me nor did I feel the roughness or smoothness of the journey. I was completely alone on that particular portion of the road, hearing and feeling nothing; I was motionless. This is a unique part of my life in which someone else is to account for.

To correctly reconnect my life story, just like somebody waking up from a deep sleep in an empty room, I suddenly opened my eyes, looked around but seeing no one except hearing some talks in my vicinity. I did recognise that I was alone in an empty truck, and I knew that it was in Zinc because I was familiar with its environment. I gathered my strength, stood up and tried to climb down from the truck. But like a ghost, people did not believe their eyes and joyfully rushed to help me to come down. Some of them were shedding delightful tears while thanking God and calling my famous name: "C.K! C.K! C.K!" I smiled with them and thanked God too for allowing me to see the sun once again.

Those who were with me on the journey narrated what had happened. They told me that I lost consciousness on the way, and when they informed the driver, an Ethiopian, the vehicle stopped immediately. After seeing that I was completely dead, he told the others that they were not going to do anything to my body there along the road but to take it to Zinc where it should be buried. So to bury me in Zinc became part of the reason that took the truck there.

I suppose that while lying dead on the truck in Zinc, people were conferring about the process of my burial. Nevertheless, the Lord, the only source of life, was not in that deal but was rather conferring on how to restore my life. 'The Silent Hand' was really upon me. I at last realised that the fate of my illness was no longer the issue of getting better quickly and continue with my military training, but rather it became a matter of life or death.

The following day, we proceeded to Itang, not knowing where and with whom I was going to stay with as none of my relatives was there. Upon our arrival there, some of the people in the camp came to see whether some of their own people were among us. It was in this process that the Lord brought Paul Tiopich Liet and Jol Kuol Jiel into my life. Of course, we knew each other before. After greeting me and finding out what had happened to me, Paul politely asked me whether there was one in the camp to take care of me, and my answer was no. He then requested me to stay with them, and I gladly accepted his offer. They took my baggage and led me to their homestead where Jol joyfully offered to share his small tent with me. The hospitality accorded to me by all members of the family at that time is commendable.

Later on my maternal uncle Paul Alier Nyok requested me to go and stay in his newly built hut. And this became like my own house where I ended up hosting many friends and relatives, especially when they were sick.

My Life in Itang

I followed up my medical treatment in Itang Hospital and recovered slowly. But it was now too late for me to return to Bonga, for the training was over, and people were just waiting for graduation. Since the sickness caught me before I successfully finished the training, I considered it not honourable for me to graduate with those who had done it completely. Thus, my aim was to recover and join Mormor batch, which was waiting to replace Khoriom in Bonga. But some people were not comfortable with this idea because they believed that the training that I had had both in Tiger and Timsa as well as in Khoriom was enough to qualify me as a good SPLA fighter.

The Death of Stephen Kut Bol

Stephen Kut Bol Leek was a handsome, strong, courageous, sociable, intelligent and wise young man with undeniable, inborn leadership traits. While at Rumbek

Secondary School, Kut focused on additional mathematics and finished successfully. He hoped to pursue an engineering career. He wisely served as the chairman of the students' body in 1981–1982 in the same school. He was a very patriotic man and ready to sacrificially pursue with others the noble cause of the oppressed people. According to what he told me, before we left Bor for Ethiopia in August 1983, his elder brother who had participated in Anyanya One war strongly advised him to pursue his educational studies instead of going to the bush. But Kut vehemently turned down his advice. In a nutshell, Kut is one of our gallant young men who sacrificially poured down their precious blood before sowing their own biological seeds to emancipate the poor Sudanese masses from the merciless jaws of the oppressors.

In August 1984, some battalions, including Rad, were released from Bonga and sent to Sudan to confront the enemy. To show our intimate relationship and his love for me, Brother Stephen Kut convinced the leadership in Bonga and took my gun with him with the hope of giving it to me somewhere near Itang, for he did not like to see me return to Bonga for the third time for the same military training. But because of the lack of proper communication network at the time, I did not get the information in time to join the battalion en route to Sudan, and so they went with the gun.

Upon their arrival inside Sudan, particularly around Waat area, these battalions were repeatedly attacked by their own brothers from Anyanya Two of those of Akuot Atem and Abdullah Chuol. Stephen Kut was commissioned as second lieutenant and put in charge of a platoon during their graduation in Bonga. While leading his men, he died heroically in the battle of Rim, fighting a senseless war. Yet I call it a senseless war because it was not a real fight between SPLA and Khartoum troops but rather an unfortunate and a senseless fight among the sons and daughters of the same mother and father, the Southerners. Also among the fallen heroes was Herjok-Abuchok.

This unfortunate news about the heroic death of Stephen Kut and other beloved friends and associates reached me in Itang, and it was like a bitter pill for me to swallow. And, of course, I did swallow it because this was the route we had chosen to liberate ourselves from the long bondage of oppression and mental enslavement. Anyway, this was the beginning of a series of unbearable tragic news from different parts of Sudan, especially Southern Sudan. Surprisingly, this news heightened my patriotic spirit, making me take up my gun officially and join the rank and file of the movement like my dear brothers and sisters to carry on a sacrificial war to enable us realize our undeniable aspirations of the oppressed Sudanese people.

Beer Machar Deer

In December 1984, some armed Murle men launched an organized raid, killing more than 30 people and taking away thousands of cattle. Those who died on the side of Deer include Aguto Gol Deng, Majer Guet Mach-Jiel, Deng Magot Let, Garang Mach Mayen, Joh Ajak Mach, Yuor Lual Yuor, Aret Guut Mayen, Alier Garang Leek, Kuol Jam Aleng and Kucha Guut. This was a devastating, savage fight because the precious lives lost from both parties was not nearly equivalent to the loot taken. It is one of the senseless, tribal struggles, which were of no benefit to our people in the south of the country because these are some of the deeply rooted obstacles to peaceful human co-existence and developmental activities. It is time for our people to learn how to live together as brothers and sisters for the common good of mankind. They must know that their major, real problems include disunity, illiteracy, poor infrastructure, disease, insecurity, poverty, inhumanity, etc. Let's love each other as we love ourselves, while we respect and cherish our ethnic and geographic uniqueness. This was also one of the bitter pills that I painfully swallowed in Itang.

My Pastoral Works in Itang

Many people wisely convinced me to drop my dogmatic idea of returning to Bonga for the third time for an infantry training. Instead, they advised me to wait for the next batch of shield three training. I took this counsel and waited there to go to Bilpam during the time of interviews and general screening.

John Madit, an evangelist and a trained military soldier of Battalion 105, was in charge of the Christian church in Itang. It was a kind of inter-denominational church. It was through John that in 1985, I began my pastoral work, especially the sharing of God's word on Sundays. While working for the SPLM in Itang from 1986 up to 1987, I spared sufficient times to do my pastoral work. Besides preaching the word, I was given the chance to teach the books of wisdom to the interested members of the church in particular and the public in general. I also started an adult literacy class in the church to teach English language. As a major part of my gifts and talents, and because of the backing of the Almighty God, I was successful in my pastoral work.

My Christian Faith vis-à-vis My Patriotism

Although I had been discharging my revolutionary work to the best of my capability, Alternate Commander (A/CDR) Dr. Amon Wantok, a SPLM camp administrator, was not happy to hear that I was also involved in the church activities. He might have been informed by one of his anti-Christ personnel. But he did not openly express his displeasure to me until one day, after official business hours, when he tactically and diplomatically cornered me, and I walked with him to his house. In the course of our short conversation in his home, he asked me how the work was progressing on, especially the ideological class, and I gave him a definite answer that it was fine. He then politely explored whether it was correct that I was involved in some church activities, and I said yes. He further asked whether the ideological class of Marxist-Leninist philosophy was not good with me, and I told him that it was good. Then he lamented that if people like me were still associated with the church work, then it was not good.

Initially the SPLA/M Marxist-Leninist ideology was taken seriously to the extent that those who maintained their Christian faith were openly ridiculed and discriminated in one way or the other. They were named names. Those wearing the newly acquired communist uniforms, although they were not true communists at heart, were applauded and favoured by the movement. In order to attain the leadership's favours, many people dropped their Christian names and despised Christianity openly. As one of the diehard followers of Jesus Christ, I refused to be swayed like a little baby by the unhealthy winds of intimidation and human favours. My religious faith was not in any way conflicting with my revolutionary duties.

After listening keenly to Dr. Amon's revolutionary and ideological concerns, I told him that I truly love the Marxist-Leninist philosophy that the movement had embraced, and so I was still loyal to the movement. Then he questioned why I still maintained my loyalty to Christ if I was really interested in the new ideology. I told him that I did not actually have faith in those comrades who tended to have faith in Christ but turned away overnight, abandoned their Christian beliefs and deceitfully said that they were real communists. Furthermore, I pointed out that for one to be grounded in a new faith, it always takes time and a personal decision. I told him that faith is not imposed on people but is a free choice, not imposed through ideological intimidation. I went on to explain that I was born into and grew up in the African Traditional Religion, the religion of my forefathers, until the time I got exposed to Christianity. But as ATR was deeply rooted in my life, it was not just replaced at once with Christianity. It rather took about six years, a duration of complete exposure and personal conviction, before I made an individual commitment to Jesus Christ as my Lord and Saviour.

However, in comparison, I elaborated further that if I were not convicted enough about the essence and the lifesaving power of Christianity, I would have turned it down and continued with my faith in the ATR. In conclusion, I told him that I was going to follow the same procedure by vigorously and thoughtfully studying the Marxist-Leninist philosophy and comparing it with Christianity before I made an informed-personal-final decision of whether to accept or reject this new belief. And in the process of examining the essentials of this new belief, I had to continue with my Christian faith as the way of life so as to avoid creating a spiritual void within myself. After spiritually and logically disarming him, Dr. Amon smiled at me, we shook hands, and I left him for my home.

Although I went on with my work and studies on the Marxist-Leninist philosophy, I did not see this ideology quite useful to displace Christianity in my life. For Jesus Christ says: "I am the way and the truth and the life. No one comes to the Father except through me" (Jn.14:6). My main focus in life is to return to my Creator when my life ewes away from this world. And so since Marx and Lenin did not promise in their communist ideology to be the truth and the life and the way to God, I scornfully turned it down and went ahead joyfully with my Christian life.

In principle, one of the very essentials of communist ideology argues that religion belongs to an individual but the state belongs to all nationals, and hence, there should be a separation between state and religion. It further argues that people, irrespective of their individual beliefs, should not be discriminated against but accorded equal opportunity by their government. That is, an atheist and a religious believer should have equal rights before the national law. But in the SPLA/M, the newly half-baked communists did not adhere to these core principles. So what we had was not the genuine Marxist-Leninist ideology but a kind of weird communism.

My Works for SPLM in Itang

In 1985, Dr. Amon Mon Wantok, maybe because of our being together as hostages under the leadership of Akuot and Gai Tut or the like, requested me to work for the SPLM, especially in the library. I told him to give me time to think about his offer. I was very reluctant to work in the camp simply because it was not my choice to be there, but I was there due to my sickness. I preferred to be in the battlefields. After making some consultations with my closest associates, especially Elijah Alier Ayom and Jacob Biar Mach, I took up the job on a voluntary basis.

My work consisted mainly of looking after the library as the head librarian and helping with the organization of the Marxist-Leninist ideological class. In addition, I was to register all the educational elite among the new recruits and keep the records well for easy future reference. Comrade Johnson Thon Reng, a political commissar, was my immediate boss, and I had some men under my jurisdiction. I loved my job and did it well. It was in the course of my work there that I came to know Comrade Peter Aduok who replaced Johnson Thon, and hence, became my immediate boss. I was also involved in the publication of the SPLM Newsletter, headed at the time by comrade Chagai Matet. In the course of this work, I published some of my own writings, and the following poems are parts of them.

Comrade

Comrade!

Comrade!

Comrade is a language commonly spoken in the realm of ants.

Comrade is a language commonly known in the kingdom of bees.

Comrade is a tongue commonly spoken in the realm of love.

Comrade is a language commonly spoken in the realm of progress.

Comrade!

Comrade!

It is absurd for Mr. Darkness to call Mr. Light comrade.

It is mere foolishness for Mr. Light to call Mr. Darkness comrade.

It is absurd for a tongue that flows with hatred and lies

To dive the lake of comrade.

It is absurd for a master to call his slave comrade!

It is absurd for a slave to call his master comrade!
It is totally absurd for Mr. Tiger to call Mr. Goat comrade.
Comrade is a strange language in the realm of hatred and lies.
It is absurd to call a person you despise a comrade.
Comrade is unknown speech in the kingdom of jealousy and selfishness.

Comrade!
Comrade!
Let's practise what we preach!
Let's practise what we preach!
When we perish together for a common goal,
We are comrades.
When we toil together,
We are comrades.
When we cry together,
We are comrades.
When we laugh together,
We are comrades.
When we rejoice together,
We are comrades.

Comrade!
Comrade!
Let's practise what we preach.
Let's practise what we preach.

The Woman in the War
Why am I in this unjust world?
Why am I born to live and die in disgrace?
Why is my beauty my problem?
Why am I forced to prostitution and defilement?
I am a woman in war, an object of shame.
Why do I live?

Am I created merely as an object of sinful man's sexual desire?
If I am gang-raped in broad daylight in front of my crying kids

By shameless and wicked men, where is the essence of humanity and goodness
in this world?
Am I the real cause of man's wars?
Do people fight to rape and humiliate me?
What are the real causes of the wars in the world?
Who is my creator, I the woman in the war?

O, my rapists are the killers of my husband and relatives;
O, my rapists are the looters of our properties.
Why do you rape, torture and kill me in cold blood?
You take nine months in my belly;
I endure painful labour and nurture you to be a real man;
Alas, you turn around and rape me shamelessly.
Shame on you; shame on you, bunch of criminals!
Is there any help under the sun for I the woman in the war?

Why do you take my daughter and make her a sex worker?
Why do you take and force her into shameful prostitution?
If you love her, marry her.
If you love her, marry her to live in dignity as a descent wife.
O, I the woman in the war am unlucky, very unlucky.

Why do I carry the sinful man's child in my womb?
Will I endure the multitudes of disgrace in the sight of God and man
Until I bear this illegal child?
Will my rapist come back for the child? Not at all, not at all!
Unfortunately, my beloved children have different colours of skin,
For I am the woman in the war.
Because of my being raped, my husband shuns me.
Am I the actual cause of the problem?
O, what shall I do? O, what shall I do?
I the woman in the war live a miserable life.
I am not worthy to live.

Why do you infect me with your chronic STDs?
O, unkind man, why do you infect me with HIV/AIDS?

Why am I to suffer and die of someone else's sinfulness?
Why am I to pass the same wickedness to my faithful husband?
I the woman in the war am not worthy to live,
For there is no justice in this world.

I don't know the fate of my husband in the battlefield.
Yet I pray that he is alive and not raping other women in the war.
My children and I are constantly insecure like rats among merciless cats.
My kids and I live on wild fruits and leaves,
And drink dirty waters to see the next day.
My kids and I cover our shameful and shivering bodies with leaves.
My kids and I lie on rough and dirty ground as our mattresses.
I the woman in the war am all in all.

I am among the millions of unlucky widows because of the war.
I am vulnerable like a city without a wall
Because for the sake of war.
I have many lovers against my will because of the war.
I am the unfortunate widow who doesn't know the grave of my husband,
For he died in the war.

I the woman in the war don't enjoy life.
I the woman in the war live without human dignity.
I live against my will, for I am the woman in the war.
I endure numerous hardships and burdens,
For I am the woman in the war.
My worst enemy is the war.
Where are the peace lovers to stop the wars?
May all human's wars end!

The Cry of the Child
O, I was born along the road,
In the harsh, open air.
I grew like the child of leech.
I grew in war and fear.
I am like a chicken born and reared in the realm of the hawk.

O, where is the happiness of life?
Are man's children in the same boat worldwide?

O, no! O, no!
Man's children aren't in the same boat.
Some children enjoy life.
And some children hate life.
Some children bless the world.
And some children curse the world.
A child elsewhere enjoys the calm, blue sky,
And the love of a dad and a mom.
Alas! I live in the darkest den,
For the constant fear of raining, merciless bombs and bullets.
No mom; no dad.

A child elsewhere sleeps warmly, comfortably in a bed;
Yet I sleep and stay in the rain and sun.
O, bird has a nest and fox has a hole,
But the son of man has nowhere to lay his head.
A child elsewhere drinks milk and eats honey.
Yet I eat the most bitter leaves and poisonous roots
To see the sun and stars.
I sing hunger and disease always.
I am only bone with no flesh on.
O, death is my best friend.

A child elsewhere gets fatigue by circling dad and mom,
By enjoying the world of toys.
Alas! My bones are out of joints;
My blood is streaming hot;
My feet are blistering and full of sores,
All because of hard, helpless journeys.
Across marshes and rivers full of unmerciful crocodiles,
Leave alone the fear of drowning beneath the deep waters.

But where do I go?
O, to the Promised Land, to the harsh hills and mountains of Ethiopia,

Across cruel and wild forests,
To the dusty, windy desert of Kenya,
Across unfriendly jungles, hills and mountains of Uganda,
Across dense, vast forests.
To the thick, wild jungles of Zaire,
Across wild, arid forests,
To the harsh, inhumane concentration camps in Northern Sudan.
O, where is help under the sun?
O, where is help under the sun?
The help is only from the Almighty God.
This is the cry of the helpless child.

God Division Is No Solution to Man's Problem
There is but one God!
There is but one universe!
There is but one man!
One Son but God!
One Holy Ghost but God!
Only three but One!

Through one God,
The universe rejoices and dances,
The sun warms all the planets heart and soul,
The stars visit the night all long,
All are cooperative and humble.
There was a stream of truth and peace.
God was and is still in control.
Man was gold in God's hand.
Man swam in God's heart.
Man wasn't black, white, red or brown but man.
Man was just a man.

The black cloud emerged sadly.
There came lie and fear.
By one's pride,
The universe got spoiled and polluted.
The darkest wall appeared between God and man.

The man began to crave and crave.
The man began to want and want,
But in vain, in vain.

There was emptiness and emptiness,
But God's merciful eyes were still on Enoch.
Still man sinned and sinned.
Again God's love was on Noah.
God opened a new page with Abraham.
Yet man desired and desired.
There was thirst and thirst.

Man divided and divided.
So there was black man, white man, brown man and red man.
Even others thought of becoming "green man."
Still there was death and poverty.
Some laugh but some cry.
There are wars and no peace.
The more man divides himself,
The more he craves and kills.
Man is no longer a man.
Man to man is no longer brother and friend.
But God is still on his throne.

O, a child from Bethlehem,
Brought peace and reconciliation between God and man.
Though man runs faster towards darkness,
Still God's love shines over there.
God is on his throne.
Again there is hope and despair.
There is joy and sorrow.

No black God.
No white God.
No red God.
No brown God.
No even blue God.

God remains God.
God is love, life, truth, and righteousness.
God is good; God is good.

O, God is divided again!
O, God is divided again!
So there is Christianity and Buddhism;
There is Christianity and Islam, etc., etc., etc.
There is God and gods.
Yet God is not divided, only man.
Yes, division of God is no solution to man's problems.
As God is one,
Let man be one.

Birds' colours unite.
Animals' colours unite.
No beautiful rainbow but varieties of synergised colours.
Why do man's colours breed hatred and death?
Why do man's colours divide and divide?
Why does Paul cry while Mohammed laughs, and vice versa?
Why does Deng starve while Ruth is satisfied?
Is God not all in all?
Is Adam not all in all?
Is Jesus Christ not all in all?

God's division is not a solution to global problems.
Let God remain one.
Let man unite.
Let man share joys and sorrows together.
Then peace shall rule.
Surely, the Son shall appear again.

No Straight Road in the World

At the end of the road,
Thousands of miles away,
We do see freedom over there.
But the road has twists and turns.

Of course, there aren't straight roads in the world.
Only if we aim correctly,
We will hit the point;
We will hit the target.

But who will lead the way?
O yes, we must do the task.
We must take the bull by the horns.
We must lead the way
Till the end,
Till the end,
Till the golden end.

But the task needs patience.
Surely, we must endure hardships.
We must surmount all the difficulties,
And march ahead,
Step by step, slowly but surely,
And sooner or later,
We shall reach over there,
And we will say,
O yes, this is what we want.
O yes, this is what we want.

And the dead will praise the living.
And ignorance will eventually realise
The genuine freedom paid with sweat and blood.
And tiger will live in peace with goat.

Labour Is the Life
Everything in existence is mainly due to hard labour.
Human life should have ceased to exist on earth,
Had it not been the power of labour.
Through hard labour,
Man has subdued the wild nature.
Because of the power of labour,
The fragile bees built their beautiful city of honey.

Sudan is too rich to feed all the Sudanese.
Sudan is too rich to feed all the Sudanese.
Sudan is too large to accommodate all the Sudanese.
Africa is too rich to feed all Africans.
Africa is too large to accommodate all Africans.
The world is too rich to feed all mankind.
The world is too large to accommodate all mankind.
Let's live in peace but not kill one another.
Let's help one another.

O, world of the poor!
There is an immense ocean of the poor in Africa.
There is a vast sea of the poor in Asia.
There is a large sea of the poor in Latin America.
There is a lake of the poor in Australia.
There is a lake of the poor in North America.
There is a lake of the poor in Europe.

O, land of the poor!
When hunger strikes, it is the poor who die.
When epidemic erupts, it is the poor who die.
When the rich causes war, it is the poor who die.

Where is the land of the poor?
Who will help the poor?
Let your mind heal your heart.
Let your heart heal your mind.
Let your energy save your life.

What a Good Day Africa!
What a good day Africa!
What a good day Africa!
The day when the sun shines
Upon the whole land,
The day when the moon shines
Upon the whole continent,
The day when the rain falls

Upon the whole land
For the betterment of mankind.
O yes, this is the most beautiful day.

How should a golden soil
Yield no fruits to its people?
But if it feeds birds, animals,
There is something wrong with the man.
There is something wrong far beyond us.

How long should the poor dying masses
Remain awaiting their neighbours' aid?
How long should Africans depend on foreign loans?
Don't we have minds to think?
Don't we have energy to work?
Africans must learn to work.
Labour beautifies the life.
We want freedom to work,
But not freedom from work.

We aren't warmongers,
But we love peace.
We love the world peace.
We have faith in peace and man,
But dependency paralyses the legs.
We must stand alone.
Africans must stand alone.
We must stand alone.

Peace Is Life and Soul
Sudanese must know who and why to fight.
Africans must know who and why to fight.
Mankind must know who and why to fight.
I never feel at peace

If hunger always knocks at my door.
I never feel at peace
If I always swim in a dirty lake of poverty.
I never feel at peace
If disease deprives me of my grey hairs.
I never feel at peace
If the world around me is an ocean of strange.
I never feel at peace
If the wall of stone age constantly surrounds my squalid cave.
I never feel at peace
If my own brother collaborates with my brother-in law
To bury me alive.

Sudanese must know who and why to fight.
Africans must know who and why to fight.
Mankind must know who and why to fight.
I shall never feel at peace
Unless I tear into pieces the basket of evil.
I shall never feel at peace
Unless all rivers of Sudan flow with justice and integrity.
I shall never be at peace
Unless the kings of genuine peace
Wear the linen clothes of truth
And ring the bell of humility
For all peace lovers to gather
And sit on unity chairs in peaceful atmosphere
Around the equality and equity table
To discuss the matters of life and death.

Only then shall I feel at peace.
Only then shall all the animals and birds feel at peace.
Only then shall the whole land
Swim in the peaceful sea of brotherhood.
Peace is life and soul.

When Doing Right Becomes Wrong

In 1986, I asked Dr. Amon Wantok to give me a letter of recommendation and release me to go to Bilpam to attend interviews for those going to Bonga for shield three officers' training. But he convincingly turned my request down by saying that he was going to recommend me to the top leadership of the movement to allow me to join the next batch of political training, obtain my commission and go to any officers' training in the future. I wisely tried to persuade him to permit me to go to Bilpam by explaining to him at length all the hurdles that I had had along my revolutionary way. But he adamantly refused to leave me by saying that what I was doing there was very vital in the ideological life of the movement. I reluctantly but politely consented to his advice, although I was not completely convinced.

Since I was not officially commissioned and assigned to do that political work by the top leadership of the movement, I knew very well that I was carrying out a sort of donkey's work because, apart from Dr. Amon, no one was going to appreciate and promote me for my honest, patriotic work. My concealed decision was to take a 'French Leave' and go to Bilpam without any authentic permission or letter of recommendation from him and try my way out personally, for I knew that the leadership there was not going to turn me away.

But before I executed my decision, I consulted Elijah Alier Ayom to hear his opinion about the whole matter. He advised me not to do so in the fear that if Dr. Amon were to write a letter against me to authorities concerned, explaining how I deliberately disobeyed him and abandoned the SPLM work, it might not go well with me, given my track record in the movement. On the contrary, he asked me to proceed with my work, abandon the desire to join shield three training and insist instead on Dr. Amon to honour his promise. In the end, I took his counsel and remained there doing my work with the hope that Dr. Amon, a powerful member of the movement at the time, was going to fulfil his promise.

The Untimely Death of Brother Ayoor-Goigoi

In 1986, I received bad news from Pricilla Nyankot Kuot, a relative of mine, concerning the untimely death of my eldest brother Ayoor-Goigoi, which occurred in April 1986 in Nyueny cattle camp in Bor, Southern Sudan. He died after a short illness. I mourned him deeply and dearly. His death was one of the shocking messages that I received while in Itang. At the time of writing these memories, his wife, Alok Malual Deng, has passed away, leaving their two married daughters, Nyang and Yom, and one son, Mading. Death is always very unkind and unfriendly, although it lives with people on a day-to-day basis.

Fighting on the Frontline

My Life in Bilpam, 1987

Around the second quarter of 1987, things changed drastically within the SPLA/M system with the so-called progressive officers being put behind concrete bars by the leadership of the movement. Among them was Comrade Dr. Amon Mon Wantok. He seemed to be one of the formidable vanguards of the movement, and so his arrest took many people by surprise. Because of his arrest and drastic leadership changes in Itang, a new management came to power. Anything that was connected with Dr. Amon was subjected to critical scrutiny by the security personnel. As a result, the promise he had earlier made to me concerning my going to political school was jailed with him. What was funny about the policies of the SPLA/M was the manner in which they boomeranged and recoiled on its best loyalists, leave alone the unknown nine men.

Someone later asked me how I missed being arrested with those of Dr. Amon since I was one of the people working with him. But I told him that, first of all, I was not one of the so-called progressive officers. Secondly, I told him that Amon and I were neither age nor political mates, and we did not share any ideological similarity. Furthermore, I informed him that Dr. Amon and I came to know each other in the bush as comrades in the army, and so our working together did not automatically imply our thinking, acting, talking and being arrested together. However, Dr. Amon was and still is my good friend, although each of us is capable of carrying his own cross if need be.

Within the second quarter of 1987, I took my bag, the only property I had in the world, and went to Bilpam. Upon my arrival there, I reported myself to the authorities concerned, and they gave me a warm revolutionary reception. Because of my library experiences, Captain Ngang Lazarus, a political commissar, put me in charge of the library therein. I discharged my work nobly while waiting earnestly to join shield four training in Bonga.

A Nominal Officer

In the course of my staying in Bilpam, heavy battles took place between SPLA and government troops in Southern Blue Nile, especially around the Kurmuk and Gezan areas. At the same time, fierce fighting took place in many areas in Southern Sudan. Due to the intensity of war and a lack of enough trained officers, the leadership of the SPLA/M suspended shield four training and sent us to the frontlines, especially Southern Blue Nile to engage the enemy.

Chagai Atem Biar, Commander in charge of Bilpam, commissioned me with the military rank of a sergeant and put me in charge of a platoon. I gladly took my patriotic role. My friend and relative Ateny Kuol Aluong was also put in charge of a platoon. Other non-commission officers who were waiting with us to join shield four were given the same positions. After this quick organization, we hurriedly left Bilpam for Blue Nile through Ethiopian territory in November 1987 and arrived in Kurmuk on 29 of the same month.

Fierce Battles in Various Fronts

When our forces reached there, Kurmuk was already captured from the government forces by the gallant SPLA on 12 November 1987. Our reinforcing troops were quickly broken up and sent to different fronts to face the incoming enemy soldiers. Those of Ateny Kuol, Deng Chol Ngueny and Bior Deng-Wiel went to Gezan and captured it. Our forces went towards Mayak and Challi Phil, while others went towards Khor-Amer.

The capturing of Kurmuk and Gezan and other small army garrisons by the SPLA was seen as a direct slap in the face of the government. Hence, its thousands of soldiers were hastily mobilised and sent to Southern Blue Nile with the sole mission of recapturing those places and expel the SPLA/M from Southern Blue Nile.

Our company was under the leadership of Captain Mayom Deng Biar. In the process of engaging the huge government troops, Alternate Commander Ateng Alier Kuany met his death when our combined forces under the direct command of Salva Kiir attacked Challi Phil in a broad daylight. Due to some shortcomings in our military plans, our enemies outwitted and defeated us, leaving us to retreat from there.

In the course of fighting, our valiant officers, including Garang Mabil, Garang Malual, Majok Mach Aluong (Buongajoh), returned from Cuba and proceeded right away to give us needed reinforcements. But despite our braveness, the huge, well-armed government troops overwhelmed us by recapturing the strategic towns of Kurmuk and Gezan plus other minor garrisons.

Since it was difficult to maintain our solid footing there inside Sudan, the SPLA/M leadership commanded all the forces to withdraw to some places inside Ethiopian territory along the Sudan – Ethiopia border. Our company and other forces moved to Dul where we spent the dry season of 1988. Prominent among our officers were Captain Mayom Deng Biar, Captain David Ngare, Captain Kong, Captain Mabior Nhial Makol, Captain Chol Abednego Majok, Captain Chol Abraham Kuchkon and Captain David Oboch. First lieutenant Magoor Ajang Duot was also with us. Because of his seniority, Captain Mayom took the overall command of our combined forces. I worked as an adjutant in the headquarters.

After the fierce battles in Southern Blue Nile at the time, all the nominal officers, including myself, were told by the SPLA/M leadership to maintain their previous ranks of non-commission officers until further notice. As there was a lull in the fighting, particularly during the wet season, we, the supposed candidates for shield four, eagerly waited to go to Bonga for the training.

Heroic Death of Ateny Kuol Aluong

Ateny, my distant cousin was my age mate; a very brave, loyal, wise, humble, strong, unselfish, sociable, caring and patriotic man. He sustained a wound on his right arm in the war of Thiaijak in which Commander Francis Ngor was killed. As mentioned earlier, he was one of the nominal officers who vehemently and bravely engaged the enemy in Southern Blue Nile. Ateny was not only a relative but also a dear friend to me. In January 1989, Captain Majok Mach sent me some bad news through Comrade Deng Chol Ngueny about the heroic death of Ateny, which occurred on 7 December 1987 when SPLA captured Gezan from government forces. He met his death while leading his platoon.

At My Spiritual Height

During our lull in Dul, I studied my Bible and prayed earnestly before the Lord, and it strengthened my intimate companionship with him. All the comrades knew my unconcealed loyalty to Jesus Christ, and so I was free to share my faith openly with those in need.

In my entire Christian growth, the time I spent in Dul was one of the happiest moments I had with the Lord because I felt at my spiritual height in many aspects of life. The Most High was shining in and through me. I used to take my gun, venture into the surrounding forest and have my quiet time with Him. One day, while I was burning in my spiritual mood, singing hymns and songs of praise, I suddenly saw a partridge trying to get away from me but falling back to the ground. It was scared to death, but before long, I knew that it was entrapped.

Getting meat regularly for our meals was very uncommon, for we had no funds to buy it from the neighbourhoods, and it was also difficult for us to get some wild animals for meat. This situation forced some clever soldiers to trap birds and other small wild animals. It was in this way that this unlucky bird found itself in this unbreakable snare.

I was in the ethical dilemma in that the fate of the bird was totally under my control. I had the right to free it from that trap to enjoy its life and attract ceaseless curses in return from my unknown comrade and wildlife's enemy. On the other hand, I had no right to violate the concrete laws of the jungle. And for me to act as a man of the jungle, I had two righteous options: the first option was to tell my God to leave me alone for a little while so as to kill and steal the bird from the trap and run away with it to enjoy the meat with or without my friends. Second option, was just to leave the bird struggling alone in the trap for its predators to come and feast on it.

I slowly caught the bird, disentangled and held it in my hands for a little while, and it stayed there motionlessly, looking at me helplessly with begging eyes, not knowing that it was free. Then I asked it to go in peace, threw it into the air, and it flew away without a word of thanks. My spirituality compelled me to take this unusual option, although I knew very well that that owner of the trap would have fought me if he were around.

However, I am not saying that killing a bird or any other animal for food is evil. Instead, I am rather pointing out the fact that, being at my spiritual height at the time, I saw the glory and beauty of the Lord in that bird, although it was not created in his own image and likeness. In terms of environmental conservation, human beings have a divine mandate from God to produce, multiply, dominate and rule all other creatures but not to destroy them (Genesis 1:26-28). In fact,

I rarely kill any living, edible creature for food, although I am not a vegetarian for that matter.

It was at my spiritual height that the Almighty God gave me spiritual power to compose and sing some soul-searching songs, although some of my spiritual songs came later on. All the songs are in Jeng language.

The Sudan's Coup, 1989

Omar Hasan Ahmad al-Bashir toppled Sadiq al Madhi's government on 30 June 1989 in Khartoum. His military government promised to talk peace with the SPLA/M. As a result, it sent a peace delegation to Addis Ababa and met SPLA/M representatives between 19 and 20 September 1989. The movement knew very well that this Islamic military regime was going to try first to defeat the SPLA/M by force before talking genuine peace, and it really did.

A/Commander Simon Gatwich's Complaints

Within the second quarter of 1989, A/Commander Gatwich Dual was the head of our army forces around Kurmuk. One day, we were talking, and in the course of our conversations, he openly expressed his displeasure on how things were done within the SPLA/M leadership. I quietly and surprisingly listened to him. Thereafter, I politely asked him whether he would be permitted to see and share his viewpoints with Dr. John Garang if he wished. He said it might happen, although those around him often refused to allow people to see him. To show him my deep concerns, I told him that if people like him were to complain against and criticise the movement in public, what would happen to junior people? I encouraged him to see Garang personally so as to air out his concerns and find possible solutions to them.

Comrade Gatwich talked as if he had lost hope in the SPLA/M, and that was my concern. To prove my own feelings right, two years later, he withdrew his allegiance and pulled out from the movement. And the counsel that I took from that event and more of a similar nature is that the moment people stand aloof from their system and begin criticising it, or one person connected with it in terms of leadership, they have lost hope in it. And unless something is done urgently to regain their confidence, the system will automatically collapse.

1989's Military Offensives

After being to Addis Ababa briefly on medical referral, I returned to Southern Blue Nile. Our forces started engaging the enemy in preparations of attacking and capturing Kurmuk for the second time. Our Cadet Task Force under the leadership of Captain Garang Malual left Gatawerga base inside Ethiopia for Khor-Amer on 16 and laid an ambush there on 22 August 1989. Then we patiently waited there to attack government troops that were returning to Damazin town. In this ambush, despite the dispersing of the big convoy of government troops, Captain David Ngare was fatally wounded and later died in Asosa Hospital inside Ethiopia. He was one of the devoted revolutionary officers.

Kurmuk Under the SPLA Siege, 1989

In desperate attempts to rescue Kurmuk from the merciless jaws of the SPLA, the Khartoum Government mustered and sent a series of reinforcements from Damazin and other areas to Kurmuk. The government reinforcement was ambushed and repelled on 15 October 1989 along Surkum-Mayak Road by the SPLA. Again the government sent a big reinforcement, nick-named Aman el Kurmuk under the leadership of Lt.Col. Said Jamal el Din. It left Damazin on 9 October 1989 for Kurmuk but fell into a severe ambush of El Punji el Jidit on 16, and fighting continued up to 23 of the same month when it was repelled. Another enemy's reinforcement under the command of Col. Mohammed Ali el Haqih was stationed in Dedoro, awaiting further instructions.

Mountaineers' Attacks on Kurmuk

In order to engage the entranced government forces decisively and up root them, our commanders devised some sort of aerial attacks in support of the usual ground incursions. They sought ways and means of sending some mountaineers on one of the cliffs that overlook the town of Kurmuk from its northern part. On that rocky cliff, there is only a very small, narrow place, about fifteen metres long and five meters wide, where one could clearly see the military garrison, the one towards the Ethiopian border. Despite its strategic location for the mountaineers to launch surprise air attacks on the garrison, it is quite exposed and vulnerable to all heavy artilleries, especially mortar launchers. What is also funny about it is that there is only one horizontal bulge, descending gradually away from it up to the foot of the mountain, in a north-north east direction, a great distance from the town.

Since this strategic location is visible to those inside the town, particularly the military garrison, the mountaineers were to ascend to and descend from it only by night. This means that even if mountaineers were defeated, they had to ceasefire and remain there vigilantly until the next nightfall. It was also very difficult to evacuate casualties from there, and so the dead were to remain there unburied. Because of the insufficiency of that location, only two squads were allowed to carry out such an attack. In order for the mountaineers to launch their attacks on the garrison beneath, there had to be a friendly ground assault on the same garrison to act as a cover to the mountaineers. The entrance from the foot of the mountain was also to be properly secured by the friendly forces to allow safe passage for the mountaineers; otherwise, the enemy would trap them on their way from the top of the mountain.

In the course of the SPLA attacks on Kurmuk, some of our security personnel surveyed the mountain and disclosed their findings to the commanders in charge of the operations. Around 18 October 1989, the first mountaineers went to the mountain in support of a ground attack on the town. But the government troops bravely repelled us, and so our forces retreated to their location, just along the seasonal stream, marking the Sudan-Ethiopia border. But what happened to the mountaineers was hidden until sometime in the evening when they sadly came down, leaving their six dead comrades behind. During the fighting, the enemy shelled their position, and in the process of that, one mortar shell fell over there, killing six of them instantly.

Before daybreak, on the following day, Captain Moses Dhieu Kiir led the second mountaineers to the same cliff. I happened to be one of them. We hiked it strategically and carefully, avoiding deep valleys and bottomless pits on the way to that historical location. Unfortunately, we met our smelling, decaying heroes lying motionlessly in the same place. We slept there with them, polluting our oxygen with their remarkable odour until the morning's joint attacks on the enemy garrison.

To give our advancing ground force a military cover, like a hungry hawk wanting to devour its preys, we staged a severe in-flight attack on the enemy garrison, although it was no longer something new to them, having being attacked from the same spot the other night. In return, we received concerted fire exchanges from the garrison. As we were swamped with whispering and echoing bullets, we fell headlong and flat like a helpless child, not knowing where to run for assistance. But since there was no room for escape or possible shelter from the enemy's fires, we took the bull by the horns and fought back valiantly.

The purpose of our aerial attack was not to capture the enemy post from the air but to help our ground force to take added advantage on the enemy, up root and capture its post. Unfortunately, the enemy bravely fought us both on the ground and in the air and repelled our ground forces. We saw our men retreating speedily towards our border location, carrying their casualties, both the wounded and the dead.

The situation forced us to ceasefire, although the enemy kept shelling our place with some heavy artillery. We kept mum but vigilant like a rat entrapped by its foe. After some time, they took good counsel not to waste their precious ammunitions on cowards hiding and dying on the rock like badger. And subsequently, they stopped firing on us. We sustained no single casualty. They fired no single mortar shell on us. We came to discover that our luck was largely due to the fact that the enemy had run out of mortar shells in the course of a series of attacks between the SPLA and their forces.

We sneaked out at dusk and rushed to our small clinic to seek medical treatment. In fact, the strong smell of the decaying bodies made us very sick. You can imagine, everything about us, including our clothing, terribly smelled like the dead, and even our own breath was no pleasant smell either. After receiving some medical aid, we recovered steadily, not lying on sickbeds, but rather moving up and down, engaging the enemy. We were the last mountaineers at the time.

The Ineffectiveness of Anti-Personal Mines

In our Cadet Task Force, mine was the first platoon in the first company. This means that if our task force was the one to first stage an attack on the enemy, I would be in the forefront, leading my men.

One day, in broad daylight, our forces launched concerted attacks on the enemy's outpost, the usual post near the foot of the mountain on the way to Ethiopian border, in Kurmuk. Ours was on standby as reinforcement to the attacking force. The attacking troops bravely fought and captured the enemy's garrison, forcing them to retreat into the town. But within no time, the government rushed in some troops, backed with some tanks from their headquarters, which was situated near the foot of the mountain on the western part of the town. As a result, our men dashed out with some booties from the enemy's garrison.

The Cadet Task Force was ordered to launch another attack on the same garrison so as to dislodge the incoming government reinforcement. I led my platoon and bypassed our retreating soldiers. We charged in and took cover, charged in and took cover again under heavy fire from the enemy. Again I commanded the force to move and charge in, but I heard two voices behind me, saying, "Stephen, Stephen, Stephen... not there, not there, not there but to that small rock, that... that... that rock, rock, rock and take cover." I heeded them and within no time, we found ourselves under that small rock. We breathed heavily and bewildered. The enemy pounded our formidable rock mercilessly, although we tried to fire back on them.

I was bewildered because I found myself with only two comrades, Joseph, a young man from Tunji, and Michael, a young man from Juba. When I commanded the force to move and charge in for the last time, the entire force found it hard to move a bit forward under the enemy's heavy fire. Hence, three of us found ourselves in the very killing zone of the enemy. Neither was it simple for us to return to our men nor was it wise for us to march foolishly toward the enemy to meet our collective death before their trenches.

As we stooped there behind the rock, Michael pulled my leg slowly away from that spot and told me to beware of anti-personal mines. As a precautious measure, the enemy planted strategically some anti-personal mines in and around some suspected locations as deterrents and deadly traps on the attacking enemy like us. Although they planted such deadly traps around that small rock, the Lord took good care of our feet.

Having sustained some heavy casualties, our troops withdrew and ran away with their victims, especially the wounded. Then the enemy turned their vigilant eyes upon us and rained our rock regularly with bullets. It was dangerous to retreat towards our previous advancing route because it was very open and clearly within the killing zone of the enemy. Our left-hand-side was unfriendly for us to run to while our right-hand-side was very rocky with big pits and possibly mined by the enemy. But militarily, this was the possible route for us to withdraw to despite such hurdles.

After agreeing on the escape route, I cautioned my colleagues to be ready to move. Then we tried our luck under the heavy gunfire with our helpless feet missing some mines here and there before we took cover. The angered enemy pounded our hiding place with bullets and rockets, but we remained there like some rats in a cave, gulping for fresh air. After gathering enough energy and surveying the next route of move, we dashed out like flying arrows, irrespective of danger both on air and on the ground. The echoing sounds of heavy shells and exploding mines were very deafening. Upon reaching the next cover, I surprisingly found myself alone. I looked behind to see whether my colleagues had been at last devoured by the enemy's fire but saw nothing.

Now I was out of the enemy's vision but among larger rocks divided by some sort of bottomless pits. If I were to fall into any of them, that would have been the end of the long story, a kind of everlasting grave. So I took absolute care of my life and rifle until the danger was completely behind me.

The rain started pouring down heavily. I moved around to join the force and found 1st Lt. Deng Antipas commanding the soldiers to evacuate the wounded to the rear base. We reached our seasonal stream and found it overflowing with water from the rain. Our squalid belongings were not there, for they were rescued and moved away to a higher ground by some soldiers.

Upon my arrival to the new base, I saw Michael with bandages on his thigh and arm and Joseph in good health. They amazingly narrated that during our last move, while retreating from the enemy, I stepped on anti-personnel mine, which immediately exploded without harming me. Instead, it injured Michael in the process. By experiencing this unusual event, they decided not to follow me but rather to use a different route. They assumed that I had some divine protection which made me immune to such dangerous anti-personal mines and/or bullets for that matter. Of course, being a Christian, I have unswerving faith in the protecting divine power of Jesus Christ. Hence, God has done it to many people, including myself, and He is there to do it to others in line with His will. The 'Silent Hand' was very much on me.

The Fall of Kurmuk to SPLA

At 8pm, on Saturday 28 October 1989, Kurmuk fell to the SPLA forces of New Punji, and we triumphantly marched into it in the darkness. The following day, late afternoon, a strange plane came and hovered over the town. And we innocently looked at it until orders came from our headquarters, ordering the artillery unit to shoot it down. After receiving some shots, it increased its longitude and slowly moved southward dropping bombs, which burnt the nearby bushes. We realised that it was an enemy's military plane, which later became commonly known as the Antonov medium and long transport aircraft.

On 31 of the same month, our force moved from Kurmuk to Dammunsur, and we moved from there to Ura on 4 November. Then we moved strategically from Ura and besieged Challi Phil on 6th of the same month. In the course of the attacks on Challi Phil, we captured it on Thursday 8 November 1989. Commander William Nyuon Bany came to congratulate our troops on this significant victory, for this was the first time for it to fall under SPLA.

The Expulsion of SPLA from Southern Blue Nile

The fall of Kurmuk and its surrounding towns to SPLA was a big blow to the Khartoum Government. So it organised and sent waves of reinforcements, one after another, to Southern Blue Nile to recapture those places. But the SPLA forces vehemently engaged them in various fronts but in vain.

On 29 November 1989, the government troops recaptured Kurmuk. On 30 of the same month, SPLA General Headquarters ordered us to withdraw from Challi Phil and move towards the Ethiopia-Sudan border so as to avoid being trapped in by the enemy. So our army moved from Challi Phil to Ura and proceeded to Khor-Yabus on 2 December 1989. Here we found stores full of huge bags of coffee. Being a border town, some traders used Khor-Yabus as an exit point to Ethiopia to sell their goods like coffee. Those of us who took coffee tried to drink as much as they could. Since there were no nearby markets for us to sell it, it became as useless as something of no value. It was very amazing to see soldiers pouring the precious coffee down and taking empty sacks to put in their belongings.

I took good counsel in this important instance that where there is no demand for anything, no matter how precious it is like silver and gold, there is no significant value attached to it. And that is why empty sacks, because of their demand, were more valuable than the coffee itself. We in fact left them intact when we departed from there, for we had nothing to carry them.

Between 3 and 4 January 1990, the government troops, with the help of Ethiopian rebels, attacked and overran Longkuei Refugee Camp. This led thousands of refugees, with terrible, flea-bite wounds, to move aimlessly along unfriendly hills and mountains of Ethiopia. Some of them found themselves in the town of Makelek inside Ethiopia and eventually landed in Khor-Yabus. Others found no better options to resort to other than to surrender to the nearest government towns, and probably not to return to SPLA/M areas again.

Tiresome Journey to Bilpam

On 7 January 1990, the Commander-in-Chief ordered our forces to move from Khor-Yabus to Bilpam, and this marked the temporal departure of the SPLA/M from Southern Blue Nile. Highly demoralized, the majority of our combined forces disobeyed the orders and headed for their respective areas. Yet a few of us trekked back to the General Headquarters. We took the route leading from Khor-Yabus to Maban and curved a little bit eastward towards Ethiopia and found ourselves in Wengkech, a small Ethiopian border town. Then from there, we moved to Itang en route to Bilpam.

In a state of loose leadership or no law and order, our forces broke into smaller groups of like-minded people who could share their joys and bitterness together along the rough way. Common and obvious hurdles were lack of food, insecurity, sleeplessness, exhaustion, a lack of drinking water in some places and foot-sores, among others. Boots stayed on our feet for 24 hours per day, non-stop, during that month. It became common for the soldiers, including myself, to lose toes. Then they got healed, and the new toes grew in the course of the journey before reaching our final destination, Bilpam.

At the Verge of Dying of Thirst

Between Maban and Wengkech, there was a vast No Man's Land, which could take a serious day's walk. It was hard to find water in this land during the dry seasons, although it has a lot of seasonal streams. Nearer to Wengkech from Maban, there is one large pool. And to reach there, people needed to draw some water to quench their thirst along the way and move vigorously the whole night to arrive there at around 7am. Among us there were some people who knew this route very well and were the ones to guide us.

We filled our small water bottles and left our last point in Maban area at around 4pm and headed for that large water point. From the onset we determined to travel the entire night and reach there in the cool of the morning. But because of the hardships we had confronted on the road since the commencement of the trip, almost all the troops found it too difficult to walk the whole night.

Before 8pm, the weaker people started spreading over along the road and refused to move an inch farther. As time progressed, people proportionately lost their strength in relation to their varied physiological make-up and willpower, and they rested here and there along the way. Others and I staggered until around midnight and took some rest by the roadside. But the officer, who guided the way, being well aware of the imminent danger, travelled the whole night with his men and arrived at the water point early in the morning.

At around 3am, people started staggering along the road with the hope of reaching the water point before thirst claimed their lives. Although we tried to walk very fast, we seemed to regress on our journey. The sun came up brightly like an ember out of the horizon, and the sign of the desired pool was beyond our pale hope. We knew that the danger was merely around the corner.

To soften their cracked lips, soldiers reached for unripe tamarind fruits and leaves and chewed them as they moved. At around 7am, I gulped the last drops of water that I had in my water bottle and moved on with others. My personal decision was to find a good shade and rest there when it became too hot for me to move and then move on later during the evening. However, I was neither the head nor the tail of the journey.

As people tried to move away from danger, you found the walkers bypassing one another along the road, leaving the weak to lag behind. Despite our snail-like-movement, we staggered along the narrow path under the scorching sun. That day the sun seemed to have doubled its strength because the sky was totally cloudless, with no wind blowing but only the sun burning out of control. It was our 'D Day', and we feared the worse.

We heard the sounds of gun shots at around 9am in front of us and, as there was no exchange of fire, we believed that the firing was peaceful. It could have been something to alert the ones behind of good news. At first, we assumed that the expected pool was near. We regained our hope and rushed ahead to find out what was happening. Upon our arrival there, we found people in great jubilation after having satisfactorily quenched their thirst. They directed us to where the water was, about one hundred metres off the road. We headed straight there and drank to the full. Then some big water containers were hurriedly filled, put on donkeys' backs, and the animals were chased backwards to rescue the last groups. Finally, the whole force was out of danger.

How did people find the water in that place? As you know, experience is the best teacher in life. As people staggered along the road, one of the soldiers spotted a certain bird on a tree. So he stood and looked at it carefully and told his colleagues that there should be water there because that bird cannot live where there is no water. But since the place was totally dry, people attempted to dispute him, but he insisted on his viewpoint based on his wildlife knowledge. And instead, he took off and went towards the bird. Before reaching the tree where the bird was, he joyfully shouted back, "Water!!!!" and fell headlong to satisfy his thirst.

We discovered that elephants moved there during the last wet season and left big cracks and holes on the ground. Hence, these holes turned out to be the blessed water catchments. Without this miraculous event, most of us would have died of thirst. This is another important event whereby the 'Silent Hand' was not only upon me but upon all of us. We spent the day there and later moved to the pool where we found our road guide with his few men.

From there we moved to Wengkech. On 1 February 1990, we left Wengkech for Itang where I met my brothers and sisters in Christ. I left there for Bilpam on 5 of the same month. We spent about one month there, struggling with sand fleas.

On 13 March 1990, our force left Bilpam for Pinymor. Then we went to Meketa on 14 of the same month en route to Pagak. On 27 of the same month, we left Pagak for Maiwut. But I became sick and got referred to Itang Hospital on 2 April 1990 by Dr. Dan Aleer Abit for a further medical check-up. This moment came to be the last time my gun left my hand.

First row from Left to Right: Bior Bariach Bior, Biar Mach Deng-Beny, Stephen Mathiang Kuch & the one behind is Bair Pandiar Biar Itang, Ethiopia, 1991

First row, Left to Right: *Late Manyang Deng-Alangjok, Alier Chuit*
Second row, Left to Right: *Late Akuei Jok, Late Biar Mach, Achiek Ayomthiei*
Itang, Ethiopia, 1990s

PART FOUR

Big Life Changes, 1990–1996

CHAPTER SEVEN

Shift in Career

The Choice for a Wife

By the late 1980s, it was the right time for me to marry because all my elder brothers were married by that time. But marrying in exile was not easy due to two primary factors: firstly, girls from our ethnic community in places like Itang were very few; secondly, I did not have sufficient wealth to cover the entire cost of my marriage in terms of bride price plus other expenses. The better option for me was, therefore, to return home and marry a lady from there. This was my plan but not God's, as it turned out. For it had been difficult for me to return home anytime between the mid-1980s and 1990. As I pushed on with my normal life, my relatives and closest friends knew of my marital plan; yet it was not a big concern because I was approaching my 30s.

In April 1990, I attended a church service on one of the Sundays in our church, Itang. We came out after the service and interacted and greeted each other outside the church. There Rachael Aluengi Mawut, one of my relatives, approached and greeted me warmly. Then she said casually, "My cousin, why don't you marry now before you return to the frontline since the Lord has brought you back." I smiled at her and said: "It is a good idea, but is there a girl?" Then she smiled and nervously said: "Sure, even the little daughter of my brother, the daughter of Deborah Nyaluak, is now big, and there are young men eyeing to compete for her hand in marriage. They have moved to Pinyudo Refugee Camp." In conclusion, she promised to pay us a visit in the course of the week to confer further on her suggestion, and I nodded in agreement. At that time I already knew that girl, her mother and two of her brothers.

Aluengi's mother and my father's mother are sisters, daughters of the same mother and father. Because of her relationship to both the girl and I, she had to weigh her recommendation carefully and sincerely so as not to offend any party or both parties in the marriage.

In fulfilment of her promise, Aluengi came one day and had a good, intimate time with me. In the course of our conversation, right in the beginning, she mentioned what has since then stuck firmly in my mind. She looked at me lovingly and said: "My cousin, your way of life always deters one from proposing a marital mate to you because no one knows the right girl to meet your desires and aspirations." I appreciated her suggestion and encouraged her not to worry very much as the right choice for marriage or anything else belongs to the Almighty God. As a matter of fact, Rachael was a real lover of Christ. We then continued with our frank conversation. In the end, I told her that I would give it a thought, follow up my medical treatment, and see whether to pay a visit to Pinyudo to meet her and her mother.

Then I shared this suggestion with my best friend and relative, Jacob Biar Mach. Jacob's mother and my father's mother are the daughters of Biar Akol; so Biar and I have dual blood relationships. After sharing with him the idea, we committed it into continuous prayer.

A Letter to My Expected Mother-in-Law

In order to follow up on Aluengi's suggestion, I wrote an introductory letter to Deborah Nyaluak Kuol Yak. In the letter, I made it clear my desire to marry her daughter, Elizabeth Agot Leek Deng. But I made it categorically clear that although I knew her daughter personally in the church, I had not courted her or even shared this marital idea with her. I requested Jacob Biar to see how to convey this vital letter to her personally so as to back it up with his words. This was also because I was planning to return to Sudan on a church mission. I promised him that I was not going to take any girl in Bor as my wife. Instead, I was going to come back to Ethiopia in time to pursue and see how this marital proposal was going to unfold.

On a Church Mission to Sudan

The New Sudan Council of Churches (NSCC) was formed in 1990 in Torit in parallel to the Sudan Council of Churches (SCC) so as to champion the needs of the churches operating in the SPLA/M liberated areas. After its historical formation, there was a need to call a general assembly. The assembly at the time consisted of the representatives from all Christian denominations in different geographic locations with the task to go and deliberate upon, amend and eventually approve all the vital operational documents of the NSCC. This first General Assembly was scheduled to take place in May 1990 in Torit.

Churches in Itang, Pinyudo and Dima Refugee Camps inside Ethiopia were requested to send their delegates to Torit. My church council met in Itang and nominated their representatives for the meeting. My role in the church at the time was only to preach the word of God whenever asked by the church leadership. I was not involved in day-to-day crucial decision-making in the leadership. As a result, I neither participated in the church council meeting nor influenced in any way the process of the selection of the Torit's delegates. Above all, since the importance of this newly founded para-church agency was still in the bud, the curiosity of who would or not go here to Torit was very low in the minds of the church members.

One day, while I was taking my leisure time in the shade of a tamarind tree in our homestead, Angelo Biar Wech paid me a visit. Angelo, a young Christian devotee, was a member of the church council in Itang and also a member of the SPLA. He was one of my distant relatives. Before he sat down, he asked me whether I had heard of my being nominated by the church council to go to Torit for the NSCC General Assembly, and my answer was no. He told me that the council had selected me. However, he asked me to wait for the official information from our pastor, Rev. Peter Bol Arok.

I am sorry to mention here that Angelo lost his life in the last quarter of 1991, while engaging the military enemy in Pochala, a town on the Sudan-Ethiopia border. In the course of our conversation, Rev. Bol came and told me the decision taken by the church, but I asked him to give me time to think about it.

I shared with A/CDR Majok Mach Aluong and Jacob Biar Mach, my closer relatives and friends, the suggestion advanced by the church for me to attend a church meeting in Torit. They collectively concurred with it. Besides, they proposed for me to proceed to Bor after the meeting so as to see our relatives. I took their advice and gave a positive response to the church.

Departure for Torit

The journey between Itang and Dima Refugee Camps took us three days, 1–3 May 1990. Rev. John Machar Thon, the priest in charge of the Anglican Church in Dima, hosted us very well. We were 70 in number from different denominations. Among the delegates were Rev. Peter Bol Arok, the late Job Adier Jok, Rev. Michael Deng

Anuol, the late Peter Yuang Mach, Elijah Biar Mathiang, Abraham Mayom Athiaan, Rev. John Jok Chol and Joseph Maker Atot. We waited there in Dima for about three weeks for transportation. Dr. Atem Nathan, the camp commander, tried to find for us a vehicle, but he failed.

Biblical Church vis-à-vis Human Church

This was my first time to live in the site of church compound and to closely monitor church activities and the behaviour of leaders. I used to hear with great displeasure and surprise, leadership wrangling in the church. To me, the church structure and leadership must be biblical in nature, and so unnecessary strife and bad governance should not be associated with it. My mental picture of the church was and still is directly based on the way I read my Bible. Unlike the political arena, I envision the church to be peaceful, understanding, loving, trustworthy and Christ-like in all its mannerisms. For the Lord demands the church to be an oasis of genuine love, operating as the salt and the light of the world.

However, in the course of our waiting there, I discovered that my assumption was totally wrong because my colleagues, especially some of our church leaders, were on each other's necks like un-cooperative chickens. Almost each day was spent settling petty disputes among them. Such intermittent settlements were punctuated with unheeded prayers.

Engrossed in deep thinking and reflection, my daily place was the shade of a tree in the church compound. I sat there tuning into my radio for the world news. Whenever people were called to attend reconciliatory prayers in the church for those who had half-heartedly repented, my repeated response was no. I refused to join them in what I termed to be childish behaviour. Because their feuds were not accidental but something deliberately planned and executed without any slightest fear of the Lord. And after a little while, you found the same people calling people to pray for them and asking God to forgive them. I do not think that God or people of sound mind like premeditated wrong actions.

It was at that time I came to reinforce my belief that Satan overtook people and occupied the church sanctuary in his desperate attempt to chase God-seekers away from the church. But is there any comfort zone to resort to in the world apart from the glorious presence of God? He is the only source of life, the solid vanguard, formidable refuge, everlasting saviour and a reliable friend. Hence, despite such unwarranted leadership wrangling, unfriendly and unloving atmosphere in the church, my resolute decision was to stand steadfastly in my faith and maintain my unshakable spiritual ground in the church and hold my Bible firmly for the evil one not to snatch it away. This is called spiritual warfare, which involves all Christian believers. The journey to heaven is not, of course, an easy and smooth sailing one.

The NSCC General Assembly took place while we were in Dima because it became obvious that it was hard to find a vehicle to take us to Torit in time. Then we were told to return to our respective places and wait to be served with the minutes of the meeting in due course. My hopes to go to Bor and see my people were ruined again.

A Journey to Bor

Despite being late for the NSCC General Assembly in Torit, Abraham Mayom and Joseph Maker insisted on proceeding to Sudan for private issues. Peter Yuang and I decided to join them and go to Bor. My main interest was just to go and see my people, share with them my marital proposal and return to Ethiopia to pursue it before going back to my battalion.

On 25 May 1990, we left Dima by a military truck for Khor-Chum. We had to cover the distance between Khor-Chum and Jabel Boma on foot under military guard because of security issues. Strategically, the right time to walk the road was by night, for armed robbers seldom walked that route in the dark. It was also good for us to walk in the cool of the night to curtail the high level of thirst and also to minimize our visibility along the road from the nightfall armed gangs.

Narrow Escape from a Gangster

The authorities in Khor-Chum gave us a five-man armed escort, and we left there on 26 May by night for Nyilongre, a SPLA base. We carried our small belongings, and so we had to rest frequently along the road. After resting somewhere, we gathered strength and decided to move farther, but, as we started to walk, my things got loose. Thus, I decided to put them down in a hurry and tie them properly. In the course of doing that, my colleagues were already ahead of me in the dark. I put them on my shoulder and hurried on to catch up with them. As I walked, I heard some footsteps behind me and looked curiously. Then I saw somebody following me. For sure, all my colleagues were ahead of me, and hence, I took him for an enemy. I increased my walking speed, although I maintained absolute calm, while looking frequently over my shoulders. We walked steadily for about fifteen minutes. On the way, I descended and ascended a small valley and continued along the road. Then he reached the same valley, stood there and cleared his throat. As I moved on, I did not see him behind me anymore. He was looking for an easy opportunity to brutally attack me and take away my humble belongings, although there was nothing worth my life with me to loot. But is a human's life valuable in the merciless eyes of robbers? The 'Silent Hand' was heavily upon me.

Finally, I caught up with my colleagues and asked them whether any of us had remained behind apart from me, and the answer was nil. For the sake of not causing any fear among my team members, I kept quiet and continued on with our journey until we arrived at Nyilongre. The escort from Khor-Chum left us under the security of those in Nyilongre and returned to their place, using again the night cover.

On 27 of the same month, we were given another SPLA escort and left Nyilongre for Boma and arrived there safely. While in Boma, I narrated to my colleagues what had happened to me along the road. Mayom responded by saying that he knew something might have occurred on the way, and that was why I asked such an inquiring question. We thanked God for his protection.

Mr. Russell Nobel, an American employee of ACROSS (Association of Church Resources of South Sudan) and a former teacher of Rumbek Secondary School, drove us by a car from Boma to Kapoeta on 31 May 1990. Mr. Nobel was my teacher, teaching physical geography at Rumbek.

The SPLA/M authorities transported us from there to Torit on 1 June 1990. We met Bishop Nathaniel Garang there, and he warmly received us. Bishop Nathaniel told us to wait for him while wrapping up a few things so as to go to Bor with us. He was constantly with Abraham Mayom Athiaan, although some of my colleagues and I did not know what they were planning.

Narrow Escape from a Deadly Antonov Bomb

On 5 June 1990, the Khartoum Government sent some military planes to raid the town of Torit. In the course of these horrific air bombardments, a huge shell fell on our church compound. It fell just 8m from a hut where Bishop Nathaniel and other priests were having lunch and 18m from a tree under which I was sitting with other youth members. I clearly saw the shell as it parachuted on us from the sky and cautioned my colleagues to quickly lie down. But although I took care of them, I delayed throwing myself down from the bench on which I had been sitting. The whole area was enshrouded completely with dust and falling branches of trees. A huge branch fell on us and slightly hurt my forehead.

Within no time, I rushed to the bishop's hut and saw two pastors dashing out from it like small birds escaping for their lives. Then Abraham Mayom followed them, meandering on his knees, and I asked him how he was; he showed me the burn in his hand and asked me to find out if Bishop Nathaniel was still alive. As I tried to enter the hut, he crawled out, totally covered with dust. I told him to remove his white T-shirt and run with others to the nearby river for extra protection in case more bombs fell.

The hot particles of the bomb pierced through and made many holes in the bishop's hut. It cut into pieces a cloth line hanging in the house and tore some clothes. Mayom's hand got burnt from a hot shrapnel. All the occupants were saved with the exception of the slight burn suffered by Mayom, and such a huge furnace did not torch the hut in spite of its grass-thatched roof.

It is amazing to note here that the blaze burnt the roof of a lavatory room, although it was 30m away from the site of the bomb. That type of bomb explodes in circles, leaving nothing in its way, all around, up to a distance of about 300m. It fell at a distance of 18m from the church building, which was also a grass-thatched roof kind of shelter. Like a threshing floor, littered with cereal grains, the church was full of dust, but its entire structure was miraculously saved from the destructive bomb.

Everything on the church compound was in a total mess with some big branches thrown here and there. While sitting by myself on a wooden bench by the church, the air raid was on going, with aeroplanes dropping bombs randomly and indiscriminately. Civilians continuously poured into the small stream and ducked down for their own safety. One of the by-passers, a Jeng woman, came running, reached our church and was surprised to see the mess. With deep concern in her voice, she asked me: "Hii, pieth koc?" Which means: "Are people alright?" And I told her that people were fine; then she went on running and murmured: "Ne cak akɔn malɔu ke ye kɛŋ loi e lɛ?" This means: "Can even dark-grey elephant do things like this?" The raid lasted for about three hours with more than ten people killed and many wounded.

Bishop Nathaniel and Abraham Mayom made some plans and told us to wait for them in Torit, while they rushed to Kenya on an official visit. So we remained in the Episcopal Church there. After a little while, they returned to Torit from Kenya.

Family Reunion

On 16 June 1990, I left Torit for Bor by a humanitarian plane and proceeded on the same day to Palabach Cattle Camp and spent the night there amidst the restless and mooing cattle. It was good time to reconnect with my people and the cattle way of life. Some of the children I left in 1983 were now adolescents. We knew each other merely by names but not in person. Moreover, it was now for the first time that I was able to get acquainted with the young ladies that were married to some of my relatives after I had left the village. The night was short, fantastic and remarkable. In fact, one day in the cattle camp was not sufficient for me to reunite with my people. But I had been compelled to rush to the village for the sake of seeing my mother and father and other relatives.

Nevertheless, since Palabach is somewhat near the village, we understood that we were going to see each other quite often during my stay there.

After enjoying some fresh milk, I left the cattle camp on 18th of the same month for our village of Werkok. I was accompanied by some youngsters and we moved along, enjoying our traditional forest. All my senses reconnected not only with my people but also with other common environmental features. My respiratory system enjoyed the varieties of aroma from the vegetation to insects, etc. Despite the absence of almost all our traditional birds and animals, my eyes reconnected again with most of our unique geographic features. Being born and brought up in Bor, my physiological systems automatically adjusted to the climatic patterns of the local area. Everything about Bor greatly appealed to my whole being.

From the first homestead in the village, along the meandering path to our house, just a distance of about two miles, it took us more than two hours because it was too hard for me to bypass any of my relatives on the way. Both the young and old, males and females, embraced each other with me and shed tears of joy, and we praised God together for having kept us alive. Those waiting for me with my parents in the house were almost running out of patience, for they also wanted to satisfy their love for and curiosity to see me. Upon reaching our house, just like the prodigal son, all people ran, embraced and kissed me lovingly. It was the first time to meet the wife of my brother Bech because their marriage took place while I was in the movement.

My parents had organized a homecoming feast to mark our family reunion. One of the amazing impressions I encountered upon my return home was the lack of clothing and medicine. By that time, people living in the SPLA/M liberated areas lacked access to some vital social services such as health care, education, clean water, etc. People were in rags, and as a result, women felt ashamed to appear before men in any social gatherings. I shared my few clothes with others, although they were not enough to meet their grave needs. I really wished I had magic might to supply all their needs. Yet the worst time was still around the corner by then. We had a good time with my parents and relatives. My father and I slept in our luak during my time back home.

My Ordination to Priesthood

My trip from Ethiopia to Bor culminated with my ordination as a pastor in the ECS Diocese of Bor. While enjoying my time with my relatives and friends, Bishop Nathaniel and Abraham Mayom were enjoying their exclusive time, strategizing and planning all things that eventually led to our surprised ordination. Mayom and maybe other colleagues of mine, Peter Yuang and Joseph Maker, knew what was going on pertaining to our final ordination. But on my side, I did not put much interest in that due to two primary reasons: firstly, my aim of coming to Bor was focused on a reunion with my people; secondly, becoming an ordained priest was out of my mind, although my pastoral work was beyond any reasonable doubt.

Immediately after coming to Bor from Torit, Bishop Nathaniel and Abraham Mayom went on a brief visit to Kenya to solicit some humanitarian and relief assistance. Thereafter, they returned to Bor sometime in July 1990.

Abraham Mayom broke the news to us about our proposed ordination. A lot of things came into my mind. The first question was about my military career – will the movement, relatives and friends be happy with this choice? Is it what the Lord has called me to do, or am I imposing my own desires against his will? These and other better questions cropped up in my mind and heart. But, as a God-fearing person, I put everything before God in prayer and sought his will to be done. Some of my friends and relatives were in support of my ordination, and their arguments were based on my recognisable spiritual values. What about the opinion of my colleagues? Of course, Abraham Mayom was in favour of our ordination. Peter Yuang and Joseph Maker did favour it, too. Lazarus Dhiop Manyiel and Reuben Akurdid Ngong were ready to be ordained with us and had no any single hurdle before them, for they were civilians.

With Mayom, Maker and Yuang the issue of us being officially released from the army was not a big deal. However, I insisted that the diocesan bishop should send an official letter of request to the SPLA/M leadership, seeking my official release from the army before the ordination. As people sometimes confuse truth and opinion, I did not want some people to miss the truth, speculate and place their narrow judgments on my sincerity.

The Diocese of Bor was in need of skilled personnel and thinking of placing a request before the leadership of the movement. Hence, instead of launching such an important request in my name alone, they included the name of Gabriel Atem Manyuon and Daniel Matiop Anyieth who later died in a road accident in Nairobi.

In preparation for the ordination, some senior priests properly screened us. In the course of screening, our military background was thoroughly checked because the church did not want to enter into possible disputes with the movement for having ordained us, the SPLA soldiers. Abraham Mayom defended our position strongly. To me, any outcome –being ordained or not was good with me, for I knew God's will was to prevail in the end over our personal desires. Thus, I did not stage any serious defence before the panel.

However, I remembered paraphrasing two parables in the Bible: firstly, in response to the fear of the church not to ordain SPLA soldiers, I referred to the blind man that was miraculously healed by Jesus Christ in John, chapter 9 and ended up causing excommunicable problems between his parents and Pharisees whereby the former, because of fear, responded to the latter by saying, "Ask him. He is of age; he will speak for himself." I meant that if the movement was to question about our ordination, the church should ask us to talk as adults. Then I proceeded with another parable of Jesus Christ in which He says in Matthew, chapter 9: "The harvest is plentiful but the workers are few. Ask the Lord of the harvest, therefore, to send out workers into his harvest field." Based on this parable, I told the panel that we thought that the harvest was still plentiful, and so workers were still needed, that is why we did not refuse to be ordained. But now if there was no need for more workers, then it was fine. I even told them that after ordination one might return to and do some pastoral work in the army, as was the case for me. After responding slightly towards my biblical arguments, the discussion came to an end. So the panel approved of our ordination and gave their findings to Bishop Nathaniel.

Surprisingly enough, during their recent visit to Kenya, Bishop Nathaniel and Abraham Mayom bought and brought some priest's uniforms with them. And this justified the fact that although we had a glimpse of the whole picture, the two leaders were the real architects and executers of the plan. We were shown all the procedural steps to follow during the ordination ceremony and asked to keep on praying unto the Almighty God for his blessings. Bishop Nathaniel fasted and earnestly prayed before the actual day set for this significant event. The church authority fixed the venue and the time for the ordination – the place was Kapat Church, and the date was Sunday, 12 August 1990.

During the war, Kapat was the seat of the Anglican Church Diocese of Bor because Bor town was repeatedly contested between the SPLA and the Khartoum Government. But it was under the SPLA at the time of our ordination. It was captured from the government troops on Monday, 17 April 1989.

On Sunday 12 August 1990, the bishop and some of his priests ordained us in Kapat Church. Abraham Mayom, Reuben Akurdid and Lazarus Dhiop were ordained as full priests; while Peter Yuang, Joseph Maker and I were ordained as deacons in line with the order of priesthood in the Episcopal Church of Sudan. Now we were empowered to preach the word and carry out other pastoral duties in our respective dioceses as well as wherever the Lord placed us. Many relatives and friends warmly congratulated us on our ordination. The church asked me to come and work within the Diocese in Bor.

This was unintended shift in my career. To me, my ordination into priesthood was clearly under the divine influence of the Almighty God, the constant 'Silent Hand' upon my life. He patiently, graciously and lovingly fought and won the war of my destiny. Hence, I personally view August 12, 1990 as a clear point of division between my past and future life.

After the ordination, I requested the church leadership to permit me to go to Ethiopia and pursue my marriage, and it was automatically granted. I did also promise to return to Bor to work with my diocese after my marriage.

Sharing My Viewpoints with the Relatives

With the consent of my parents and other family members, I called some of my relatives to have a meeting with me in our luak. Since I had returned home from the exile, I had been talking with my parents, sharing the word of God with them and trying to convert them to Christianity but with no success. Father told me that there was no problem burning the family shrines if other members of our extended family were in agreement. The significant shrine in the family was Alok, which was famously in the form of drums. Alok was brought home from somewhere in Tunji by my great grandfather Mathiang Ajoh. He brought it, for it was believed to have some divine power which could, besides others, help people win any battle. Although it belonged to the entire family of Mathiang Bior, it was in our home. This is because, tradition-ally, my dad being the first son of Alier who was also the first son of Mathiang had the ultimate responsibility to look after it on behalf of other relatives. But he had no right to disown or throw it away without the duly given consent of other family members.

The agenda for the meeting was, therefore, twofold: firstly, to share the idea of my marriage and secondly, to share the Gospel and see how to persuade the rela-tives to abandon their shrines, burn them and turn to Jesus Christ as their Lord and Saviour. The second agenda was not an easy task because most of the people, not only in our village but in the entire area of Bor, were still devoted worshippers of their African Traditional Religions. And so, as part of the whole community, my people were not ready to part with their shrines, especially Alok.

In the course of our discussion, my parents and others seconded my marital pro-posal and asked me to go ahead and keep them posted. Although some of them tried to persuade me to abandon my returning to Ethiopia for marriage, which was not yet ascertained. Instead, they asked me to look around in Bor for any possible girl of our collective choice to marry. But, in order not to break my marital promise done in Ethiopia, I turned down their advice and kindly asked them to give me a chance to go back to Ethiopia before I made another promise for a different marriage. So they all wished me journey mercy back to Ethiopia.

Coming to the second agenda, I categorically explained to them, using some key biblical verses, the dreadful consequences of following Satan along the broad road that leads to death vis-à-vis trusting and believing in the only God of creation through his only begotten Son Jesus Christ. I told them that believing in Jesus is like following the narrow path of life that leads to everlasting life. I took absolute care to discuss this theological paradigm with them with much persuasion, in love and deep concern by avoiding any condemning or rhetoric language because I knew very well that my main purpose was to sow the seeds, water them and leave their germination and growth entirely in the hand of God. As one of their own, their response was very polite, cunning and elusive.

Bestowing some tantalising spirit upon me, they clearly took advantage of my returning to Ethiopia by requesting me to put the whole issue off until I came back from Ethiopia. I became nervously concerned because spiritual issues are not deliber-ately deferred but timely dealt with as they are matters of life and death. For the Lord says: 'Today, if you hear his voice, do not harden your hearts' (Hebrews 3:7b-8a).

Paul also tells the Corinthians in his second letter: "I tell you, now is the time of God's favour, now is the day of salvation" (2Corinthians 6:2b). I pleaded with them not to put their decision off but to take an immediate decision with regard to their personal conversion, yet they refused to respond to my altar call. In the end, I asked them to think about it and make their personal decisions, even while I was away. I pointed out that the church and pastors were there to take care of their spiritual needs during my absence. Apart from my mom and dad, my other family members were converted to Christianity. I left everything in the hand of the Lord.

My Marriage

In September 1990, I left Bor for Kapoeta and left from there for Nasir by plane. Since it was the flooding time of the year, I planned to move from Nasir to Itang by motorboat. Unfortunately, I waited for about two weeks there for any possible chance of a boat ride but in vain. Peter Makuach Nyiek, a Presbyterian leader in charge of churches therein at the time, took good care of me.

After running out of patience, Peter Makuach organised my mission to move on foot under a well-arranged escort from one church to another. It was a journey of about two weeks. All the churches along the route were to render all necessary assistance to me in terms of feeding, accommodation, transport and security to make my journey successful. From Nasir up to Itang, I passed through and was hosted by various churches situated in the following locations: Kot, Rokrok, Zekzeek, Dauguar, Bol, Nyak, Wak, Mayen, Pakur, Pialguop, Makuei, Wuriang, Dhardhar, Kiech, Pagak, Kuorjieny, Thuer and Koukou, a total of eighteen churches along the route. I am very grateful to both the church leaders and other members whom I met during this long and tiresome journey.

The journey between Koukou and Itang normally takes about two days on foot, and at the time passed through a kind of No Man's Land. In Koukou, there was a need for volunteers to show and help me with my baggage from there up to Itang. Two young men, Peter Mut Wieu, James Duer Bechiok and Mary Nyanguet Tueng were planning to go to Itang from Koukou. Thus, they were requested by their church to take care of me on the way. Koukou is in Yom Nuer. One of these young men proudly narrated that from time immemorial, no alien, even from other Nuer groups, dared to cross the land of Yom without being killed, leave alone someone volunteering to carry his luggage. He went on and said that such a traditional norm had greatly changed because of God's Word and modernization. So he agreed to help me with my bag up to Itang.

Thus, we left there on 8 October 1990 for Itang and arrived there safely. From Nasir to Itang, a certain SPLA officer joined me, and he also benefited from all the help given by the above churches.

In one of such fellowships between Nasir and Itang, one man asked me as to what we, the Sudanese, were to pray for before God in regard to the raging civil war. I took a child and said, assuming this child was yours and did something bad to you, what would you do as a parent? He said he would discipline him. Then I said if he continued disobeying and insulting you, what would you to do? He said he would beat him even more severely. Then I asked him why, and his response was the child was stubborn and needed more discipline. Again I said if he were to plead with you, asking you to forgive him with the hope that he would not do it again, what would you do? He said he would forgive and leave him. Finally, I told him that we should respond to God in the same way, asking him to forgive and restore us to himself. He nodded in agreement. His naïve question taught me that some of us easily know how to make mistakes but do not understand how to repent and make some restitution to such mistakes.

Having mentioned the churches that helped me accomplish my long journey from Nasir to Itang, I just want to honestly once more underscore here that the hospitality I got from my Christian brothers and sisters, irrespective of our ethnic and denominational differences, was very commendable and worth sharing here in appreciation. Like other people under the sun, the Nuers are God-fearing and hospitable people, especially in relation to church folks. I refused that they slaughter bulls and sheep or goats for us in many churches, simply because we were in a hurry and also saw no good reason to do that since we were just two of us. I extremely enjoyed my fellowship with them, sharing God's Word and interceding together in all the churches I passed through.

My Marital Procedures, October 1990 – May 1991

I found out the letter which I had left earlier with Jacob Biar for my expected mother-in-law was not delivered. He failed to convey it due to two main factors: firstly, he did not have sufficient time to travel to Pinyudo, and secondly, Jacob and other relatives of mine were not in support of my coming back to Ethiopia from Bor to pursue such a marital pledge of which its futurity was very uncertain. Since I got that golden chance to be at home after seven years, they were, therefore, of the opinion that I should find a wife right there in Bor. To fulfil their suggestion, Jacob and other relatives such as Alier Chuit Agou met and agreed to send me an urgent radio message. The content of the letter was for me to forget my earlier marital promise to Leek's family, and instead, look for a girl of my choice there in Bor to marry before returning to Ethiopia. However, all their concerted arrangements took place while I was already on my way from Bor to Itang, and so my arrival in Itang took them by complete surprise. They, as a result, abandoned their idea and solidly stood with me as I pursued and gave a chance to my marital promise.

Marital Competition

I withdrew my letter from Jacob Biar and went to Pinyudo Refugee Camp to present myself before my proposed bride and her relatives. Upon my arrival in Itang, I received some heart-breaking news that some capable men had already presented themselves both to the girl and her relatives, each wanting to marry her. So there was already a very tight marital competition. In the culture of Jeng people, marital competition is quite normal because it boosts the social status of the girl and her family background. Also it is a useful means to lure the competing youngsters for a higher bride price. But normally, the final evaluation for the best choice in terms of bridegroom lies with the bride and her relatives.

Some of the obvious yardsticks or merits for evaluation include but are not limited to the good physical appearance, dignified moral character, respectable family lineage and sufficient wealth in terms of cattle. Wealth is not the primary winning factor in this particular culture because it is believed to be temporal in comparison to some acceptable, enduring moral values. Also the girl's parents and other relatives, given their enormous social and other cultural experiences, are not only after the wealth or bride price but also after the brightest future for their daughter. They are the ears and eyes of their daughter in that they help her to make the right choice.

As an ordained priest, I didn't feel like competing with some of my church members in marriage. Nevertheless, the honour of my earlier marital promise and the recommendation given to me by Rachael Aluengi compelled me to join the tight marital competition. Withdrawing in the marital race in Jeng culture creates some unnecessary speculations both on the side of the bride as well as on the side of the bridegroom. For example, some people can foster some shallow conclusions by saying the man is afraid to compete because he lacks some admirable credentials, or he detects something wrong about the girl. So since I heard nothing bad about my expected wife as well as knowing nothing wrong about my family lineage and me, I wholeheartedly decided to join the race and see what the Lord had in store for each of us.

Without breaching the holy canonical rules of holy marriage, and without alienating the cultural marital norms as well as sacrificing my Christian and pastoral traits on the marital altar, I promised myself and others to take and lead a clean path of competition from the beginning to the end, irrespective of final consequences. Normally, in any area of competition, competitors always try to push each other down in the process through pride and all sorts of character assassination. For instance, in marital competition, common and obvious words from the mouth of weak-hearted competitors are: "You see, I am better than so and so... my family background is the best" and so on and so forth. This is the unhealthy type of language that I sincerely promised to avoid in the course of the competition. As we know, it is biblically correct that pride comes before the fall, and humility leads to glory.

Disclosure of My Marital Idea First to My Church

Since Jacob Biar failed to deliver my introductory letter to my expected mother-in-law, I did not know whether they knew my marital intent or not. Like any leader, a priest is a figurehead who is constantly under a close surveillance by both his subjects and outsiders. He has to take maximum care of his personal character not to commit unwarranted mistakes that will stain and bring his spiritual leadership into disrepute in the eyes of the people. He must make sure that his private and public lives do not conflict with each other – what he does and says in private must be the same as what he does and says in public. This is especially the case in terms of sexual behavioural patterns; when an unmarried priest frequently associates himself with ladies, particularly the young girls, he gives wider room to unhealthy conjectures among his church members. The best thing is to let them know your intent so as to allay any justified fear from their minds and hearts as well as to protect your own image and the word of God.

So in order to fill and smoothly level all the unnecessary pitfalls along my marital path, I called for a meeting with the church council on one of the Sundays' services in Pinyudo. I thought it wise to keep the agenda for the meeting very confidential so as to maintain the right forum in terms of curiosity sake and also to avoid some possible prejudices and premeditated feelings towards the subject. Almost all the council members turned up to hear something from their respected pastor. My expected mother-in-law, as a member of the council, was sitting right in the meeting, although she was not quite sure of what was happening. The members looked at me suspiciously as they waited to hear the purpose of this extraordinary church meeting.

I excitedly told them my marital purpose but cautiously added that it was just a plan, for both the girl and her parents and other close relatives knew nothing about it. I explained to them that the reason why I called the meeting, as their priest, was to inform the church about my marital intent. This was in order to dispel unworthy thoughts in the minds and hearts of the people whenever they saw me paying frequent visits to the girl's home and talking to her.

Then I looked around and tilted my ears, trying to hear and observe their both verbal and physical expressions and reactions towards my idea. Their general response was very positive and welcoming. One of the encouraging responses from the members of the council came from a very wise Nuer guy who was, unfortunately, blind. He told me that what I did was very unique, exemplary and in direct line with my spiritual leadership. He commented further by saying that the only thing that might cause me to fail the race could be due to my priesthood as many people wrongly associate the pastoral role with poverty. In other words, those looking from a worldly point of view would not be comfortable with the idea of me marrying their daughter into a sort of poor economic status. However, he encouraged me to go on with my plan. Some of the members of the council who were related to those competing with me were not pleased with my proposal for the fear that the race was going to be in my favour. Yet they kept quiet and boiled inside slowly. In short, this church council meeting endorsed my marital competition and earnestly prayed for God's guidance in the course of the race.

Letting Her Know My Intent

Following my cultural patterns of marital procedures, I individually presented myself to the girl and shared with her my intent. This is not always a one-day event, for it may take weeks, months or even a year, depending, among others, on how the man properly presents himself before the girl and also on the girl's perception of him. Although the girl internally likes and is willing to accept him, she is not to do so personally and individually. Because the best, culturally accepted way, is for her to share her feelings, either negative or positive, with her friends and blood-related sisters who will in turn break the news to the man and his friends and blood-related brothers. Always both the men and girls put up a fierce verbal fight, arguing among themselves for and against the marital idea. Here the talks, especially from the side of the girl, focus on the physical stature and moral values of the expected bridegroom. If the girl and her sisters dislike the man, they will adamantly reject the proposal by clearly and aggressively explaining why they do not like him. They use aggressive and abusive language so as to embarrass and defeat the man and his fellows and deter them not to dream of coming back again or proceeding to girl's parents and relatives to lobby with them. The talks between the ladies and gentlemen sometimes take some days to allow the girls to seek some additional consultations from relevant sources. At this juncture, if the men are completely defeated and rejected humiliatingly by the girls, there is no headway. But if there is room for agreement, the ladies can politely tell the gents to go ahead and present their case to the mothers of the girl for further deliberations and approvals. These 'mothers' include her biological mother and other wives of her uncles and other relatives.

At this particular level, the young men are to show a high level of respect and politeness as they are dealing with people akin to their own mothers. Even at the point of disagreement, they have to use a lot of diplomacy and persuasion. Pertaining to the side of the mothers, although they portray recognisable standards of respect and accommodation, they are proactive, investigative and examining in their approaches, especially by analysing the moral character, family lineage and socio-economic status of the expected bridegroom. The mothers, of course, have the utmost interest of the futurity and general wellbeing of their daughter at heart, for they correctly know what it means to be a wife in a foreign land. Their opinion is highly appreciated by both men and girl, especially when it comes to issues pertaining to marital relationships and family management. Like the first group, they have no final authority on the whole issue, though their comments are valuable and commendable. If they are satisfied with their own findings, they refer the young men to the fathers of the girl for further deliberations and final resolutions. Fathers include the biological father, if still alive, uncles and other members of the extended family.

At this final level, the fathers vigorously launch their investigative discussions with the young men by investigating the family lineage, socio-economic status of the expected bridegroom. One of the key questions is to find out whether he has been officially released by his parents to marry. And of course, when one is officially told to marry by his parents, it means that he has some wealth to do so. Here the meeting is very brief and to the point because the level of respect is very high between the two groups. At this level, there is no room for any romantic and unnecessary talks during the discussions. If the fathers of the girl have some valid reasons for which they do not want the marriage to go ahead between this man and their daughter, they categorically explain to the young men why the marriage should not progress on, warn them not to return again and send a word of warning to the relatives of the man, telling them not to allow their son to insist on the marriage. Something contrary to this final decision on the side of the girl will lead to some social feuds between the two sides. But if the girl's fathers have nothing bad to reject the young man from marrying their daughter, they ask them to go and make a request of their parents to send an official message to the parents of the girl, indicating their approval of their son to marry this particular girl. This is to crosscheck whether the young man's claim to marry is realistic or not.

In the event that the young man's claim to marry is official, his parents or relatives will immediately send an emissary with an official family message confirming the marital claim of their son. The envoy is nicely hosted so as to give him the positive impression of the girl's family in the eyes of the man's family. After receiving the official message, they give their final decision, either approval or rejection, to the emissary to take back to the man's parents and relatives. If the response is positive, then the primary message from the girl's parents and relatives is to invite them to go and see their wealth allocated as bride price for this marriage. But if the answer is negative, the girl's parents will not have a desire to go and see the young man's wealth. Instead, their opinion will shift to any of the other competing men.

If the man's parents and relatives want the girl's parents to examine their wealth meant for the marriage, they will invite them. The primary role of the young men from the side of the girl is to go and see the cows from the cattle camp of the expected bridegroom. The bridegroom and some of his relatives show them around to see and nominally select the cows of their choice. If the wealth is not appropriate in their eyes, the girl's brothers can bitterly protest and reject them, meaning that their daughter should not be given in marriage to him due to his low socio-economic status. They may even refuse to eat and leave on an empty stomach. Whether positive or negative, the young man from the side of the girl will report back to their relatives of their findings and give advice to them. Their advice will either allow or prevent the marriage from going ahead. In case of a positive report, the youngsters will, in most instances, advise their parents and relatives to conduct the marriage in terms of the bride price – giving the wealth to the girl's relatives – before the final marital ceremony in which the girl will be blessedly passed over to her bridegroom and his relatives.

Having certified all or most of the above preliminary marital procedures, the first phase of my marriage was conducted between Thursday 14 and Saturday 16 February 1991 in Itang Refugee Camp and marked by the slaughtering of a bull for the girl's relatives. Presiding over the marriage was my late cousin Jacob Biar Mach and other esteemed relatives and friends. Then the bride was taken back to her mother and other closest relatives in Pinyudo Refugee Camp, Ethiopia where the final marriage ceremony took place.

Why Not a 'Sacred Marriage'

Rev. Andrew Mayol Ajak planned to conduct and bless our marriage ceremony in the church in Pinyudo Refugee Camp sometime in May 1991. He was the pastor in charge of this church. But in the course of our preparations, some church leaders, including Rev. Andrew Mayol went to Addis Ababa, Ethiopia on an official visit. While in the capital city, the political situation of Ethiopia drastically changed making the Communist regime be at the verge of complete failure and collapse. In terms of ideological and political connections between the Mengistu's regime and SPLA/M, the imminent death of the Ethiopian Government created some nervousness and confusion in the minds and hearts of all the supporters of our movement. This is because they believed that the staying of the innocent Sudanese people in the refugee camps inside Ethiopia was now not going to be possible. Hence, the SPLA/M leadership alerted its supporters to be on full alert and ready to evacuate all the camps and flee back to Southern Sudan in the event of any possible danger.

Therefore, the Sudanese church leaders were cut off from their flocks, especially in Itang and Pinyudo Refugee Camps because of the raging battles between government troops and rebels along most of the routes leading towards the capital, Addis Abba. Chances of their reuniting with us while still in Ethiopia were very remote if not completely impossible.

Given this terrible scenario, I was confronted with two options: the first option was to adjourn the wedding until further notice, although I did not know whether my bride and her family and I were going to run to the same destination inside Sudan. It was very probable that in the event of escaping back to Sudan from Ethiopia, my in-laws, including the bride, and I were not going to see each other for long if not forever because the consequences of war are difficult to ascertain. The second option was to let some church laity oversee the marriage ceremony outside the church while it is conducted in a traditional way. By traditional way, it does not mean doing it in an unbiblical manner. But it rather implies that reading of canonical verses plus other doctrinal procedures usually done by an ordained minister were not going to occur during the ceremony simply due to the lack of a pastor.

The unanimous decision from both sides of the marriage fell on the second option, that is, to finalise the marriage ceremony outside the church before the final exodus from Ethiopia to Sudan in order to enable my wife and I to run together. Hence, Paul Deng Chol and other laity, including Philip Biar Mathiang, took charge of the marriage ceremony and conducted it in a colourful celebration which occurred after the normal church services on Sunday 10 May 1991 in Pinyudo. Despite the absence of an ordained priest to oversee the marriage, outside the church such unique marital verses were read by Paul Deng Chol who was an evangelist in the church.

The ladies, over forty in number, who accompanied the bride returned to their respective homes on Saturday 16 of the same month after spending a remarkable moment of joy and jubilation. I became one of the winners of the year, and it shows that all plans belong to us, the human beings, but the end result lies with God.

Marriage, a Shared Responsibility

In Jeng culture, marriage, like other communal events, is very inclusive in that it involves all relatives and close friends from both sides. It is like a very long, big and heavy pole being relentlessly carried from one end by the side of the bridegroom and from the other end by the relatives and close friends of the bride, while the middle part of the pole is left for the husband and wife to carry wholeheartedly. For it to remain in the air until the entire journey is finished and the final destination is satisfactorily reached, all the parties involved are to diligently and sincerely carry their parts of the pole. I call this joint sustainability or success of marriage. Or else, the moment it is left to one or few of the instrumental carriers, the load will automatically come down heavily on them on its way to the ground. And this leads to divorce, separation or family breakdown. It is because of this communal nature of marriage that the Jeng culture views it from an inclusive perspective. It takes all the important in-laws from both sides to build it up. But it also squarely rests on them to continually repair, uphold and keep it up perpetually until it is smoothly passed over to the very offspring born and brought up in the same marriage and on to the next generations. It is because of this inclusiveness of the marriage that the Jeng people are able to mentally record and keep their long genealogies up to more than thirty or so generations.

Cultural Marks of Marriage

One of the funny but vital things about Jeng marriage is the way in which there are no written documentations involved. Apart from the case of some of the urban Jeng people, our marriages are not marked with the so-called legal certificates. To the best of my memory, there are no unmarried couples or people who can live out of traditional wedlock in Jeng culture. In addition to being an embarrassing thing to both the girl and young man's parents and relatives, living together as husband and wife out of matrimony is degrading and not acceptable to the young man and young girl, even if the young man's economic status is below zero. This is because it will continuously affect the social status of the children born and brought up in such unhealthy marital circumstance. Culturally, it is far better to be in debt than to be given or to take someone's daughter freely, for Jeng people own one another. Irrespective of your age, you are either legally married or legally and solely unmarried; therefore, there are no short cuts to marital status in Jeng culture.

The prominent marks of Jeng marriage include, but are not limited to: the bride price, exchange of gifts, slaughtering of some animals at different levels of marriage and designated feasts and articulated swearing by both sides of the bride and bridegroom during the wedding ceremony, which is carried out by elders from both sides. All these and more are highly respected more than a written certificate by people from both sides. However, because of the current globalisation of mankind, people from our culture are forced, against their will, to seek legal and marital certificates in justification of their marriages. I have now acquired such a document, especially in case of global travel beyond our cultural domain.

Prominent in the wedding on the side of my in-laws were Mother, Deborah Nyaluak Kuol, Leek Majang-Adiit, Edward Chuol Leek, Deng-Madot Leek, Ayen Kon Deng, Leek-Matany Aleer Deng, Malual-Maguar Deng, Aleer Leek Deng and Makuei Leek Deng. On my side, some of the prominent relatives and friends were Jacob Biar Mach, Elijah Alier Ayom, Jacob Wuoi Mach, Jacob Wai Mach, Deng Garang Deng, Ajoh Garang Makuach, Ateny Makuei Piok, Maker Lual Kuol, Chol Manyang Makuach, Nyankot Kuot Mach and Paul Anyang Manasseh.

Aluengi's advice was finally realised. Unfortunately, my dear Rachael Aluengi had left us in this rough world in the 1990s to be with the Lord.

The Sudanese Exodus from Ethiopia to Sudan

The Fall of Mengistu's Derg

In May of 1991, the level of panic alarmingly increased among the Sudanese people both in the refugee camps and SPLA/M. This occurred after the fall of Mengistu Haile Mariam's Military Junta and the ascension to the political power in Addis Ababa by an Ethiopian Government that was widely believed to be pro Khartoum regime. The new Junta ruling the nation was the Ethiopian People's Revolutionary Democratic Front and Tigrayan People's Liberation Front (EPRDF/TPLF). It was under the leadership of Meles Zenawi (President), Tamirat Layne (Prime Minster) and Siye Abraha (Minister of Defence).

Rumours of unfriendly Ethiopian forces advancing from different routes to the camps of refugees became very common. The SPLA/M leadership took a very keen notice of such unhealthy political development in Ethiopia and so advised its citizens to be on high alert and run back to Sudan whenever necessary.

Disorganized Exodus

Just after seven days from the date of my marriage, the order came from our leadership, asking the camps authorities first to evacuate none essential staff, things and vulnerable refugees to some areas inside Ethiopia along the Ethiopia-Sudan border. The first vulnerable group to be evacuated was of the unaccompanied minors, that later came to be known as the 'Lost Boys', and disabled soldiers. But because of fear, the whole exodus became disorganised and voluntary in that people, especially civilians, took different routes towards Sudan and moved at their own discretion and time convenience. They broke up into smaller and manageable groups, consisting mostly of relatives and friends who had a common destination in Sudan in mind. They were to care for each other in terms of security, hunger and carrying of huge baggage, among others.

Less Becomes More

Unlike the blessed Israelites who cheated their innocent Egyptian neighbours and took away their precious stones of gold and silver, among others, on this terrible exodus, the Sudanese left almost all that they had and fled with their lives only. Each and every person was mindful of his own things, and each and every group was concerned with itself. Like little ants carrying their heavy loads during the worst inundation of their holes, SPLA soldiers were busy, carrying their armaments, food items and personal belongings. Because of the haste of the journey, insecurity and very poor logistic arrangements, SPLA left most of its valuable things along the routes.

Concerning individual preparations for the journey, maximum care and wise decision was maintained. For instance, despite the poor economic status of the refugees, in the event of the terrible exodus, personal belongings became huge, and so the choice of what to take and what to leave behind became difficult and tempting. There must be the right balance in such a choice in that one was to take a bit of food items, clothing, beddings, especially blankets, bed-sheets and plastic sheets, water containers, cooking utensils, plates, spoons, knives, shoes, etc. Yet the baggage was to be reasonable and small enough to carry; the heavier it was, the more one was likely to lag behind in the march, and thus, the more one was probably exposed to any possible danger.

For instance, my wife and I took only what we could carry and left most of our belongings behind. Precious among what we left were my valuable textbooks. Those with smaller children who could not walk alone, it was terrible because their parents and other related adults had to carry them, in addition to food items and personal belongings. The sick and the elderly got very worse as there was no Good Samaritan to assist them during such rushed hours. Although some of them survived that horrible ordeal, the rest became food for wild beasts and birds of the air.

Most of the people in Pinyudo went to and camped along the banks of Gilo River. It was at its flooding height because it was the rainy season of the year. The distance between Pinyudo and that particular site of Gilo River is estimated to be 65 miles, and it is full of some dangerous wild animals such as lions and bears. The distance between River Gilo and Pochalla, a border town inside Sudan, is also estimated to be almost the same like the one between Gilo and Pinyudo. Some armed groups, unpopular with SPLA/M, were also along the same routes, causing fears and confusion among the people. Lack of food and shelter were also some of the hurdles faced by the Sudanese masses on their way back to Sudan.

I acquired an old bicycle while in Pinyudo. It helped me a lot during the exodus, although its tubes burst and got worn out on the way. My beloved wife, a newly wedded lady, took the bull by the horns and faced the journey head on. She carried her baggage and walked fast in the course of the entire journey. When on the move, I tied my heavy load on the bicycle and pulled it along the road and trekked quicker than others; even when others rested, I kept on moving and reached the intended destination quite ahead of my fellow travellers. On reaching there, I put down my load and hurriedly returned to catch up with some of my relatives lagging behind to help them with their loads.

During my return journeys, I usually saw some bad, discouraging sights in that the weak ones were the ones behind the march, left by the strong ones at the mercy of any possible peril. With my priest uniform and the old bicycle, and plus the way I always used to return to catch up with those behind, all the people marching with me along the road came to know me very well. On my opposite direction, they usually asked me whether the destination was near at which I nodded and asked them to take courage and move on. One day, while on the move, one of the ladies praised me for the way I had handled the whole journey and said she would have given me a girl for marriage if she had one, and I thanked her and said that I already had one.

My Two Daring Trips

While in Gilo River, I made two remarkable and daring journeys. In order to lighten our heavy loads during the next trip from Gilo to Pochalla, I thought it wise to put some of the loads on my old bicycle and take them to Pochalla ahead of the time of departure. My wife reluctantly concurred with my idea. I took off one early morning walking along the slippery and muddy path on my way to Pochalla. It was the first time that my feet had touched that wild route. The blades of tall grass embraced and kissed each other across the road, reducing the visibility along the route to a minimal limit. Huge and tall trees significantly dominated the landscapes. Apart from the amazing sounds of birds, some of which were quite strange to my ears and eyes, the area was deathly quiet.

Shortly after leaving our shanty camp, something leaped out from a big bush near the road. It jumped two times only and kept quiet, not very far from the road, but I failed to see it because of the thick, tall grass. People later assumed that it was either a bear or a lion. I had no option besides pushing on along the road and putting everything squarely in God's hand. I tried to double my strides to see whether I could reach my destination the same day, but I later discovered that my imagination was short of reality. I went on and on but with no sign of hope. I sweated and sweated and sweated until my clothes became damp and started smelling horrible. My ugly shoes were very dirty and filthy because I waded and walked with them so as to protect my feet. They were the best pair of shoes that I used during the time of my marriage.

As the sign of my destination was still beyond the far horizon, I came to believe and convince myself that I was going to spend the night in the forest before reaching Pochalla. But despite this genuine resolution, I decided to maintain my walking momentum and pushed on as far as I could before I sought the best place to spend the night. Are there best places in the forest? Of course, in terms of human's habitation, there are no best places in the jungle. But if you make a sort of comparative analysis of the jungle itself in terms of safety measures and the environment, especially during the wet season of the year, the best place in this context refers to a situation whereby possible hurdles are most mitigated.

In the choice of my best place, I planned to move away from the main path to a distance of about one hundred metres and choose a dry and smooth ground. This isolated place would also avoid and/or minimize the likelihood of meeting with some marauding armed men, for they mostly used the road. This is what I called the best place, although if bad luck holds it tightly in her grip, a wild beast may stumble on it and cause terrible havoc on innocent life.

The sun fled towards the western horizon, but I refused to give up on my tiresome journey before twilight. I staggered along the road, while looking here and there to find a place for the night. I broke many self-made decisions as I moved along. For example, as I moved along the road, I said to myself, "I will go and see where to spend the night at that place ahead of me." And the moment I arrived there, I set another target and so on and so forth, depending on the slightest availability of the sunlight.

As my last hope dragged me along, I fortunately stumbled on some people preparing where to sleep by the side of the road. Recognising that they were Sudanese, I just branched off the road and joined them for the night. They were also going to Pochalla ahead of the masses. I unequivocally believed, given my solid Christian faith, that what occurred was divine intervention. When I narrated this event to a Christian friend of mine some years later, he told me that the ones I met and spent the night with along the road were angels sent by the Lord to help me. When I pointed out to him that they were real Sudanese, he challenged me that God's angels can appear or change into anything, depending on unique circumstances.

The following morning, I packed my things and put them on the bicycle quickly and continued on my way to Pochalla ahead of other people and reached there at around 11am. I was completely exhausted and hungry but very happy and thankful to God for having blessed that portion of my journey.

I spent the night and took off early in the morning on my way back to Gilo. Although my bicycle was beyond repair, it was quite light and easy to pull along than before because the load was no longer there. I was determined to complete the entire journey within twelve hours, from six in the morning to six in the evening of the same day. I pushed on relentlessly and quenched my thirst with the stagnant water I found along the way. I sweated as I moved on under the merciless sun of Africa that damped my soiled clothes. Hunger became part of our life during this exodus, and so it was very unusual for anyone to complain about it. By 8pm, I arrived in the camp to the jubilation of my impatient wife and other relatives and friends. My wife and I praised the Lord for having brought us together again in sound body and high spirit.

People were about to leave Gilo for Pochalla because the danger was greatly looming right above the people as rumours of Ethiopians' attacks on refugees intensely and alarmingly increased. There was no food in Pochalla. And the little food which people brought with them from Pinyudo was almost depleted in the course of staying in Gilo. Hence, some able people moved up and down along the Gilo-Pinyudo road to replenish their food provisions before they finally embarked on their final journey to Pochalla. As the only strong person and breadwinner in our nuclear family, and given the fact that our little food almost ran out, I stubbornly decided to proceed to Pinyudo the following morning, irrespective of my wife's opinion. Because of her love for me as well as the long and tiresome journey that I had had, she almost refused to accept my decision but reluctantly permitted me to do so. Thus, I spent the short night, half awake in readiness to embark on another long, frightening and daring trip.

One of the relatives, a woman, asked me to go with her son to seek some food items for the family. I consented unwillingly to take the boy with me, but I told his mother that I disliked putting other people's lives at risk. You see, the way in which I persevered and walked alone, even by night, made me very hesitant to permit the weak youngsters to partake with me in such daring trips. It is better for people to blame you for your own mistakes than for the wrong you have done to others.

As I mentioned before, the distance between Gilo and Pinyudo is more or less the same like the one between Gilo and Pochalla. This small boy and I took off early in the morning, crossed the river and dashed along the way back to Pinyudo with the hope of reaching there the same day. We continued on our journey, taking no rest, only except when we often stood by the roadside to quench our unceasing thirst from the stagnant waters. In terms of walking, my judgement on the boy was wrong, for he kept running beside and after me like a small calf with its mother. Although we tried and tried to overcome the long distance, our hope of reaching there before dusk became very minimal. The sun went down and sank our hopes with its demise while we were still very far away from the camp. To make it worse, the remaining section of the road was covered with stagnant water and tall grass. So we groped and waded along the meandering path. Of course, we could not see where we were placing our helpless feet amidst some floating snails, deadly snakes, pitfalls, embedded rocks and thorns, among others. It is very difficult if not impossible to maintain quietness while wading. And thus, the chance of us not being heard either by any wild animal or unfriendly human being(s) was totally out of question.

It was along this part of the journey that I confirmed my fear of not wanting to walk with such a small child on this dangerous trip. I did not fear for my own life but rather for the precious life of the small boy. I ceaselessly and silently interceded with the gracious God as we staggered along the way. We eventually and much to our joy arrived at the SPLA outpost at around 8pm and were stopped at a reasonable distance by a sentry. After declaring ourselves, we were allowed in and spent the night there. The following morning, we proceeded to the camp itself where our first agenda was to look for food.

I got what I wanted, spent the night anxiously in the camp and took off at daybreak the following morning. The boy decided to remain behind with some relatives and friends for a few days to support himself. Hence, finding myself alone I was happy to dash on for more than twelve hours with Gilo still beyond the horizon. Some of my good friends tried to lure me to take some rest and spend the night halfway and continue on my journey the following day, but I tactfully and politely turned down such nice offers and pushed on with my trip.

At around 8pm, I reached Gilo at the eastern side of the river. Luckily enough, I found some SPLA soldiers trying to ferry their armaments across the river to the western side. They used the wooden canoes. After reporting myself to them, seeking their assistance to take me to the other side of the river, they asked me to wait. So I sat there lonely and ignorantly and observed what they were doing. I was totally ignorant because I did not know why they hurriedly tried to carry out such a daring mission by night.

The river was at its flooding height, and so the current was very strong, swift and dangerous. I saw the poor soldiers doing their utmost efforts to accomplish their national duty but with little success. When all their attempts failed, they gave up and suspended their mission, most probably to continue with it the following day. They sent one canoe and took me over to the desired bank of the river where I cheerfully met my beloved and anxious wife, friends and relatives who welcomed me joyfully.

Gilo's Tragic Incidence

By around midnight, we heard the sounds of heavy gunfire across the river from the east. Very soon some of the SPLA soldiers began pouring into our shanty camp, very wet and without shoes. They came running away from the fierce Ethiopian attackers, and so they swam across the river. Elijah Alier Ayom, one of my relatives, came and told me what was happening. Then he asked me to let our people be ready to evacuate early at daybreak and move with others towards Pochalla. In other words, the entire camp was ordered by the SPLA to depart from Gilo early in the morning and move towards Sudan as fast as possible.

I came to discover that in the course of my long journey from Pinyudo to Gilo, Ethiopian attackers were also moving there in the forest, trying to cut off the route between Gilo and Pinyudo, and launch some surprise attacks on SPLA posts along the route as well as on the refugees along the western and eastern banks of the river. SPLA detected the enemy's plans, and that was why they had tried to ferry their armaments across the river by night. I walked innocently within the dangerous zone on my way back to Gilo from Pinyudo. Had I accepted my loyal friends' advice to spend the night along the way, the attackers would have cut me off from my wife and others. Also if I were not taken across the river by the SPLA soldiers by night, that dangerous situation would have forced me to swim across with others in the darkness. Yet unfortunately, not all who swam made it safely to the western side of the river. I came to confirm that patience and determination are some of the vital ingredients of life and admirable leadership. Above all, God did not want me to be separated instantly from my newly wedded wife. The 'Silent Hand' was surely over me.

We put our belongings in order, maintained serious vigilance and found ourselves on the slippery way at daybreak. As usual, I loaded my old bicycle and hurriedly moved ahead with others and left my baggage in the first rallying point and dashed back to catch up with some of my weak people. As I went back, I met a huge number of people rushing along the way, escaping for their own safety. They informed me of what took place after my departure. That is, the Ethiopian attackers came and attacked the Sudanese on the eastern bank of the river, forcing the survivors, both the swimmers and non-swimmers, to jump into the swelled, merciless river. The best swimmers and the luckiest ones made it safely right over to the western bank. The rest of the people instantly drowned and got swept along by the strong currents as the hungry fish fed on them. Huge and numerous personal belongings plus SPLA armaments remained along the eastern side of the river as beneficial ill-gotten gains for the Ethiopian troops. But as for those who managed to jump into the river with their belongings, the currents took them along with the floating human bodies. This was one of the worst parts of the exodus.

From Gilo to Pochalla

With our back completely towards Ethiopia and with little or no hope of returning there, we staggered on our way to Pochalla. Yet it was obvious that people there were feeding on some of the wild vegetation – eating certain roots, leaves and fruits of some plants and trees. Also due to the lack of proper medical facilities and medicines plus poor hygiene and environmental sanitation, some people died of different types of diseases and hunger-related illnesses. Heavy rains caused some flooding along all the routes from Pochalla to other areas. This trapped people inside the town without thinking of venturing out in search of better livelihoods. Red Army, which was later known as unaccompanied minors or Lost Boys, and other refugees were already in Pochalla.

In spite of such visible hurdles on the way as well as inside Pochalla, we marched ahead single heartedly with some SPLA troops maintaining proper vanguard and rear-guard in case of any possible attacks from the enemy. Although I made this hard journey in less than twenty four hours before, it took us about three days from Gilo to Pochalla.

Some Hardships in Pochalla

Eventually, we reached Pochalla and put up some temporal shelters in and outside the town. Some of the youngsters staying with us were Jacob Wuoi Mach, famously known by the name Magany, Nai Ayuen and Akuot Nyanwut, among others. These terrible conditions moulded and baked them like earthen, durable pots until they became better than the other weak-hearted adults. We helped each other along the rough way from Pinyudo up to Pochalla. Those of Jacob Biar Mach, Rev. Michael Deng Anuol and Ateny Makuei Piok fled from Itang and joined us in Pochalla.

Since church is not the building but people who believe in God through his Son Jesus Christ as their Lord and Saviour, we the believers prepared a place in the shade of some big trees and made it as our meeting place. As the pastor in charge, Rev. Andrew Mayol Ajak was caught up in Addis Ababa by this situation, the ones left in charge of church leadership were Evangelist Paul Deng Chol and Philip Biar Mathiang. Although Rev. Michael Deng was there, he was not given any leadership role because he belonged to the Pentecostal church. I offered to help them in their church affairs but declined to play any leadership task because our diocesan authorities did not administratively assign me to this church.

In the course of our suffering in Pochalla, UN envoys came and assessed the situation. Other humanitarian bodies rushed in their representatives to assess these alarming circumstances and promised some hope. We impatiently waited and waited for their delayed responses. We almost gave up hope on seeing any touchable feedback or hearing any responses from such envoys, although the airstrip and dropping zone were completely cleared and smoothened by the hungered masses.

One day our community and SPLA leaders were informed by the UN representatives in Kenya to be ready to receive some food and other non-food items by air transport on the following day. The people took the information lightly as they had heard such unproductive news before. Nevertheless, to their great surprise, big planes lined up and dropped down some cereals, while the small one landed and offloaded some fragile food items. The planes continued for a few days with the delivery of the basic necessities of life, and sooner or later the whole unbearable event became a thing of the past, just a mere history.

Although UN addressed the issue of hunger to some extent, the security situation, the thing that took people to Ethiopia in the first place, was not solved. People were going to face a serious lack of almost all the important social services such as education, health and potable water. Hence, Pochalla was considered as a temporal home, just a transit residence.

Our Departure from Pochalla to Bor, August 1991

My aim was to find a way out from there to Bor so as to take up my diocesan assignment. But since floods blocked all the routes, especially the one leading to Bor, my wife and I simply decided to cross our fingers and remain there until water receded and routes opened for people to move.

In the meantime, NSCC envoy, Father Matthew Haman came to Pochalla by a chartered plane on a fact-finding mission. Part of his mission was to look for and meet with the church leaders of different denominations to find out how the church was doing in such turmoil. So we met and shared our concerns with him. After the meeting, others and I shared with him about my general plans, and he promised to take my wife and I during his return journey.

We put our things in order and waited happily for the plane. One of my young relatives, Jacob Wuoi, wanted to go with us, but I vehemently refused. The reasons for my refusal were varied and useful. Firstly, since we were heading for Bor where there were no education and other social services, it was of little or no benefit for him to go there and end up without education. Instead, I advised him to remain in Pochalla and wait for and see where the SPLA/M was going to take the groups of the Red Army, for these were the right people to link up with, as he was originally part of them. I knew SPLA/M was not going to dump them as useless despite being in such a desperate condition. As a strong-willed youngster, Magany took my advice lightly and insisted, instead, to go with us, although I was not yet convinced.

As I did not mean it for bad for Magany to remain behind, he left us in our residential place for somewhere inside the town to play with some of his age-mates. In his absence, the plane came and landed on the local airstrip. With the help of our relatives and friends, my wife and I took our small belongings and rushed there where we met Father Matthew. After a short while, we nervously and joyfully boarded the plane, amidst the enormous cheerful goodbyes and warm well wishes from friends, relatives and members of the church, and took off.

We joyfully waved to our friendly onlookers. Then we looked at each other with love and thanked the Almighty God and Father Matthew and his pilot. Our joy was mixed with worries because we left behind our esteemed relatives and friends. However, we prayed that God was going to bring us together again at his own chosen time and place. Unfortunately, that was the last time we saw each other alive with my beloved cousin and friend Jacob Biar Mach. Although I left my old bicycle behind, my small iron chair boarded the plane with us, for, besides our small bags, it was the only chair we had under the sun.

Our plan was to go to Lokichogio (Loki), a border town inside northern Kenya, in order for us to move from there to Bor by road. This road was busy with relief convoys that delivered humanitarian materials from Kenya to various parts of Southern Sudan in the eastern bank of River Nile. Shortly after leaving Pochalla, we happily but strangely arrived at Loki for the first time; so as strangers, it was difficult for us to know who to meet and where to go. The airport authorities put us on a small vehicle and drove to a small SPLA garrison at Key-Base. It was a small strategic location at the foot of a mountain, off Loki-Narus road. Our SPLA troops received us warmly, gave us a small hut for our accommodation and told us to wait there for any possible transportation to our final destination or so.

From Left to Right: *Peter Yuang Mach, Joseph Maker Atot, Abraham Mayom Athiaan & Stephen Mathiang Kuch in Kapat in Bor, August 1990*

CHAPTER EIGHT

Dr. Riek's Coup and My Reactions

Dr. Riek's Coup in the SPLA/M leadership was announced over the BBC on 28 August 1991 while we were in Key-Base. Like adding salt into injury, this news was received with greater shock because the minds and hearts of the Sudanese refugees and SPLA/M were heavily laden with the human and material loses endured by the Sudanese people during their terrible Exodus from the Ethiopian soil. Also people deeply were concerned with the uncertain fate of their movement. Therefore, hearing of a coup within the leadership of the SPLA/M was just like hearing the untimely death of the movement itself. But this volatile situation was somewhat mitigated immediately when Dr. John Garang went on air, denouncing the coup and reaffirming his full grip on the SPLA/M leadership.

Nevertheless, I did not welcome the split within the movement at that particular moment because of the following obvious factors: first of all, the division among the Southern Sudanese was always a sign of doom on their part but a victorious gain to their common enemies. It was in the favour of the racist policy of divide-and-rule, while it contradicts the obvious principle of: "Divided we fall, united we stand." My second objection was that waging a revolution within a revolution is just like waging a coup d'état within a coup, which logically leads to weakness and, most probably, the final collapse of such an entity. Thirdly, the horrible expulsion of the SPLA/M and its supporters from Ethiopia was to the undeniable benefit of the Khartoum Government, for it weakened the movement to a greater extent.

Immediately after our expulsion from Ethiopia, the primary concern of the movement was to see where to solidly put down its roots and continue with its protracted war against its enemy. The movement was also concerned with where to find suitable refuge for its loyal supporters, the expelled refugees, in order to continue receiving some vital social services from the UNHCR and other humanitarian agencies. Given these unfavourable circumstances of the movement, the Khartoum Government was preparing to launch some serious attacks on the SPLA/M, most likely, to destroy it once and for all during the next dry season.

Hence, having said the few points above, the timing for this coup was wrongly planned and meant to kill the movement rather than to strengthen it. It was not also for the general welfare of the destitute Southern Sudanese masses who were aimlessly moving up and down in the unfriendly environments of Southern Sudan.

It is always my firm belief that any capable person is fit to rule anytime anywhere under the sun when given a chance by his own people. As a result, Dr. Riek was not exceptional were his timing and other mannerism not ill planned. To me, this unsuccessful coup was, unfortunately, the second terrible blow next to one of those of Anyanya Two in the historical life of the SPLA/M.

The Bor Massacre, September – November 1991

Saddened with this news, my wife and I proceeded on our way from Key-Base to Kapoeta and put up with the leadership of our Episcopal church. We narrowly missed boarding some lorries going to Bor with relief supplies, and this made us quite unhappy. For the time being, Bishop Nathaniel found us in Kapoeta while on his way to Kenya on an official visit. He advised my wife and I to go and wait for him in Torit before proceeding to our final destination in Bor. So we went and waited for him there.

Why Bor for Enmity?

In the course of our waiting in Torit, Dr. Riek's followers made some heinous plans to attack, plunder and uproot the entire community of Bor because of reasons known only to them. However, some of the obvious causes shared by many people were: firstly, since his rival leader of the SPLA/M, Dr. John Garang was from Bor, and because some of the strong supporters of the movement and of Dr. John himself were from Bor, the entire Bor was taken for enmity by Riek's groups, despite the fact that his aborted coup was also backed by a few soldiers from Bor itself. It was a well-known fact that some Southern Sudanese as well as those from the side of the common enemy hated people from Bor. And hence, that was the right time to give them a terrible knock and disperse the remnants from their geographic, ancestral homeland.

But apart from the above revolutionary reason, why in the first place did other people hate the people of Bor? They are the only ones who can provide a genuine rationale for their actions. Nevertheless, this is still my personal viewpoint: part of the general equation is that people from Bor have been in the political, socio-economic, ethnic and religious forefronts both at national and regional levels in Sudan since the colonial era. So it is a common factor that anyone involves in any kind of business always makes friends and enemies innocently in the process. That is why the Holy Bible makes a strong warning that "When words are many, sin is not absent, but he who holds his tongue is wise" (Proverbs 10:19).

Based on this proverbial quotation, should people of Bor have held their tongues and be wise even when others cheated Southerners of their rights, or should they have tactfully and lovingly used many words to defend others and themselves and leave others to term them sinners and fools? We must, however, understand that the Bible is categorically clear about the sin of omission and the sin of commission. We should also bear in mind that when one vocally and physically defends his own rights, his opponent considers him to be a real enemy, and so, if given a chance, he will tirelessly work to turn his own naïve brothers and sisters against him. Above all, people sometimes hate others for who they are rather than what they have done. But all in all, the worst was looming over the innocent people of Bor and their meagre possessions.

Merciless Attacks on Duken

Before my wife and I reached Bor, some unfortunate news reached and shocked us in September 1991 in Torit concerning the merciless attacks on the innocent communities of Duk Padiet and Duk Payuel by the forces of Dr. Riek. With loss of human lives and property, the remnants of these communities ran and sought refuge among their brothers and sisters in both Twic and Bor areas. Those who took refuge in Bor were accommodated in the former Malek Church Mission base on the eastern bank of the Nile, along Bor-Juba road.

My parents and other relatives heard of our arrival in Torit and were anxiously waiting to receive us, especially my wife, for it was going to be the first time for both parties to meet each other. Although we accepted Bishop Nathaniel's second request for us to wait in Torit, our patience was running out because of our great desire to go and meet our anxious parents and relatives in the village before I took up my new assignment with the church.

I took two trips from Torit to Bor town in which I escorted some church visitors to see the displaced people and SPLA/M authorities. In the last journey that took place sometime in November 1991, I asked those of the NSCC to take my wife and I to Bor together with the visitors in order for us to remain there after the visit. But when they saw our baggage and the number of the people in the car, they turned our request down but promised us to wait for another chance. We were not happy but put everything in God's hand. In the course of these two visits, I met my brother John Bech inside Bor town, and he told me how they were eagerly expecting to receive us. I promised that we were going to come home very soon. At the time, my wife and I knew our plans very well but not God's plans, especially for us.

The Danger of Underestimation

But why were we insisting to go to Bor while war was raging on therein? In spite of such huge destruction and displacement of the two communities in Bor, the rest of the people both in Twic and Bor underestimated the seriousness of the problem. These communities logically and correctly considered the split within the movement to be entirely an issue to do with the SPLA/M itself and not with them, the innocent civilians. Although they supported the movement wholeheartedly, they had no part to play in the leadership wrangling between Dr. John and Dr. Riek. Instead, they were willing and ready to place their allegiance in whoever was to prevail in the end. On the other hand, they strongly argued that the people from Nuer community had no specific problem with the people of Bor, which could lure the former to invade and attack the latter. As to why the attackers invaded and attacked the two communities in northern Bor, the rest of the communities believed that since they shared a borderline, they might have picked a quarrel that had triggered their Nuer neighbours to attack and uproot them.

Based on this noble belief, the remaining communities believed that Dr. Riek and his supporters were going to march along the road, leaving the innocent civilians enjoying their life in the rural areas, to Bor town and other SPLA garrisons as they continued with their political fight. My wife and I also shared the same viewpoint and so did almost all the SPLA soldiers. It was because of this common argument that my wife and I were forced to look continuously for ways and means to proceed from Torit to Bor. Therefore, as the war continued in northern part of Bor, those in the southern part innocently relaxed and went on with their normal ways of life.

On the side of Dr. John and his supporters, some of their forces were heavily involved in a series of fighting along major routes leading to Juba. For the particular reasons known to them, they, however, underestimated the seriousness and magnitude of Dr. Riek's incursion to Bor. Because of their ignorance of this alarming situation in Bor, Dr. John and his colleagues failed to send urgent reinforcements to Bor to fight off the attackers and save the general masses.

Around 19 November 1991, I went to Bor with some church visitors to examine the appalling circumstances. At this time, the entire community of Twic was pillaged and uprooted, forcing the remnants to flee and sought refuge in Bor. While in Bor, fierce fighting took place between the attackers and SPLA forces around Jalle area, a distance of twenty-six miles north of Bor town. In the course of this fighting, Captain Anyar Apiou was badly wounded and hence, evacuated to safety with others. The visitors and I returned to Torit on the same day. Although the civilians lately understood that the merciless attackers were sparing no one and property on their way, it was too late for them to seek better safety. And so they decided to hide in the thick bushes, far away from Bor town and the main road.

The Final Signs of Bor Massacre

On 20 November 1991, the attackers launched wide and concerted attacks both on the SPLA and the whole community of Bor plus the displaced people, pillaging and uprooting all the inhabitants. They overtook the fleeing civilians in the bushes and pursued them together with the SPLA soldiers up to Magok-Kolong, a cattle camp, nearer to Mongala along Gameza-Mongala road. The attackers killed thousands of innocent civilians, looted thousands and thousands of their livestock, destroyed crops and other valuable properties and abducted many children and women.

Although Dr. John and his groups turned a blind eye to Riek's incursion in Bor and kept on fighting their common enemy at the very expense of Bor community, they took some urgent counsel when the danger was just on the threshold of their house. So they vigorously attacked, repelled and pursued Riek's followers back to and beyond Bor town.

Immediately after the repelling of the attackers, I went to NSCC (New Sudan Council of Churches) and asked them to give me a car to rush to Bor and see for myself what had happened. This final attack on Bor took place while Bishop Nathaniel was on another visit to Kenya. He went there to solicit some relief assistance from some humanitarian agencies for the displaced people. He left his family in Bor, and so part of my mission was to go and see what had happened to it.

Right away they gave the car to me, and I took off hurriedly at daybreak from Torit with Rev. Philip Akuok Chol, Michael Roger Medley, a British Consultant working with the Diocese of Bor, and others. We met a huge number of destitute and demoralised, displaced people trekking along the road between Ngalngala and Mongala. We could not see the end of the march. And I still remember clearly, seeing our driver, a middle aged man from Equatoria, shaking his head, leaving the steering wheel, raising his hands and saying with a cry, "O God, what is this?" He reduced the speed of our car and went slowly among the crowds as we passed on to them our sympathy and love. It was embarrassing and heart-breaking to see helpless, malnourished children and aged people. Most of them had sores and blisters over their bodies, particularly their feet because of the long, painful journey and thorns, thistles and other sharp objects during their plight. All were completely exhausted, hungry and in rags. Almost all of them had lost their loved ones and properties. As we moved slowly along the road, some of them narrated to us what they knew about the whole ordeal.

Right after reaching Magok-Kolong, we saw many signs of the war as the ropes and sticks for tethering cattle, sleeping materials and other personal belongings were littered here and there along the road. Thereafter, we met many human and animal corpses along the road, and so our vehicle had to dodge them now and then, making a bit of a meandering journey. It was the first time for me to see what they called mass killing whereby innocent people were tied together or separately and butchered mercilessly in one place and left in their own blood. Almost all the dead we saw were killed in cold blood with their hands tied behind. The smell from both human and animal bodies was terrible. To our surprise, it was quite amazing that the human's corpses smelled more awful than the corpses of cows. You could see the traumatized survivors walking and holding mieth (a local perfumed plant) around their noses to avert or mitigate the smell.

As for the animals, most of them died of exhaustion because they suffered from severe flooding and flood-related diseases in Bor in that particular year. As a small calf dies slower than its mother, we saw some calves standing or lying innocently beside their filthy mothers along or by the roadsides, while waiting for their slow and eventual death. We became totally mum but left our eyes to observe this terrible event.

We met Abednego Aboot Riak at Malek by the side of the road, and in the course of our talk, he told us that we had not seen enough of the carnage because the enemy had killed and done destruction in the villages and bushes, too. From there we proceeded to Bor town, encountering a similar situation en route. We saw an elderly woman lying dead in the shade of an acacia tree, off the road near Pakuaw Airstrip in Bor. We stopped the car and approached to have a closer look at her and saw that she had no wound on her body. She lay down properly with her bed sheet spread over up to around her knees with her walking stick lying by her side. She might have died of exhaustion and hunger. Amazingly, there were no beasts or birds feeding on the corpses, and we did not know why.

We arrived inside Bor town and proceeded to our church compound, which had been turned into a residential place by the attackers. There were human and animal corpses here too. With no one in town to feed us with better information, especially concerning the bishop's family, we decided to venture to Kapat in the rural area where his family lived. Shortly after leaving the town, we met Commander Salva Kiir on Pakuaw road on his way back from Baidit, and he stopped us to find out our mission. He permitted us to go but asked us to be very vigilant as some of the attackers were scattered in the bushes. We reached there safely and found that one person was killed near the Kapat church. We heard his family was okay, although they were still hiding somewhere in the nearby forest to make sure that things completely returned to normal before coming to their home.

The Death of My Father

People were returning to their places from the bushes where they were hiding at the time we were there. While standing with people by the roadside in Kapat, one of my relatives, Kuol Ayom or Kuol Ayen Mathiang approached me, greeted me and broke the unfortunate news about my father's death during the incursion. He was murdered at his home. It was just a matter of time for each of us, the Sudanese, in that car to hear bad news concerning member(s) of the family, close relatives or friends, for there was no single homestead that was not bereaved in one way or the other during the massacre.

Our village of Werkok is about four miles north of Kapat, and so we took off from there to see my bereaved family and other relatives. I alighted from the vehicle and rushed home on foot, leaving colleagues waiting for me along the feeder road. When my mother saw me, she embraced me and broke down in tears, and I comforted her by saying that my dad was even better than those killed in the bushes because he had had a decent burial in his home. It was unfortunate that I did not see his body before burial, for I found my brother John Bech and cousin Alier Mathiang compacting the soil on his grave. Hence, dad and I saw each other physically for the last time when I left home for Ethiopia in August 1990.

As people were streaming back from their hiding places, I took a pen and note-book and registered the names of those killed in our village. I wrote more than ninety people, including my beloved dad. I came to learn later that those who died during the massacre were over two thousand. But those who passed away later on in different places of various causes related to this massacre were in tens of thousands. The majority of them were children and elderly people who used to depend mostly on cows' milk.

People of Bor Outside Their Homeland

In order to alleviate our family's suffering, I decided to take my brother Bech's chil-dren, Yar and Thon with me to Torit and promised to come back in due course for my mom and other vulnerable members of the family, especially after the funeral rites for my dad. We rushed back to the vehicle to return to Torit. Brother Bech put his children in the car and looked at them and told them: "My children, your uncle is now your father. As your cows are now taken by Nuer, the vulture was going to eat you if he had not taken you." I almost wept at his heart-felt words. The hope of coming to Bor with my wife was ruined. Instead, other members of the family were going to join us outside our homeland because of this man-made catastrophe, just a calamity caused by a merciless brother to his own innocent brother.

We said goodbye to each other and rushed on our returning journey. We reached Ngangala at 8pm, very much exhausted. Michael Medley requested that we spend the night there and continue on our journey to Torit the following day, and I gave in to his request. Most of the displaced people spent the night there with us. We slept merely in the open air with nothing soft to lay our bodies.

These people ended up in displaced camps including Amee, Atepe and Lab-one, among others. The majority of the other remnants still in Bor at that time fol-lowed their own brothers and sisters and resided in these camps. Also many people went to Khartoum and other towns in Northern Sudan in search of protection and some social amenities. Others crossed over the national boundaries to neighbouring countries such as Kenya, Uganda and became refugees. Unfortunately, some of the remnants did not return to Bor, their traditional homeland, because they died and were buried in those foreign lands. The Bor massacre marked the beginning of the meandering and dreadful journeys of the masses of Bor, with some ending up happily or sadly outside Africa on a resettlement basis.

We continued on our journey from Ngangala to Torit the following morning and arrived there safely. My wife hardly sustained the unfortunate news of my dad's death. Her hope of seeing him alive was lost forever and ever.

After some time, I went back to Bor and brought my mother and two children of my eldest brother Ayoor-Gogoi with me to Torit. My brother Bech requested to leave Bor with his wife and their suckling baby, Amor and go with us to Torit because he correctly predicted that the same attackers and government troops were going to return to Bor during the dry season to continue with their unmerited destruction on the few remnants. But, unfortunately, I played down his fear and told him to remain behind to maintain our family name in the area. I promised to look after them in any way possible while in Torit. It did not come to my mind that the government army was going to recapture Bor town from SPLA. Bech and his wife reluctantly accepted my advice and remained there. Before having her own biological child, my wife became like a real mother to the four disadvantaged children. She was a very young mother of a big, extended family.

Varied Reactions to Bor Massacre

Reactions from the People of Bor

People in Bor generally believed that what Dr. Riek and his groups did to them was far worse than what the Arabs had done to them in their historical memories of the two civil wars in Sudan. They failed to sustain the shock of the massacre and its aftermath because they totally did not understand the logical and justifiable reasons that had led them to execute such unbearable mass murder and barbaric destruction of their innocent lives and meagre possessions. They did not take Riek and Nuer people for their enmity as such, and so until the time of this writing people from Bor do not comprehend why their own brothers and sisters did inflict such inhumane atrocities on them and their land. Due to a lack of proper justification for the massacre, most of the people are left with no better conclusions than to say that Riek and his followers were used by the Khartoum Government to achieve its primary objective of the total annihilation and dispersion of any possible remnants of Bor area. To make it worse, people from Bor and other well-wishers seem to be bitter towards Riek for the manner in which he turned a blind eye to the real carnage and failed to apologise officially for the event. It is good to underscore here that this ethnic strife later engulfed other sections of Nuer and Jeng communities, causing numerous human deaths and destruction of property.

My Personal Reactions to the Bor Massacre

On 22 January 1992, I met some white people in the residence of Roger Shrock, a former American Secretary General for the NSCC in Torit. Without being prepared, I found myself in a sort of interrogative and investigative conversation with them. They sought my personal opinion by storming me with a lot of questions and possible, justifiable reasons surrounding the Bor massacre. In my response, I totally denied Riek's involvement in this historical, unhealthy event, for I totally failed to understand the actual connection between his coup and the life of the innocent civil population of Bor.

In fact, I shared with them that if the SPLA/M was and is still pursuing the cause of the oppressed Sudanese people, of course, including those in Bor, any possible changes in its leadership should not negatively affect any section of such oppressed civilians. According to me, Riek tried to take over the leadership from Dr. John simply not to punish any groups of people but rather to put things right, if at all he and his followers were not happy with some issues, within the movement so as to achieve its primary objectives. So given this prelude, if his coup was to make things better for both the SPLA/M as well as for the general masses for which it was originally created to liberate from all forces of darkness and serve them thereafter, then I saw no logic and reasonable argument for him to turn his guns against innocent people. It was just like a merciless parent turning his deadly force against his innocent child. Otherwise, one is left to wonder about the genuineness of the coup itself.

Then they asked me that if Riek was not behind the massacre, who was in charge? "God knows", I told them. Otherwise, Riek was the right person to justify his inhumane actions in Bor.

In conclusion, they asked me whether those from Bor were going to avenge themselves on Nuer people. I gave them a yes answer by pointing out that, just like any hurting human being, some people were going to seek ways and means to get even. But to me, despite the fact that I lost my beloved dad, relatives, friends and valuable possessions during the massacre, the spirit of revenge was just like adding or rubbing salt in a deadly wound. This is simply because it would drastically block out the road to the emancipation of the oppressed Sudanese masses, for instead of fighting the real enemy, these ignorant brothers and sisters would mistake themselves for enemies. I also pointed out that Nuer people would not benefit if they killed and wiped out Jeng people from the face of the earth and vice versa. Even the on-going fight between the Northerners and Southerners in Sudan was not meant to annihilate each other in the process but to share the national cake equally and equitably, or else separate each other agreeably and live mutually in separate geographic locations.

The spirit of revenge is not in me, but rather I have the spirit of reconciliation because the former spirit is very destructive and recurring. It is biblical to forgive one another.

God's Plans vis-à-vis Our Plans

God always has ultimate plans for His own people, and such plans are more worthy than their own. For instance, my wife and I had one primary goal of going home to meet our parents and relatives and friends before I took up my new church assignment within the Diocese of Bor. For that reason, we were not happy with all kinds of delay we met on the way, regardless of the fact that they were meant for me to carry out some useful church services while in Torit. Our people at home were not happy also with such a very long hold-up. But after having seen what happened in Bor, we understood that the omniscient God had pre-knowledge of the Bor massacre. So he conscientiously used Bishop Nathaniel and others to frustrate and prevent us from reaching Bor according to our human plans and be part of the whole ordeal. Of course, His ways are not our ways, knowing for sure that all plans belong to us but their ultimate end rests with God. Definitely, the 'Silent Hand' was upon us.

With the death of our dad and uncertainty of going to Bor in the near future, my wife and I squarely put everything in God's hand and rested assured on His way forward for us and other members of our family. Torit became our temporal home with other members of Bor, and so even Bishop Nathaniel brought his family there.

A Series of Events

A Foretaste of Educational Hope

In the course of our staying in Torit, Bishop Nathaniel got an important chance from ACROSS for one member of our diocesan priests to go to Daystar University, Kenya for a bachelor degree study. The criteria for the candidate to fulfil were: firstly, he should have the Sudan School Certificate with an average of seventy per cent and above. Second, he must be willing to return to and continue with his services within the diocese in Sudan. These were the primary requirements.

At that particular time, I was the only person, especially with regard to those priests who were working with our diocese in the SPLA/M liberated areas, with such a certificate, for mine was seventy-one point two (71.2%) from Rumbek Secondary School. My commitment to serve our people and readiness to return to Sudan after the studies were quite unquestionable. For my diocesan bishop and other colleagues plus myself knew my aim was to come back to suffer with our people immediately after my four-year academic studies.

It is an odd thing to note that in our earlier escape from Abdullah Chuol's groups, all copies of my Sudan School Certificate and other essential documents were taken by those merciless soldiers. But the Lord saved the original, knowing very well that it was going to be one of the major requirements for my future education. And despite the ruthless years that I went through prior to 1992, it remained in my bag, waiting for that day in line with God's will.

Of course, our people knew that I did successfully finish my high school studies and had a good certificate. Yet they wondered whether I still had it in spite of such turbulent circumstances under which I went through. Hence, they called and asked me whether I had it, and to their amazement and joyfulness, my answer was yes. Then I was given the form to fill quickly to be returned to Kenya in time for the forthcoming August semester of 1992.

At that time, Daystar offered major programmes in Business Administration and Management, Community Development, Communication, Accounting and Bible Studies. Since this was the only door the Lord had opened for me, I forsook my previous aim of law related studies and asked the Lord to lead me in my choice. With regard to the intensity of the above course, my aim was primarily of what would be of greater benefit to the Diocese of Bor in particular and Sudanese people in general. As per the level and depth of studies, I knew that I was going to manage them well, irrespective of my being away in the forest from academic circles for such a long period of time. With God's help, the bishop and others advised me to choose Business Administration and Management as my area of study. As a result, I filled in the forms and gave them to Russell Nobel to take them to Nairobi for processing and possible admission. Like a net thrown into the water to catch some fish, I put the whole process in God's hands and went on with my life.

The Death of Biar Mach Deng-Beny, 1992

Jacob Biar and I intimately grew up, as real cousins and best friends, both in rural area and urban centre before the beginning of the 21-year civil war in Sudan. He was very strong, wise, valiant, tall and handsome, hardworking, sociable and a good wrestler. He was one of the best singers, with admirable leadership qualities. Because of his worthy braveness, he graduated from Bonga and was assigned a 46 automatic machine gun, which he handled amusingly in many battles until he was fatally wounded in the chest in the famous battle of 'Achara alip' – ten thousand government troops marching to Bor from Juba and caught up in a nasty fight with the gallant SPLA forces of Khoriom division along Bor-Juba road in 1985. After receiving his serious wound, he married Mary Achol Jok Kut and went to Ethiopia, Itang Camp to seek some further medical treatment. Because of his hardworking spirit, he managed to acquire some cattle while there. Jacob Biar met his unfortunate death in the hands of some raiding Murle bandits while protecting their wealth in Gumuruk area in 1992. He left his wife and children behind. His death was tragic and unforgettable.

More Unfolding Events of 1992

Military plans and incursions: while in Torit, we regularly shared whatever little we had with my brother Bech and his family. In the early part of the year, I made several trips to Bor on official church missions. SPLA/M and Khartoum Government carried out a series of military plans to attack and counter-attack each other. The primary aim of the government was to launch some decisive, fierce and concerted attacks on the SPLA positions to recapture them and push them away once and for all from the Sudanese soil. On the other hand, despite its current weaknesses, SPLA/M aimed at maintaining its current positions and capturing more territories from the government forces. To fulfil its purpose, government troops launched a deadly attack on 13 January 1992 on the SPLA garrison at Bilnyang, east of the Nile, and overran it in spite of gallant resistance from the SPLA.

Dine Wit's visit: Dine Wit, General Secretary of Church Mission Society (CMS) and a member of Christian Aid, UK at the time, came to Torit from Nairobi on 31 January 1992 on their way to Bor to see how the church and the survivors of the Bor Massacre were doing. They were joined by a member of ACROSS and left Torit for Bor with Bishop Nathaniel on 1 February of the same year. On the following day, I led another church team to Bor so as to catch up with those of the bishop to visit some parishes in most of the Bor areas. We returned to Torit after two days, and the bishop and the visitors proceeded to Nairobi to see how to address some of the appalling needs of the people.

Bol and Mayol's return: Rev. Peter Bol Arok and Rev. Andrew Mayol Ajak, since their separation from us in May 1991 due to political upheavals in Ethiopia, found their way out from Addis Ababa through Kenya and arrived in Torit on 2 March 1992. Another significant event that took place while in Torit was the convening of the NSCC General Assembly, which was attended by some pastors from our diocese and took place between 16 and 19 March 1992.

Unsuccessful farming: to fight against the chronic dependency syndrome and to lead others by modelling, I selected a good sizable piece of land near the church and began to clear it on 1 April 1992 in readiness for cultivation in the onset of the rainy season. Hence, other members of the church followed suit and started clearing their pieces of land. Although we took this acceptable choice of farming, the rapid escalations of the war in favour of government forces were very alarming in the minds and hearts of SPLA/M and its strong alliances. For example, Bor town fell to the hands of government soldiers on 4 April 1992, indicating a possible threat along Bor-Juba road. And it meant that the few survivors, including my own brother and his family, in Bor were about to lose contact with us. On 7 April, government troops recaptured Ngangala from SPLA and cut Juba-Torit road into half.

Bor Diocese in Nimule: seeing the unfolding events, Bishop Nathaniel called and met with some of his priests on 6 April 1992 to strategize on how to continue with the church works in such turbulent circumstances. Because of the military threat, Bishop Nathaniel's family, Rev. Reuben Akurdid's and Kur Amom's left Torit for Nimule on 8th of the same month in pursuit of better safety.

The families of these two gentlemen went with the one of the bishop because of their administrative roles within the diocese – Rev. Akurdid was the diocesan secretary and Kur was a logistician. My family and I remained in Torit with others for some time, while waiting to see the clear picture of the whole ordeal.

A series of defeats on the SPLA: on 11 April 1992, Yirol fell into the hands of government forces. Also the SPLA lost the important port of Sambe to the government soldiers on 17 of the same month. In a different warfront, the advancing government army recaptured the town of Pibor from the SPLA on 22 of the same month.

My family in Upper Talanga: I took none essential members of my family to Upper Talanga for their own safety. I took them there because my maternal uncle Paul Alier Nyok was in charge therein. Seeing the rapid scale in which SPLA garrisons were falling under the government army, within a short period of time and as a complete setback for those of Bor, the strategic small town of Mongala fell to the government militia forces on 26 April. And just a day after that, the government streamers reached Bor from Malakal. Bor was then cut away totally from Torit and all the camps of displaced people.

Cultivating for others: despite such government incursions into the SPLA/M territories, I went on with my cultivation in Torit with one solid aim: if I don't reap what I sow, somebody else will benefit from my energy. So I finished the clearance of my garden on 6 May and took advantage of the heaviest rain in the month by sowing the seeds on 9 of the same month.

More defeats on the SPLA: again the government troops recaptured a strategic town of Lierya, situated along Juba-Torit road, from the SPLA. In fact, the Khartoum Government planned to accomplish its military task before the heavy rains that mostly impede land transport almost all over Southern Sudan. And to do that, recapturing of significant towns such as Torit and Kapoeta from the SPLA were on its top agenda. To stage a fierce resistance, SPLA forces laid a proper ambush and destroyed government troops between Ngangala and Lierya on 17 May.

On 28 May 1992, the strategic town of Kapoeta was recaptured by the government troops. They penetrated through the wilderness from Pibor. The road between Torit and Kenya through Kapoeta was totally cut off for those wanting to flee to Kenya through that route. With Torit sandwiched by the government forces, the SPLA/M believed that it was likely to fall into the hands of the government. Thus, all non-essential people were advised by the SPLA/M on 30 May to leave it immediately in search of safety towards the Sudan-Uganda border.

Juba attacks by SPLA: in order to distract government troops from their strategic offensives on the few remaining SPLA positions, SPLA launched a desperate attack on Juba on 6 June 1992.

My pastoral work in Upper Talanga: prior to this attack on Juba, I eventually abandoned my hope and left Torit for Upper Talanga on 14 May and continued with my farming there. We turned our small house into a chapel to nourish our souls. Our Sunday's attendance was between 20 and 50 people.

More attacks on Juba: on 3 July 1992, Rev. Akurdid and others paid us a visit. On 6 July, SPLA gallant forces launched another attack on Juba and managed to demolish a portion of the bridge with the single aim of cutting the town away from the eastern bank of the Nile. But the government was still able to use the remaining section of the bridge in its operations and other activities.

The fall of Torit: finally, to the greater happiness of the Khartoum Government, the strategic town of Torit fell into the hands of the government at 4:30pm, on 13 July 1992. The SPLA troops retreated towards the Uganda border to nurse their heroic wounds and think of the next course of action. The SPLA war on Juba virtually stopped after the recapturing of Torit by the government. Instead, the SPLA/M reorganized its forces and vehemently defended its remaining garrisons along the Sudan-Uganda, Sudan-Kenya, and Sudan-Zaire borders against continuous and solid government onslaughts.

The expulsion of the SPLA/M from Ethiopia, the terrible split within the movement and the series of deadly attacks of the government on the SPLA/M were profound blows that left one to wonder sincerely how it sustained such heavy tremors. 1992 was one of the darkest periods in the historical life of the SPLA/M but one of the most opportune times for the Khartoum Government.

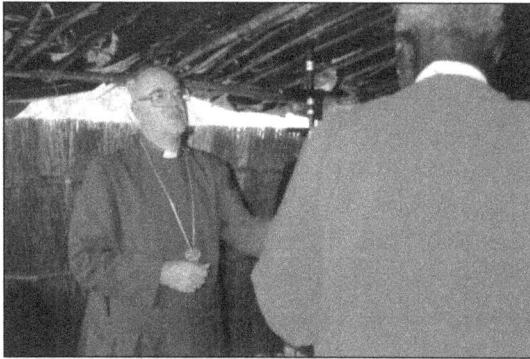

Bishop Nathaniel Garang with Archbishop of Canterbury George Carey
In Atepe Camp of IDP, South Sudan, 1993

The reception of the Archbishop of Canterbury, George Carey
In displaced camp by the youths of the ECS Diocese of Bor, 1993

The reception of the Archbishop of Canterbury, George Carey
In a displaced camp by the Church and the entire South Sudanese Community, 1993

Left to Right: *The late Achiek Anot and Gabriel Gai Riak*
South Sudan, photographed sometime in the 1990s

CHAPTER NINE

Back to School

Given the turbulent circumstances under which we were facing, I totally forgot about the academic papers that I had filled earlier and sent to Kenya for possible admission to Daystar University. There was no communication system between Upper Talanga and other places in and outside Sudan, especially Kenya. Getting in touch with my diocesan bishop and those with him in Nimule was not possible.

However, one day I had a dream while asleep. In the dream, I found myself on a trip. Then I arrived at a certain place where I met some people who surprisingly welcomed me and said, "You are Stephen Mathiang? You have been accepted to go to school, and the bishop has been looking for you; he is sitting over there; you go and hear more from him." I woke up and did not put it into my heart, for it was an impossible dream to me, given where we were and the prevailing situation at the time. I shared it with my wife and left it just as a mere dream.

Life in Upper Talanga became very difficult both in terms of insecurity and the scarcity of food because, first of all, it was not under the UNHCR authorities, and secondly, the local citizens, especially none SPLA/M supporters, were not happy with the presence of people from other places in their area. Although we tried to cultivate some cereals there, the cold climatic condition of that place could not permit them to grow well. My family was quite big at the time because other relatives joined us before we left Torit for Upper Talanga. Apart from hunger, the number one problem was the security of the entire family.

We agreed to leave there and go and seek refuge in one of the camps of displaced people. But, as a priest, I could not do that without first seeking the advice of my diocesan bishop. Thus, I decided to leave the family behind and travel to Nimule to get his blessing. I took a bicycle and left Upper Talanga for Nimule on 11 August 1992 and spent the night in Palataka. I left there early in the following morning with the hope of spending another night at Amee. However, upon my arrival at the

Amee road junction at around late afternoon, very tired and exhausted, I got a lift with a relief truck preparing to return from there to Uganda via Nimule. The driver consented to give me a lift. The lorry arrived Nimule at 9pm, on 12th of the same month, and that was my first time to go there.

The Ethical Quandary

Upon my arrival at the bishop's compound, I was received warmly and even asked before I sat down whether I had gotten any information concerning my admission to Daystar University, and I calmly said no. As a matter of fact, I found out that my school admission came back to Bishop Nathaniel some time ago from Nairobi, asking me to report to school in the middle of August for studies. But unfortunately, it was kept without being dispatched to me in Upper Talanga. Although there was a car in the diocesan headquarters, the bishop and his assistants failed to send it hurriedly to my end because they said that the car was not in good condition. As a result, they were looking for somebody coming to my end to convey it to me. But their suggestion was not going to work, for people rarely used that route at the time. And so if the omniscient God had not intervened and touched my heart to come to Nimule, I would have forfeited that golden chance. Thus, the dream that I had and dismissed just as a mere dream in Upper Talanga came to be a reality.

Having arrived in Nimule by Wednesday 12, Bishop Nathaniel told me to be ready to proceed to Kenya the next Monday 17. I accepted to go there, but since I was simply on a short, preparatory visit only to Nimule, I requested of him to give me the car so as to rush back to Upper Talanga and share with my family members about my going to school and how they were to cope with life in my absence. My primary objective, as I told the bishop, was to go and put some of the weak people into the vehicle and take them to one of the displaced camps and leave the strong ones, including my lovely wife, to follow them on foot. Of course, without such arrangements, it would be unkind, inconsiderate, irresponsible and unwise on my side, as the sole breadwinner, security provider, husband and family leader, just to proceed from Nimule to school to enjoy my studies and some social amenities and dumping my family in such turbulent circumstances.

Bishop Nathaniel accepted this suggestion happily and told me to wait for the vehicle. Days passed by without his lordship backing his yes answer with action. I persistently kept on knocking at the door and reminding him and his assistants, but the answer was the same, telling me to wait.

It is always frustrating and intellectually challenging when you deal with a very serious issue with a person whose yes or no mean one and the same thing or totally opposite. Of course, telling nothing but genuine truth is like a bitter pill, but it is biblically worthy to be forthright because the Holy Book admonishes us to tell the truth always if we want to be freed. As a result, I was not freed because my diocesan bishop and his assistants failed to tell me the truth.

Honestly, I do not know what was in their minds and hearts to treat me like a small, naughty child, although they had total authority, as my church leaders, to give me an absolute no answer despite my being one of their priests. Maybe, the answer was simply no, but because of Bishop Nathaniel's usual nature of not wanting to injure someone's feelings, he chose to give me a negative yes without realising that this kind of response did greater harm to me than if he had given me a proper answer.

It was now Sunday, but there was still no proper answer from my authorities; yet I knew that even if they were kind and honest enough to give me the car on that particular Sunday prior to my departure on the next Monday, it would have been impossible. This is so because of the unworthiness of the road at the time – it was impossible to reach my family in Upper Talanga and return to Nimule on time, leave alone transporting some family members to one of the camps. Facing this kind of ethical quandary, I was left with nothing but to make a critical personal decision. My decision was to decline from going to Nairobi until further notice and return to Upper Talanga, instead.

While in Nimule, I shared a small hut with uncle Agany Aguto and Rev. Andrew Mayol Ajak. So in the course of our conversations, I told them my final decision. But collectively they objected to it and advised me to leave the family and go to school. Although I tried to let them understand the crucial reasons behind my refusal to go to Kenya, they adamantly asked me to go. Uncle Agany lamented that since we, the Southerners, especially people from Bor, had missed education opportunities due to the war situation, as a community elder, he would not agree with me to lose this noble chance. Instead, he advised me just to rush to Nairobi, register my name, defer until the next semester, and return to Sudan and join my family.

Then I went back to Bishop Nathaniel and gave him some other conditions to fulfil for me to go to school. Firstly, I told him that I would write a letter to the family, explaining what had happened to me, put it together with some little money I had and give them to him to send to the family after I left for Kenya. Again I requested him to try his level best to send this letter with the diocesan car to go and ferry the family to one of the camps of displaced people for their own safety in terms of insecurity and feeding. If he promised to take care of these requests, then I would proceed to school. Without the slightest hesitation, he completely agreed to do that.

So I happily wrote a detailed, apologetic letter to my dear wife and other members of the family, even mentioning how the vehicle was going to transport them from Upper Talanga to one of the camps, depending on their own choice. I handed everything to him in the presence of Rev. Reuben Akurdid and Daniel Kur Amom and prepared mentally to leave there for Kenya the following day. I fully hoped that his lordship and his assistants were going to honour their promise thereafter both on humanity grounds as well as on the fact that I was going to school not merely due to my personal benefit but as a representative of the diocese – the education benefit was going to overflow to the diocese itself and the Sudanese nation at large. Above all, as my church leaders, they had an unavoidable obligation to look after my family during my absence.

On Monday 16 August 1992, I left Nimule by an ACROSS chartered plane, piloted by Mr. Martin, for Nairobi via Loki. I spent the night in Loki and arrived at my final destination the following day where I was met at Wilson Airport by Mr. Joseph of ACROSS and taken to a certain hotel in down town Nairobi for the night. As it was my first time there, I do not know the exact location of that hotel now. On 19th of the same month, ACROSS took me, a real student from the forest of Southern Sudan to a metropolitan school in Kenya. As Daystar Athi River Campus was still under construction, and because there were not enough facilities to accommodate the entire student population on its Valley Road Campus, we were temporarily accommodated at Kenya Science Teachers College, along Ngong Road. It is now a branch of Nairobi University.

The Sudanese students I met there include Atilo Okoth, Jervasto Okot, Lokosang Wani Lemi, Santino Makur, Benjamin Gimba and Arkanyjilo Wani. In September 1992, the construction of the first phase of Athi River Campus was completed, and so all resident first year students were moved there. The place was very conducive for studies and we had as our neighbours roaming giraffes, zebras, hyenas, varieties of antelopes, just to name a few.

Scholarships at the Expense of My Family

Victims of rigid sponsorship policy: ACROSS, most probably reacting on past precedents, had a rigid policy of sponsoring only a married candidate without covering his/her family. That is, such a family was to remain under the jurisdiction and responsibility of the sending church or agency, irrespective of the prevailing circumstances of both the family and the sending institution. According to ACROSS, most of its former sponsored students who went for studies with their families failed to return to Southern Sudan after their graduations by saying that there was no need to do so due to the on-going war. Thus, its principle was to train and send back such needed candidates to their sending churches so as to help in their fields of expertise and not to end up roaming along the streets of metropolitans in search of greener pastures elsewhere. To ACROSS, if married students were to leave their families behind in Sudan while pursuing their education outside Sudan, that would be a meaningful factor to force them to go back to them after their finishing. This policy was not very much successful according to what I came to know.

Unfortunately, my family became a victim of this rigid policy. Logically and in principle, it meant that my diocese was to take full care of my family during my studies in spite of the on-going predicaments of the civil war. But was the diocese really ready and willing to shoulder such responsibility as an employer and spiritual obligation and not as an added burden? The future was the right judgement to answer that question.

Communication between my family and I was not very easy, given the modes of communication in Southern Sudan in those days. The only way of hearing one another very often was through written letters conveyed by any known person passing between Kenya and Southern Sudan. Bishop Nathaniel became our reliable medium of communication as his business made him a sort of frequent visitor in Kenya. The contact person on behalf of my family in Sudan was Samuel Deng Maguet, for he was young and educated.

Registering my name in the school and postponing my studies to the next semester was not possible in relation to ACROSS standing orders of scholarships management because they did not want to see a sponsored student wasting a single cent. In other words, since I had spent much money in the process of my coming to and staying in Kenya during my registration in the school, and because my returning to my family and my returning to Kenya later would also require sufficient amount of funds, it would show a lack of seriousness and wastefulness on my part in the eyes of the sponsor. Otherwise, I would forfeit the scholarship if I were to insist on returning to Sudan. Therefore, the only option left for me was to put my family faithfully in the hands of God and proceed with my studies and see them, if possible, during the next school holiday in the second quarter of 1993.

Culture shock: my years in the thorny bushes of Sudan made many things new to me in the school environment. For example, most of my student colleagues looked younger than me. Some of the modern technological gargets looked peculiar to me, and so I had to speedily adjust myself to cope with my academic activities. It took me time to adjust to the sounds of aircrafts in Nairobi by trying to convince myself and re-programme my whole being, to consider them as peaceful and not harmful, unlike the unfriendly Sudanese war planes. I quickly absorbed these and other culture shocks and went on smoothly with my studies.

The tragic death of my niece: in the course of my studies, all the information I often received from Bishop Nathaniel concerning my family was okay. Even the letters sent to me by Samuel Deng indicated that things were fine. However, one day I heard the arrival of Bishop Nathaniel in Nairobi from Sudan, and so I scheduled myself to see him in his residence during one of the weekends. After greeting each other and exchanging pleasantries he gave me a heart-breaking letter, written to me not by Samuel Deng, the family contact person, but by a brother in the Lord, Rev. Peter Bol Arok. Bishop Nathaniel did not tell me the content of the letter, for he might have not known.

But as somebody usually thirsty for family news, and as part of my nature, I deliberately interrupted the conversation, read the letter, and wept loudly and uncontrollably. Other people poured in to hear what had happened, and bishop calmly broke the silence by trying to appease and convince me to stop crying. But I turned a deaf ear to him and continued pouring my heart out. After crying and running out of tears, I silently took out a pen and paper and wrote two letters, one to Rev. Peter Bol, thanking him for conveying to me such bad and unwelcoming news, and another letter to the family, consoling them to take heart and put everything before the Lord and push on with their life until my return to them.

After that I gave them to the bishop himself because he was returning to Sudan very soon. Then I broke my silence. First, I apologized to the bishop for having ignored him during my crying and told them the reasons of my mournfulness. I told them that I cried not because I considered my beloved niece to be more important than all those who were dying in Southern Sudan but rather because a human being had unfortunately passed away at her prime age, about five years old, purely due to negligence. I went on and said that it made no sense to me individually for others to carelessly and irresponsibly permit people to suffer and die simply because death had visited Sudan. Despite all the upheavals happening in Sudan, I explained that the Lord expected us, the living, to do whatever we could to alleviate unnecessary sufferings and death among his people. As I continued with my talks, I informed them that I cried terribly because I took full responsibility of her death upon myself in that when I took them, the deceased and her younger brother, from their parents in Bor right after the Bor massacre of 1991, my brother, their father, looked at them and said: "My children, your uncle is now your father. As your cows are taken by Nuer, the vulture was going to eat you if he had not taken you." I showed the bishop and others my wristwatch, Seiko 5, which came to Kenya with me. Then I told them that since the child died of malnutrition, I let my brother down and dishonoured his trust in me because if I were with my poor family in Sudan, I would have bartered all my clothing and wristwatch and other available belongings with any type of food items and saved her dear life. I further elaborated that you educate yourself to help your family and nation but not at the very expense of both, especially your dear family. Getting education at the expense of one's family is very useless, I added.

I felt cheated by the church for allowing me to come to school and neglecting my family. This death would have been avoided if I were with my family; it would have been avoided if the church upheld its moral and spiritual responsibility and authority to take care of its flocks. And hence, in the absence of that, it was a tragic death uncalled for, a mere negligence that was why I cried. I betrayed my family, although my church had negatively influenced me to do so – self-blaming, I mourned her dearly. As a leader in my own merits, it is my firm prayer that I would not do that to any of my subjects in my lifetime, and I admonish you not to do that to others either.

Nevertheless, this sad event cemented my determination to pursue my studies to a successful conclusion, return to Sudan and do something worthy for the church in particular and the Sudanese people in general. By doing that it would prove to others that such an educational outcome, which I obtained dearly at the expense of my family, was not pursued for my selfish personal goal. So I went back to school and continued with my studies.

More Unfulfilled Promises

In June 1993, I rushed to Southern Sudan through Uganda to see how my family and others were coping with life. Upon my arrival in Nimule, the church leadership gave me a car to take me to Atepe Camp where my family was. My dear wife received me warmly with much tears of joy, and I comforted her wholeheartedly. Samuel Deng was no longer with the family, for he had gone and stayed with Bishop Nathaniel's family in Nimule. Immediately, I discovered that my church leadership failed to fulfil its promises right after I went to Kenya for the school. For instance, the message that I wrote and left in Nimule to be despatched with other essentials to my family in Upper Talanga was not sent. The letter and other items were later collected by my wife when she came down from there to collect them after the family had learned from another source about my being in Kenya. The church also failed to send the vehicle as promised to me to collect some of the weak members of the family and take them to any displaced camp. Virtually, the church leadership totally turned its blind eye to my poor family.

To get the point right, the family did not need anything in terms of food items, clothing and accommodation or anything tangible from the church leadership during my absence but only transportation, moving them, especially the elderly and small children, from Upper Talanga, the scene of possible danger at the time, to a displaced camp where their security was to be provided by the SPLA as well as their food security to be taken care of by the UNHCR and other humanitarian agencies. Others and I know very well that the car was in good condition, but the will and the love, even an act of the Good Samaritan, to rescue them was lacking in the spiritual leadership of our church.

The family under more ordeals: what possible option was left for my family to undertake to run away from the danger? The only alternative was to tighten their belts and take the bull by the horns by trekking from the top of the mountain down to Atepe Camp, a distance of about 60 miles. As they approached the camp of Amee, they stumbled on some freshly dead bodies as a result of some fighting between the splitting group of a renegade SPLA Commander William Nyuon Bany and SPLA loyalists. By God's grace, they narrowly missed the retreating forces of William Nyuon. God knows what would have happened to them had he not miraculously intervened. Eventually, they ended up in Atepe Camp where the poor small girl Yar succumbed to malnutrition. I also discovered sadly that malnutrition claimed the life of another member of the family, a small nephew, the son of brother Ayoor-Goigoi in Atepe. But the information was not passed over to me while in Nairobi due to poor communication system.

Blame to correct but not to revenge: after getting all these discouraging pieces of information, I went back to Nimule, quite furious and ready to challenge the church leadership and brother Samuel Deng as well. First, I confronted and asked Samuel Deng whether he was sincere in all his correspondences with me concerning the family while I was in Nairobi. As a brother, I openly expressed my displeasure to him for having not fully fulfilled his relational obligation. Brother Deng gave me an apology that I heartedly accepted.

Then I called a meeting with the bishop's assistants, Rev. Reuben Akurdid and Daniel Kur. In fact, they are my distant relatives, for their mothers came from our village. Furthermore, we personally knew each other. I faced up to them squarely in the meeting as to why they failed to take care of my family, given their vital leadership roles as well as their blood relationships to me. I sincerely poured out my heart before them. I even promised them that despite what they had done to me, I would not do them the same if I happened to be in a similar leadership position. They both apologized, and I accepted their apology.

I went to Bishop Nathaniel in the end and confronted him also of what the church under his leadership had done to my family, although the church knew very well why I went to Nairobi. Bishop Nathaniel and I came from the same family lineage, and I call him my uncle. He has three significant responsibilities and obligations over my family. As priest and my overseer, he has spiritual and administrative leadership over my family; as my uncle in the African context, he has unavoidable responsibility for my family, even in my presence. And as a community elder, he is culturally duty bound to take care not only of my family but also others who are in need and brought to his attention.

On the basis of this precise prelude, I challenged him bravely and honestly. But as a good listener, he gave me uninterrupted sufficient time to air out my points of view. But to my amazement, he negated all my talks with just a simple statement by saying that people should not blame one another during the time of disaster. I looked at him speechlessly but with a lot of questions ringing in my mind. Should people forgive uncaring attitudes during such a time or should we do right and avoid wrong at all times, even at the verge of our death? Since we were not in a debating club or court room, I dropped my argument.

Instead, he asked me of what I thought should be done to my condition. I immediately gave him the following suggestions: firstly, my wife and two nephews, Mading Ayoor and Thon Bech could go with me to Kenya under the church support, since ACROSS refused to shoulder that responsibility. Secondly, I suggested that other members of the family be transferred from Atepe camp to Nimule so as to remove them a little bit from the Khartoum Government's threat. The reason why I proposed to take these two children with my wife was to prevent them experiencing what had occurred to their diseased sister and brother. He accepted all my suggestions, and so we parted company smiling and shaking hands.

My reason of documenting this section of my memories is not that I still hold any slightest grudge towards them, but to warn all other leaders to take good care of their employees and immediate dependents, especially when such employees are sent away on any official missions by their superiors.

My Family's Life and School

After getting consent from my diocesan bishop, I moved swiftly to put things in order because it was time to return to school for August's semester, 1993. Bishop Nathaniel also decided to take his family to Nairobi for his children to have access to decent education. Many people and my family were happy to see my wife and small children going to Kenya with me.

As the saying goes, "There is no beautiful refugee", life in Nairobi for my family and I was not comfortable in terms of feeding, accommodation and the kids' school. So my wife and I agreed for the family to go and take refuge in Kakuma Refugee Camp, Northern Kenya, while I continued with my studies. But they could not move by themselves from Nairobi to that place without my presence. This is simply because of three main reasons: firstly, my wife did not have prior knowledge of that route; secondly, she was heavily laden with our first child, and thirdly, we did not know any person, either relative or friend, who could take care of them in the camp before they could stand on their own feet.

On the other hand, my wife and I agreed to stay closer to some hospitals in Nairobi until the Lord saw her through during her first delivery. I finished successfully the 1993 August's semester, and the school closed for Christmas celebration. We celebrated the Christmas together and entered into the New Year. By the next January 1994, the school opened for January's semester. So I moved to Athi River Campus and left my family in Zimmerman, an estate on the outskirts of Nairobi.

Our First Child

To us a child was born on Tuesday 8 March 1994; the Lord saw my wife through during her trying moment of birth, and He blessed us with a beautiful daughter. Brothers Jok Aguto, Mathiang Lem and Athou Alier Leek rushed her, at her birth pangs, to one of the poorest nursing homes in Nairobi. She encountered some difficulties during and after her birth, given the standards of the hospital in question and other related issues. But all in all, the Lord saw her graciously through such ordeals.

In those days, wider means of communication, such as cell phones, were not numerous and easily accessible like now. Hence, the vital news of my wife's birth did not reach me on time. Because of my absence as well as because of my blood tie with him, Bishop Nathaniel took complete liberty and named our child after our famous great grandmother Ajoh Bior-Alak. During her baptism we named her Mary, the mother of Jesus Christ.

After her release from the hospital, she received kind services from our beloved Sudanese people. My family and I are sincerely grateful for the love they showed to us at that time. Had we not thought it wise to take the family to Zimmerman, we do not know how my dear wife would have gone through such a trying moment without the loving and kind hands of our relatives and friends extended over her. No man is an island; no family is an island, and no nation is an island. We all need each other because we are who we are because of those we interact with. We now had our own biological child among our beloved nephews.

Taking My Family to Kakuma Refugee Camp

As our school was about to close for a longer holiday, there was fierce fighting closer to Nimule between the SPLA and Khartoum Government forces. This forced all the displaced people to abandon their camps of Amee and Atepe and seek further refuge nearer to the Uganda border in places such as Mogali and Labone. Those in Nimule were in a great panic and sought some safety elsewhere.

Therefore, my wife and I agreed to see how to quickly bring the rest of our family members from Nimule to Kakuma. Since there was no one to execute such an important social task on our behalf, it was incumbent on me to rush there at the close of the school and see how to move them by land through Sudanese territory up to Kakuma. So I planned to leave my wife and children in Nairobi, and go and move those near physical danger to safety. Then I would return and take them, that is, my wife and children from Nairobi to Kakuma before the opening of the school for August's semester of 1994. But executing this urgent mission on time was not easy, given the wider geographic coverage, lack of means of transport, insecurity, etc. inside Southern Sudan.

I immediately left Nairobi for Nimule via Uganda on Thursday 2 June 1994. This was my first time to using such a long and meandering route. I left Nairobi and spent the night in Gulu in the house of Rev. Reuben Akurdid. Then I took off from there the following day and arrived in Nimule safely on 4th of the same month. Due to the urgency and the scope of my task, I met the members of my family and organised our trip together and asked the church to ferry us from Nimule up to Ikotos through northern Uganda. We took this venture, although people were terrified with the inhumane atrocities being inflicted on innocent civilians by the Ugandan rebels of the Lord Resistance Army. The road was in bad shape, particularly because of the heavy rains of the year.

On Friday, 24 June 1994, the church lent us the car, and we took off from Nimule on our way to Labone, passing through Gulu and Kitgum. Rev. Mark Atem Thuch, an expert driver mechanic, volunteered to accompany us up to Ikotos so as to assist Deng Keth, the driver of the vehicle. My family and I are very grateful to his spirit of volunteering. The journey between Nimule and Labone went on well, and we arrived there on 26th of the same month. With me on the trip were my mother Mary Areu, mother-in-law Deborah Nyaluak, uncle Daniel Dit, sister Akon Kuch and her four children, Abion Aleng Majok, Nyang Ayoor Kuch, Nyabol Aguto Nhial and Deng Aleer Deng.

On Tuesday 28 June 1994, we left Labone for Ikotos through Kitgum in northern Uganda, making a kind of curved journey, and spent the night in Thertenya, a SPLA border post along the Sudan-Uganda border. We almost slept between Kitgum and Thertenya because of the badness of the road. Mark and I soiled our clerical uniforms as we tried to help our driver pull out the vehicle in the dark from a series of mud and stagnated waters.

The loud sound of a running engine virtually betrayed our silence and secrecy. For it made our security very vulnerable to any possible human attacks if there were some armed bandits in the vicinity of that area. Because of darkness in the night and surrounding tall grass as well as our state of helplessness in terms of lack of some protective weapons, we just surrendered ourselves to God and waited for any eventuality. We managed in the end to bring out the car from such ordeals and dragged to safety where we were joyfully received by the SPLA soldiers.

By the following day, we left there for Ikotos but were caught up here and there by the same ordeals along the muddy, submerged road. Getting to our next destination became a big challenge, although our two drivers tried their level best to manoeuvre our way out from the defying road. Some big relief trucks found us on the way. And we seized that golden opportunity by pleading with their team leader to put us on his trucks and allow our weak vehicle to return. They agreed, and so we happily offloaded our belongings from our car and put them on the trucks. We said goodbye and departed each with our loyal drivers, with the hope that they were going to make it safely back to Nimule. We continued on our journey and reached Ikotos safely.

Stranded in Ikotos

Those in Ikotos received us warmly but with some mixed feelings. Some relatives, friends and close associates and others sympathised with our situation and welcomed us to stay with them while waiting for any possible means of transport to continue on our journey. But on the other hand, some soldiers, especially the unmarried ones, were grateful to receive us among their midst simply because of the young, beautiful girls who were with us. In fact, most of the inhibiting troops were either not married or had left their wives somewhere while pursuing their national revolutionary duties. As such, one of the girls was snatched away from us by one of the SPLA officers. We decided to leave her with him and deferred the marriage settlement to a later time as time was not on our side.

The few relatives we met there were Arep Ayom Achiek, Kuol Machok Jok and the family of late Awalith Leek Anyieth. The ladies were given their separate accommodation while uncle Dit and I were given ours. Because of the scarcity of the means of transport at the time between Ikotos and Chukudum, A/Commander Kuol Mayen Mading told us to relax and wait for any possible opportunity to continue on our trip. I even wrote on 7 July 1994 to Commander James Hoth, asking him to provide us with any possible means of transport, but he told us to wait. It was bad news for us, but were there any better alternatives?

The Remaining Part of the Journey

From Ikotos to Chukudum: on Tuesday 26 July 1994, we left Ikotos for Chukudum via Kadipo and Jabel Anyanya One. We were dumped on a large military truck with other people where we stepped on each other like poor chickens in a congested cage. Yet we were happy at least and at last. The journey was very rough to the extent of hearing some people crying and others opting to trek instead of riding on it. Because of the serious lack of means of transport in the SPLA/M liberated areas, the very few vehicles along the roughest roads were regularly overloaded beyond their professional capacity with people and materials and, sometimes with animals, packed to the highest maximum like sardines in a can. But all in all, on 28 of the same month, we reached Chukudum safely. Unfortunately, we had to wait further there for some days due to the lack of means of transport between there and Kenya.

The remarkable portion of the journey: the school was about to open for August's semester, and my family in Nairobi needed to be taken to Kakuma before I completely resumed my academic work. In order to strike a proper deal, I met with my extended family in Chukudum and came out with the solid decision that I should leave them there to wait for any possible means of transport, trek towards Kenya and inform brother Majok Mach to assist in finding means of transport to take the family from Chukudum to Kakuma. After the meeting, I went and shared with A/ Commander Kuol Deng my plan of leaving on foot and leaving the family behind. He accepted to take care of them and gave me some troops to escort me to the next nearest SPLA base, which would also do the same and the same as I passed along the way to Natinga.

So on Tuesday 2 August, they escorted me up to Kikilai. There the officer in charge of that base quickly organised another escort for me from there to the next base of Lotuke. Upon my arrival there, I was warmly received by the late Abel Alier Riakbai and James Nhial Anyang, the prominent officers managing that area. I spent the night there and the following day, resting and preparing mentally and physically for the next daring journey.

The distance between there and Natinga takes about ten hours on foot. And the road passes among a series of mountains and hills. It is a kind of up and down, meandering and curving road. To make it worse, it was very insecure. Thus, it was somewhat safer to walk it by night to take full advantage of the darkness of the night.

At 8pm, on Thursday 4 August, my five escorting soldiers and I left Lotuke for Natinga. We groped and dragged ourselves along the road like drunkards and blind people, falling on the muddy, slippery and rocky road. Because of the huge mountains, deep valleys and the darkness of the night, there was no sound of life. We hardly saw our footsteps. I sympathised with my colleagues, for they fell now and then with their guns making jingling and rattling noises. I was wearing my best student's shoes. But can you imagine what happened to them in the process of our taunting trekking? We reached Natinga at around 5am, and Brother Majok Mach received us cordially. My accompanying soldiers were taken by their comrades to nurse their wounds and exhaustion before they returned to their base. I am grateful to them all for their good hospitality and humane care.

I bathed and took a nice rest. But my mind was determined to continue to Kenya on time to undertake the other demanding social and academic issues. In the course of my resting in Majok's house, some relief came, empty lorries arrived on their way back to Kenya. Majok came and told me about them, although he preferred that I rest and wait for another chance of transport because, to him, vehicles were always moving along that route. But I turned down his kind advice and jumped on one of them and reached Loki safely the following day.

I put on my slippers, the only things to protect my feet, and went to the immigration office to stamp my passport. The official in charge looked at it, turned to me and asked how I ended up in Loki while my document was exited at Busia, a Kenyan town along the Kenya-Uganda border. I smiled and told him the nature of my meandering and zigzagging journey; he nodded, stamped and returned it to me.

On Saturday 6 August, I left Loki for Kakuma where I spent the night and asked some of our youngsters to go and bring the family from Chukudum to Kakuma. The following morning, I boarded a small mini bus and travelled the whole night and safely arrived in Nairobi at around 12 noon to the greatest delight of my family and I. My trip lasted for more than two months, and so upon my arrival in the house, I felt that my daughter had somewhat matured.

The Beginning of August's Semester, 1994

I arrived in Nairobi just in time to register for August's semester and to make sure that all my school requirements were met. On Monday 22 August, classes officially started. Having known my class schedules, I was in a better position to rush with my family to Kakuma and leave them there.

My Family from Nairobi to Kakuma

On Sunday 28 August 1994, we quickly put things together and left Nairobi for Kakuma and arrived there safely. We found that the other family members had reached Kakuma safely from Chukudum. My wife and Mading Ayoor went and stayed with her mother while other members of our family put up with their own people. However, she later decided and built her own home on a separate piece of land in Group 17 near our church headquarters. On Thursday 1 September, I returned to Nairobi and proceeded to Athi River Campus to continue with my studies.

My Work for the SPLM Update Magazine in Nairobi

My national zeal was still very high when I was at Daystar University. Having seen, heard and personally experienced numerous hardships and trails amidst the war in various parts of Southern Sudan, Southern Blue Nile and Ethiopia, I was very zealous and jealous for the national cause of our marginalised people. Due to such national zeal, I personally abhorred the cheap hotels and metropolitan streets' politics in which some of our brothers and sisters were busy with some unhealthy negative criticisms against the SPLA/M. To make it worse and to my ultimate surprise, some of these situational politicians had not been to the war-torn areas to personally witness the plight of their own people, the immeasurable destructions of their homelands and the alleged shortcomings of the SPLA/M. As no one, no system or anything under the sun is one hundred per cent perfect, I am not saying here that SPLA/M was Mr. Clean. But rather what I tend to underscore clearly here is that was it the right time and right place for one to sit at a very far, comfortable distance from the actual site of events and make some sincere unbiased value judgements? When the house is on fire, what must a wise person do? Should he first urgently try to see how to extinguish it before finding its cause and correctly apportion blame or vice versa? It is always wise for one to delay the conclusion until all facts are in.

The poetic works in this autobiography and others were published in the "SPLA/M Update" magazine in Nairobi. So if you want to properly understand the essence of my humane patriotism, you will need to study them keenly. I challenge you, as a true South Sudanese, to familiarize yourself with the following story.

National Saga

At one time, amidst the ocean of wealth, there was a golden land where both rainfall and sunshine divided the year equally. Beneath the ground there was a lake of milk, justice, love, equality, equity, unity and truth which were the only grass that germinated out of this soil. The land was rich enough to feed all kinds of creatures.

Upon the land there was a blessed family that wore the jewellery of love as its only clock. The family's name was known as Black.

But as time went by, the beautiful flowers began to change their colours. Both hatred and jealousy attacked and killed love, and lies swallowed truth. Justice, equity and equality were burnt down to death, and disunity annihilated unity. On the ashes of the above, destroyed moral values, sadly grew corruption, greed and deceit. Then hunger and disease began to rule; so there was death and thirst. Consequently, the greedy world's vultures started to use this hatred-prone, divided land as their nice hotel. The weak vampires of the land also joined them. The disease was too chronic to cure in time, and so the barrel of humiliation and oppression kept rolling.

However, the land began to think of the lost time with its beautiful flowers, but this was far apart like earth and heaven. As a result, all disgraced generations of the land passed along the valley of fire. But the clouds began to appear in the sky; so there was hope and faith. Yet the reality was a far distance away. The land was completely in darkness and badly in dire need of the sun to cast its light over its degraded face.

Amidst this terrible confusion, there appeared a son who was the torch guiding the path towards durable light. He was one in mind and heart and fully determined to dig out the rocks that block the road towards peace. Since his childhood, he sought ways and means to get a living medicine for the invincible disease that constantly gnaws the beloved people of the land. But his effort was just like somebody trying to demolish the rock with a piece of wood, for it has been tried in vain by those with might but not the brain. Nevertheless, his heart and mind were iron-like; so he continued with his research. Do you know the name of this liberating son? His name is UNITY.

One day, while Comrade Unity was sitting near the fire, facing his disgraced dear parents, the terrible sound of a war drum reached his ears. Although this awaking noise was too near, the drum itself was farther away. Immediately, Comrade Unity's heart began to change its course, and it started dancing with full expectation. Shortly thereafter, he called his closest uncles and asked them to escort him to attend to the national call. They responded positively. Then they started the arduous journey. But even eating produces sweat. Climbing a bit on the obstructing hills, his uncles started arguing with him about one thing or another, and sooner or later they changed their minds and began to wander back to the same, shameful village. But unfortunately, they were scattered and killed by some wild animals. So they terribly ended their weak hope, but Comrade Unity was too firm not to move even a step backwards.

Although the road was wild and thorny, Comrade Unity wore courage and hope. Leaping over few miles, he met a hungry, fierce tiger, which stood rock-like on the way. So he took a blind-like move and gave a slight push to Mr. Tiger, and thus there was light ahead. But unfortunately, his left index finger was the cost of the wound he gave to Mr. Tiger. Later on the birds of the air and hyenas thanked Comrade Unity for the best feast he had performed.

Confronted by the wild desert, he sat down and revised his brain and heart to see whether he could reverse his journey, but his will was still one. Therefore, he imitated Mr. Camel and surmounted the thirst. After some miles, while the sound of the drum increased its flavour, Comrade Unity clashed with an iron buffalo. In spite of receiving a broken leg, his might was a miracle in the buffalo's kingdom. Although his hope was very near to realise, he saw the huge Imatong Mountain, clouding all the way ahead. Nevertheless, he dangled his Kilimanjaro axe and broke the barrier into two, and so he conquered the huge clouds. Then he partially reached his hope.

Despite an ocean of fatigue, and before participating in the dance himself, his eyes caught some lasting words.

Long live truth!
Long live love!
Long live justice!
Long live equality!
Long live unity!

A beautiful girl carried these slogans. So Comrade Unity's heart began to swim faster towards her. He wanted to possess both the slogans and the girl, and eventually started to sing the following song:

I was looking for medicine to cure disunity,
And here it is.
I was looking for a drug to cure injustice,
And here it is.
I was looking for poison to kill lies,
And here it is.

I was looking for fire to burn inequality,
And here it is.
I was looking for a water tank
To take water to the thirsty people,
And here it is.
I was looking for food to save the hunger-stricken people,
And here it is.
I was looking for a beautiful girl to carry all these things,
And here she is.
What then can prevent me from saving my dear land?

Comrade Unity then forwarded all his problems to the girl's parents who positively agreed. But still there was an ocean ahead to cross. In spite of the thunders and storms, Mr. and Mrs. Unity were firm in words and deeds; so they started back home. Sooner or later there were some clouds swimming across the sky. But this reality seemed to be an unpromising dream to people of this dying land. But because facts usually grow, their flowers began to appear. And there was a spirit of relief prevailing over the land.

The rain was about to pour down, but only the poor welcomed this, while the rich were in the pool of jealousy. Justice rain was welcomed upon its arrival by:

The poor,
The animals and birds,
The plants and trees,
The soil and wind,
The fish and grass.

Therefore, the greedy world and the weak vultures of the land shook off their dust and left, leaving the poor to reconstruct the fallen house. Peace, love and unity were the new cornerstones. The land then recovered and began to sing this song:

We have unity.
We have love.
We have truth.
We have justice.
We have equality.

The light of the land was seen over the whole land. It was in darkness but now in light. It was hungry but now well satisfied. Where the road started is where the land began afresh. Hence, those who were misled by their stomach dreamed of returning to join in the construction of the new life. And there was life and light in a box of love.

Some Remarkable Events

In the course of my studies at Daystar, I devoured God's Word, internalised and allowed the Holy God to live in and operate through me. I used to take a walk in the wild with the Lord between 5pm and 6pm every evening, praising, thanking, uplifting and glorifying him as we communed together in the light of His love, grace and faithfulness. This remarkable communion with Him spiritually energised me and successfully pulled me through the academic season and some social, economic and political and other national issues.

The Inception of Church and Development

This was another historical moment and a turning point in my personal life. One evening I walked alone with my God in the cool of the day visualising, thinking deeply and praying earnestly about the plight of our people back in Sudan and the unmerited total destruction of our motherland, the Lord gave me an idea to come up with a Christian agency to help with the mitigation of the people's sufferings, especially in areas under the Episcopal Diocese of Bor. I prayed over it and waited upon the Lord for some guidance, and in the course of time, the idea developed and became what is called Church and Development (C&D).

My Peace Task in Kakuma, 1995

In December of 1995, I left Nairobi for Kakuma to visit my family and others. Upon my arrival there, I unfortunately found two groups of Jeng ethnic community, one from Gakrial and other from Anyidi in Bor, terribly involved in the bloody conflict. To show the magnitude of inter-clan strife, they were waylaying and attacking each other along the roads in the camp. I urgently called a pastors' meeting immediately after reaching our main church compound to strategize how to act as 'the salt and the light of the world' to bring peace in the camp. We agreed to put on our clerical uniforms and go and talk to the warring parties. But one potential danger before us was that the majority of us, the pastors, could be easily associated with either side of the conflict by the fierce fighting youngsters, for some of us, including myself, were from Bor while the rest were from the greater Bahr el Ghazal. Despite such an obstacle, we took the step of faith and marched ahead with the message of peace and reconciliation and came out victoriously in the Lord.

The Death of Bungajoh, January 1995

Majok and I came from the some ancestral origin; he is from Mach Bior, and I am from Mathiang Bior. We are distant cousins, but in our cultural context, we are brothers. To talk about Bungajoh, although death robbed us of him at his prime age, he deserves his own complete biography. He was intelligent, sociable, valiant, forthright and very articulate with some inborn leadership abilities, a real leader. He successfully finished his high school studies in 1993 and received a good Sudan School Certificate but failed to continue with his education because of his patriotic spirit. He obtained severe injuries on several occasions and fought many remarkable battles in the devastating war between SPLA and the Khartoum Government.

When I last met brother Majok in 1994 in Nairobi, he looked sickly as he had severe wounds in his body with some sharp objects embedded in his head and parts of his body. And that was why he came there to seek some proper medical treatment from the SPLA/M leadership. As a real brother, Majok paid a fraternal visit to our house in Nairobi and, having heard that he was around, I purposely came from the school during the weekend to meet him. We had a good time together. Unfortunately, he returned to Sudan without being treated.

Although he did not recover from the severe wounds, the SPLA leadership ordered him to command some forces in the battle of Kapoeta in January 1995. And there Brother Majok died heroically, shedding his precious blood with some of his colleagues for the national cause.

I was visiting Bishop Nathaniel's family in Nairobi from the school when I heard this bad news. I withheld my tears and returned to school. Bungajoh was married to Athok Arop Kuot and had three sons and one daughter. Mr. Maker Lual Kuol, the former Commissioner of Bor County has established a primary school in Bor town in the honour of the late David Majok Mach. It is my hope that other gallant martyrs will receive similar honour in and outside Bor area.

Our Second Child, 1996

On Friday 10 May 1996, the Lord blessed us with another child, a baby boy delivered in the dusty and hot camp of Kakuma. This was another joy in the family, and particularly our daughter who now had her own sibling to commune and play with. It is amazing to note here that the day of his birth was the same day that I sat for my last paper in International Marketing in the process of my graduation from Daystar University. We named him after my father Kuch and later gave him the name Joshua, akin to Moses' successor, during his baptism.

The Completion of My Studies, 1996

I successfully cleared all my subjects in my major, Business Administration and Management, and some courses in Community Development. In May 1996, before the actual D Day, the graduating class with their spouses, the faculty, school management and other distinguished guests had a colourful banquet in the best metropolitan hotel, Intercontinental Hotel in Nairobi, Kenya. The following Saturday 18 May, we graduated and received our certificates. Among the notable Sudanese who finished with me were Lokosang Wani, Benjamin Gimba, and Emmanuel Congo, to name just a few. Among those who came to cheer me on were Bishop Nathaniel and his wife, Marop Leek and his wife and Hakim Deng Majuch. The hard battle was won at last, and my immediate plan was to go to Kakuma to be with my family before taking up some duties for the church. The 'Silent Hand' was really upon me.

A Victim of Tribal Conflict in Kakuma, 1996

The current advancement of communication is of great advantage, especially in the area of security detection and protection on time. Unlike now, in the past walking into an unknown circumstance, be it favourable or unfavourable, was a normal occurrence.

After my school completion, I left Nairobi for Kakuma, travelling the entire day and arriving in Kakuma town at around 8pm. Private vehicles were not allowed to enter the camp at all times without the sole permission of the camp authorities and the government district commissioner. Of course, it was unsafe to walk in the camp by night because of some local petty thieves and robbers and marauding Turkana thugs. Yet due to our huge number, that is, many people who came with me on the same trip and wanting to proceed to their respective places in the camp, we ventured on foot towards the settlement. Upon reaching the Nuer community, we fell into an ambush. Nuer men beat, plundered and looted us and left some of us with severe wounds.

I was in my church uniform and carrying my briefcase and a small bag. And When they surprisingly attacked us, I was caught unaware and in my hesitation did not run. Some of them threatened me and tried to snatch my belongings in the process, but I held on to them. Seeing that their threat was fruitless, one of them tried to hit my head, but I repelled his stick with my arm.

Then God brought to my rescue some Nuer elders after hearing from others that I was a pastor. They pushed the other hostile men aside and led me into one of their homes. They asked me if I knew of what had happened during the day between their community and Jeng community, and my response was naught. They narrated that Bol Madut, a SPLA Commander came and called a Sudanese rally, and in the course of his talks, injured the feelings of the Nuer community and that eventually led into a fight between the two communities. The men who had attacked us were standing on guard around their territory in readiness to fight in the event of any possible night attack from the other community. At this time my arm had begun to swell and I was in a lot of pain so the two elders smuggled me out from that dangerous zone to the UNCHR compound where I was put on a UN vehicle and taken to our church compound. I really appreciate what they did for me, and this shows that all people are not the same worldwide – there are good and bad, war loving and peace loving people in every community under the sun.

I suffered not because of what I had done but simply because I am a Muonyjang. And as a result, in such a volatile tribal situation, the naïve could have thought that I deserved to share in that vengeance. But on the other hand, some of my colleagues who were victims did not deserve to suffer the vengeance because they were not from our community. For example, two of the victims were from Rwanda and others were from other Sudanese ethnicities. For those who like to avenge themselves, they are supposed to do so in a discriminatory manner in order not to mistake the cornflake for the weed. Another good counsel I took from this event is that careless words of a prominent person are as deadly as a sharp sword and as pouring fuel on a glowing fire. Thus, we must engage our mental intellect, weighing carefully the consequences of our words before we speak.

Late Majok Mach Aluong, 1990s

Left to Right: *Stephen Mathiang & Jervasto Okot, Daystar University, 1995*

Left to Right: *Stephen Dit & Stephen Mathiang in Nairobi, 1993*

PART FIVE

My Business Life, Further Education and Glimpses, 1996–2010

CHAPTER TEN

Business Life and Continuous Education

My Work for FEBA Radio, June – November 1996

During my last semester at Daystar University, Bishop Nathaniel, Archdeacon Abraham Mayom Athiaan and Hakim Deng approached and told me that I was selected by our diocese to work for FEBA Radio as a radio producer in the Jeng language. As this job was to come into effect right after my graduation, there was need, according to them, for me to be ready for an interview.

FEBA stands for Far East Broadcasting Association. And its broadcasting station was at the time situated in the small island of Seychelles, but the charity also had an office in Nairobi, Kenya. It is a Christian radio that aims at saturating some target areas and target audiences with the Gospel. So my role was to collect, write scripts and electronically transfer them into magnetic cassettes and send them to the station for fifteen-hour broadcasting daily. Since a Jeng programme was not in existence in that station, I was going to establish it from zero level.

I appreciated their offer but asked them as to why the church decided to give me this work of communication, although it was not in line with my field of studies. In contrast to this, I gave them some assurance that, given my basic communication knowledge and skills that I had acquired in some general courses at Daystar, this assignment was not going to challenge me anyway. I asked them whether this radio work was where I was going to realise my maximum potential. Once more, I asked them why they would not just give it to any capable Christian, not necessarily from Jeng Bor, who was fluent in Jeng language, knowledgeable in the Gospel and good in communication skills. But they insisted that I was the right person to do the task at that time. As they failed to understand my viewpoints, I reluctantly accepted their offer and attended the interview, which I won.

Another Nuer chap was interviewed and given the job of radio producer in their language. I was told to turn up for the job immediately after my school graduation, but I told them that I was going to go to Kakuma for some time to visit my family.

The management of the radio promised to each of us a gross salary of fifteen thousand Kenya shillings per month, inclusive of housing, food, medical scheme, transport, etc. Then the director, Mr. Lombo demanded, given the urgency and scope of the task, for us to bring our families to Nairobi so as to avoid unnecessary future requests from any of us to take off from the place of work with the aim of family visits. This order was not a problem with my Sudanese colleague because his family was already in Nairobi. However, given the level of salary and standards of living in Nairobi at the time, I did not comply with that order. Instead, I told him that my family was going to remain in the camp until further notice.

Before I officially signed the job contract and took up the assignment, I kept on thinking as to why I was given this work. Was it something deliberately designed to keep me away from the church leadership circle, and if so, why? Was the Lord behind that decision, and if so, should I disobey him? What about the idea, which I had had and seemed to be from the Lord to establish a church related agency? Would I just dismiss it as an illusion and take up the new job? These and other useful, soul-searching questions cropped into my mind but getting informed answers for them was not easy. My primary focus was not where to get money but rather it was where the Lord could use me fully for His own glory and for the welfare of His people. Anyway, I put the whole issue before the Lord in prayer and waited for some divine directives.

In the course of my strategic and analytical thinking, I returned to Bishop Nathaniel and disclosed my heart to him once more. I shared with him that I was still not comfortable to work for the radio programme. I went on and told him that my insisting to remain within the diocese did not mean that I had an intention to usurp or to be given one of the key administrative roles like administration secretary, logistician, treasurer, etc. Furthermore, I communicated to him clearly my dream of establishing an agency under the name Church and Development to help alleviate some of the sufferings facing our people, especially in the Bor areas.

He enthusiastically appreciated the idea and told me to go ahead and begin the work with FEBA Radio while he looked for someone to relieve me from there. As my spiritual and administrative leader, I obeyed but advised him to hurry up with his search for my replacement. I showed him and other members of the diocese the concept paper that I had written concerning this envisioned agency, Church and Development, and they all appreciated it.

I went ahead and took up my job with FEBA Radio in the beginning of June. The scope and intensity of the work posed a great challenge to me. Of course, collecting and writing scripts for the radio is not a sort of sluggish, white-collar job or something to do merely with using the Bible as the only source of content. It is a work, which demands rigid continuity the moment it is launched on the air so as to maintain the short attention span of restless and unseen audiences. Above all, the task is to share God's Word in a godly manner, not adding to or subtracting anything from it; it needs the guidance of the Holy Spirit to reach the un-reached and save the lost.

As we all know, people are gifted and talented differently. Hence, one of my obvious gifts is that I rarely fail in any task given to me, irrespective of its scope and intensity because I usually pursue my task sacrificially with God's backing. Based on this inborn gift, I came up with a signal tune, put scripts together, sent them to the broadcasting station in Seychelles, and so this useful programme went on air. I worked almost around the clock to keep it in constant progress, though it was mentally and physically exhaustive in reality. But the Lord sustained my whole being.

I kept Bishop Nathaniel in constant check for my replacement from this work. Eventually, the church asked Rev. Peter Garang Thiel to take over from me. He was a capable candidate to carry on with this radio programme.

Six months later, on 29 November 1996, I left my position as a radio producer and moved on in the pursuit of my dream of Church and Development. I must underscore here that that I firmly laid a proper and concrete foundation on which the Jeng programme with FEBA continued to flourish and flourish for the betterment of mankind and for God's own glory. In the end, the programme was phased out from FEBA Radio to MAP International with the same vision and mission.

Unfortunate Events, October 1996

Death of Dau: on 18 October, Rev. Abraham Dau Werabek passed away in Nairobi after a long illness. This was a big blow both to the church and his family as well to his personal friends and close associates. Dau was one of the earlier educated priests of our church. He was a very tall gentleman, a man of the people and full of veracity. His Christian and social maturity put him above tribal levels. He was a hardworking person hailing from Paliau Payam in Twic East County. I do not intend to write all the unique attributes of my late brother and friend other than the few things I sincerely stated above. He was survived by his wife and children.

Death of Mamer: Jacob Mamer Maluk passed on in Kakuma Hospital on 21 October after a short illness. He was an active and good evangelist, composer and singer of Christian songs and one of the devoted youth leaders in the church. He faithfully carried his own cross and followed in Christ's footsteps despite his young age and the scorns of non-Christian believers. Jacob left a deeper and wider vacuum both in the church and his biological family, and especially among our youth members. Like Brother Dau, I just want to shed a little light upon the unique life of our dear brother Jacob Mamer Maluk. He was from Makuach Payam in Bor County.

Baseline Assessments, 28 March – 5 May 1997

Michael Medley and I went to Bor in March 1997 to carry out a needs assessment. Michael worked with me as a consultant right from the inception of C&D. In order to achieve our objectives, we stayed and socialised with the local churches and other members of the community, sleeping and eating with them and sharing their concerns and our ideas among ourselves. Furthermore, we cleverly networked with some national and international agencies and local government authorities for them to know what we were doing and to help us in terms of transportation, communication and security protection. Church and Development did not aim to compete with the operating agencies, but it rather focused its efforts to complement and supplement their humanitarian activities in any way possible.

We covered most of the Bor area, beginning from Duk Padiet in the northern point up to Malual de Abiei in the southern part. We had various meetings with some relevant parties such as governmental bodies, churches, women's association, chiefs and NGOs' representatives, among others. We met them in Poktap, Duk Padiet, Panyagoor, Yomchiir, Makuach, Pariak, Malou, Panewel, Panepandiar, Chuei-Kher, Kolnyang, Anyidi and Anyang-Lengker. The primary purpose of such meetings was to inform them about Church and Development and to learn from them the existing gaps as well as the general needs of the area in the fields of their operations. In the course of our needs assessment trip, we discovered that one of the pressing needs that were not taken care of was adult literacy. Despite the fact that in all the churches we went to there were self-initiated adult education programmes, their main problem was a lack of learning materials.

In order to begin small, and because of the lack of financial muscles, Church and Development took adult literacy as its best-entrance project. And its role was to raise some funds, buy the needed learning materials, transport them to Bor by air from Kenya, hire some schools and distribution monitors to monitor and supervise the equal and equitable distributions and utilizations of the materials in all adult education centres. The community selected six adult education monitors, three in South Bor and three in North Bor. Church and Development undertook this humble project in its attempt to slightly narrow the very wide educational gap brought about by the war.

The First C&D Board Meeting, 14–20 August 1997

To put an official rubber stamp on this idea, and in order to comply with the vision and mission statements and the essence of the drafted constitution of the Church and Development, my adviser, Mr. Michael Medley and I got some funding and organized a board meeting in Lodwar, a town in northern Kenya in Turkana area. Diocesan Bishop Nathaniel Garang, Archdeacons John Kelei, Daniel Dau, the late Simon Anyang Maal, Samuel Majok Deng, Peter Bol Arok, John Machar Thon, Mary Achol Deng, Rebecca Lueth Wel, Gabriel Achuoth, Paul Tiopich Liet, Daniel Deng Lual, Stephen Mathiang Kuch and Michael Medley attended it. The nominated members of the governing board officially accepted their nominations. And thus became legitimate members and were empowered constitutionally to carry out their constitutional rights.

They discussed, amended and approved all the operational documents of the Church and Development and declared it as a legitimate para-church organization. To fulfil one of their constitutional roles, the board members officially appointed me, Stephen Mathiang, as the executive director to run the day-to-day affairs of the secretariat, and I accepted the appointment.

An Unfortunate Event, 25 August 1997

After conducting the C&D first Board Meeting, I joined my family in Kakuma to have a brief time with them before returning to Nairobi. While having our supper at around 8pm, we heard gunshots across the road in our church compound. I told my family members to keep low and not to run in panic. Before long, we discovered that Turkanan thugs had invaded and attacked innocent people, killing Rural-dean John

Majok Tuil and badly wounding evangelist Daniel Yor Deng. Yor, unfortunately, ended up in a wheelchair, although the late Rev. Dr. Mark Nikkle did his level best to provide him with proper medical treatment. The cause of the attack was unknown. And that is how some of the refugees lost their precious lives and possessions there in Kakuma.

Enthronement, 25 January 1998

Bishop Nathaniel Garang Anyieth and Bishop Wilson Arop of Torit ECS Diocese were enthroned in Narus, Southern Sudan by the former Dean of ECS Province, late Simon Zindo. The colourful occasion was attended by many people, more importantly from the Diocese of Bor. His enthronement was completely overdue because of the war situations. That is, it had been delayed because he was cut off by the civil war from the seat of the Archbishop of the ECS Province in Khartoum.

C&D Initial Manpower and Some Work Ethnics

Initial manpower: In terms of manpower, apart from my consultant, I was the only person executing all the necessary activities and representing Church and Development at secretariat level and other relevant forums. Some of my key tasks were, but not limited to, sensitizing the members of the community and bringing them on board to participate in carrying out baseline surveys throughout the entire Bor area to unearth the real needs of the people, identifying some pressing needs out of many and seeing how to find national and foreign solutions to them.

Work ethics: Church and Development aimed at achieving its targets in a participatory approach by involving actual beneficiaries and other stakeholders in the project cycle management so as to enable them take the ownership of the programmes. In order to get funding for the implementation of the key projects and win donors' confidence, this infant agency was to establish and maintain a very high level of transparency and accountability in all its words and actions by understanding that it was accountable both to the beneficiaries and donors plus other stakeholders. Also, because of its infancy, there was an urgent need to carefully and consistently market its image in and outside the Bor region. The Secretariat ended up shouldering almost all of the above and other vital tasks alone. This is because the war circumstances and the low level of education among members of the board incapacitated them from executing their constitutional roles effectively and efficiently.

Live with and Work for the People

As community workers, there was a need for us to live with and work for the target communities so as to share their day-to-day concerns with them. So the target communities and local government authorities were to show us where to establish our bases of operations.

In 1998, Church and Development adopted a small experimental project in ox-ploughing as a particular agricultural area of its concentration. Its primary aim was to empower the members of the community to address the chronic issues of food security and reduce in the process the high level of dependency syndrome.

In the church meeting which I had in Wun-Ngor on 22 March 1998 in South Bor with the majority of pastors and laity, the church selected the Werkok area as the experimental site because of three main reasons: firstly, it was relatively secure because of its concentrated population at the time; secondly, the areas around Werkok Court Centre had been recently vacated by the inhabitants and so suitable for ox-ploughing due to the lack of trees; and thirdly, the church chose it because of its central location between the Gok and Athoch community divisions. That is how Church and Development came to be in Ajading, Werkok. In Northern Bor, the choice fell on Panyagoor due to its central locality and relative security assurance.

First Recruitments

We received some funding and appointed Solomon Mabior Ruar, Jacob Maduk Deng and Abdon Machok Deng to help me discharge the immense tasks in the pursuit of the vision and mission statements of Church and Development. Solomon Mabior was assigned as project officer in South Bor, Jacob Maduk as project officer in North Bor and Abdon Machok took the role of agriculture officer to take charge of both areas in terms of training and supervision. An evangelist, Isaiah Diing Chan was our accountant. We recruited some auxiliary workers to discharge some relevant authorities and responsibilities.

We bought some agricultural and other supplies from Kenya and transported them to both our two locations. Abdon Machok, with the help of two project officers and others, organized and conducted two separate training courses in ox-ploughing, starting from Ajading and ending up in Panyagoor. The response for the training was very positive, but its implementation, as a totally new concept in the area at the time, was very challenging.

Our Third Child, 1998

We had our third child, a baby boy, on 23 July 1998 in Kakuma Camp. He was named after my grandfather, Alier-kuorwel Mathiang. My wife delivered while I was in Nairobi, and I received this important news joyfully. During his baptism he received the historic name of David, the second king of Israel.

The Second C&D Board Meeting, 1998

Fatal car accident: we organized the second board meeting to take place in Narus, a small border town inside Sudan along the Sudan-Kenya boarder. I took off by public bus from Nairobi on my way to Narus on 19 September. With me in the bus were Archdeacon Ezekiel Diing Ajang, Atem Garang Deng Kuek and others. Diing and I were in the front seat. As we approached Kakuma from Lodwar, the driver lost control on a curved section of the road. And so we found ourselves rolling with the bus until it stood up off the road in thorny bushes facing the opposite direction. I saw the driver moving at a long distance in the bushes, Ezekiel Diing groaning heavily on the ground and some passengers' belongings, including ours of course, scattered here and there. I realized that I was out of greater danger, although my body was covered with blood. I found it hard to sit upright in my seat. Atem came, holding his dislocated arm, and asked about my condition. I told him that I was okay, and he should rush and see Diing instead. One of us, an Ethiopian guy, died instantly.

While we were still struggling to take care of ourselves, another car, a pick-up truck came fast with some passengers on board. As they approached the scene of the incident, the eyes of some of these travellers fell to our scattered belongings. So we heard one of them saying: "Oh, there are pastors involved; do you know, they keep money in those small handbags." But since some of our colleagues were physically unhurt, those merciless and greedy people hesitated to snatch anything from us. The dead and some of us who were badly injured were dumped to the pickup and rushed to Kakuma Hospital.

Save donor's funds to save trust: I had the money for the C&D Board Meeting in the pocket of my jacket. The nurses at the hospital removed my jacket with the money still inside and my wristwatch too. But I clung on to the jacket in the fear that something bad might happen to the money, which would make it hard in the end for me to justify to the giving donor, given the usual unsound level of suspicion and mistrust between donors and their recipients. Atem quickly received some first aid and was discharged. Then he came to say goodbye to me. I seized that opportunity and gave him the jacket with the money in it – of course, I revealed to him that it had a sufficient amount of money inside and advised him to keep the cash until we met again. Since I operated at a high level of trust, I did not bother to count the money. He took the cash, called some church members in our church compound, counted the money and handed it over to the church leadership. Surely, all were saved, and I am still grateful for what he did that day.

Proceeding with the C&D annual meeting: the medical staff took care of my visible wounds but failed to find out what was wrong with my back. My wife and mother plus other beloved relatives and friends and some church members rushed to the hospital to see us. As people continued to walk long distances under the scorching sun of Kakuma to visit us in the hospital and because of the urgency of the meeting, as well as the fact that my recovery was not going to be quick, I decided to discharge myself on 24 of that month to become an outpatient.

After a little while, we left Kakuma for Narus and conducted the meeting on 25 September. I went back to Nairobi after the meeting to continue with my medical treatment. The x-ray revealed that I had some multiple fractures on my back. For this reason, I was put under long-term medical treatment, involving some physiotherapy and wearing of some aids to straighten my back. Now it seems to be a lifelong disability, although thankfully I can get around places with less and less trouble.

Achievements of Church and Development

Lifespan of any organization: organizations normally pass through three key stages just the same as human beings. That is, they pass through birth, maturity and death. The majority of them pass away at the early levels of birth if not enough care is taken at the level of the growth crisis. At the level of maturity some organizations stagnate and end up surviving by working hard to maintain their fixed bureaucratic standards or status quo without thinking of their further growth. If no strategies are put in place in order to let them live, they will swiftly descend from the top level of maturity down to their eternal grave. In short, NGOs are born, live and die like any living thing. I am happy to point out here that Church and Development has not yet reached its level of death at the time of writing.

Tangible achievements: despite its ups and downs, wise people do not deny history because it speaks for itself. That is, Church and Development grew from one man, its founder, to about one hundred and fifty salaried staff. These people decided to serve their people through Church and Development, and they did well. Church and Development established and staffed seventeen primary schools in the whole of the Bor area plus one secondary school at Werkok.

Before we phased over these schools to the government after the signing of the Comprehensive Peace Agreement (CPA), Church and Development used to pay about half a million Kenya shillings per month to the schools' teachers and their support staff. Church and Development focus was to provide quality education and somewhat bridge the wider educational gap created by the civil war.

Other areas in which Church and Development made some substantial contributions include water and sanitation, basic health care, relief and emergency, agriculture, etc. Church and Development also successfully facilitated the establishment of the Memorial Christian Hospital at Werkok. Church and Development raised some funds and assisted the Diocese of Bor logistically to have its historical diocesan synod on 29 April 2000 in Pakeu Zion Church. This was the first church meeting convened after the Bor massacre in 1991.

The Church's Unhappiness with Church and Development

Parental right of the church: the church's unhappiness with the Church and Development can best be comprehended in the context of parental relationship – a parent-child affinity, and the expectations involved in such relationships. The Diocese of Bor plays the role of a parent, and Church and Development acts as its child. Of course, in normal circumstances and particularly in the African context, the parent and his child depend on one another in terms of physical and moral support. And especially, when the parent is weak in relation to his advanced age or sickness or whatever the cause may be, and the child is at the point of his varied strengths, much is logically and reasonably demanded of him (child). Under such severe situations, if the child generously helps others and fails to take maximum care of his needy parent, the parent and others have an absolute right, irrespective of some obvious legitimate reasons, to blame him of clear negligence and disrespect to his biological parent.

Given the above analogy, when Church and Development was formed to participate in the shouldering of some relief and developmental activities in areas in which the Diocese of Bor was operating, it logically and reasonably aroused greater expectations from the latter in that it expected the former to meet its basic needs in the process of serving the entire masses of Bor and other communities. Church and Development also held a similar viewpoint if, and I want you to underline the word if, the unique international and national humanitarian situations were going to permit.

Uncompromising donor's policy: in the process of continuous, tedious and mind-numbing fundraising exercises, Church and Development failed to get a donor interested in some of the church's needs, especially the pastors' welfare. The donors whose confidence was won by Church and Development strongly wanted to see to it that their funds met the greater needs of the oppressed Sudanese people. Thus, some of them chose to pour their money into different activities in line with their unique organizational policies. For example, Caritas Australia put its money into a water and sanitation project of the Church and Development while others financed education, agriculture, etc.

Their funds were specifically meant to help alleviate the plight of the entire community, of course, including the church. For the church is the community of Christians who personally profess and claim Jesus Christ as their Lord and Saviour and are willing to participate in the implementation of the Great Commission in direct obedience to the Lord's command. Although Church and Development managed to serve the church with the above significant social services through its congregations, it unfortunately failed to get some funding to address some of the specific needs of the Diocese of Bor.

For those who have been involved in the world of real NGOs and donor's funding, there is a high and rigid level of transparency and accountability. In other words, there are inflexible policies and rules governing the acquisitions and utilizations of the donor's funds. To make it worse, some small and inexperienced humanitarian and development agencies such as Church and Development, especially from the third world countries, are not entrusted by donors to handle un-earmarked funds. Instead, they are given only earmarked funds based on very clear and acceptable project proposals to test their integrity and capability. When dealing with such earmarked funds, even greater deviation from one budget line to another within the same project proposal is not permitted without a proper prior request in writing from the implementing agency to its donor and written consent from the concerned donor.

Choosing the best biblical alternative: given this stiff scenario, Church and Development became totally and regrettably incapacitated to take care of the specific needs of the Diocese of Bor. It was caught up in an actual ethical and moral dilemma. That is, the first option for the C&D was to snatch some earmarked moneys, robbing both the donor(s) and real beneficiaries (which of course, consist of the entire members of the congregation) and meet the pressing, particular needs of the Diocese of Bor. If this was the better option, the C&D would, therefore, face the following consequences: the concerned donors would accuse the C&D of theft before international and/or national courts; the same donors might withdraw their allegiance from the C&D and stop their funding; having lost its good truck records and funding supports, the C&D would not continue rendering the same services to its beneficiaries. Thus, it might pass off scene.

The second option was for the C&D to serve the Diocese of Bor by serving its entire oppressed members at the expense of those particular church's needs while maintaining the donors' confidence and its good track records. Church and Development chose the latter or second option simply in the interest of the whole Sudanese people and donor agencies.

Some people within the leadership of the Diocese of Bor were not happy with it. But maybe some reacted out of pure ignorance while the rest or so did it out of mere hatred and jealousy. As a matter of fact, we are now living in a modern world where people are respected and entitled to their own opinions within the peaceful domain of their societies.

Never Fall Short of What to Do in God's Name

One day, when I was contemplating giving up my job with C&D, a friend of mine asked me as to what I was going to do in life. I told him that I wasn't sure, although I would always have something to do in God's name as far as I was still alive in this world. It is a common knowledge that the Lord does not require ability but availability in regards to his faithful labourers in his kingdom here and now. Therefore, if I should faithfully make myself available before him, he would surely abide in me and I in him, and he would work in and through me to will and carry out his own desires for the general good of his people as well as for his own glory.

Michael Medley's Resignation, 1999

Michael Medley resigned his post on 13 April 1999 as a consultant for Church and Development. His relationship with the people of Southern Sudan, especially those from the Bor dated back to early 1990 when he worked for NSCC on secondment to the Diocese of Bor. Michael had love for people. He was a competent writer, a community worker with a real sense of self-denial. As a case in point, during his work with Church and Development, we walked long distances, slept and ate with the locals deep in the rural areas while we tried to put our feet into their own shoes. His love for people made him quite a risk taker and adventurer. Michael was well educated, an intellectual person who approached controversial issues with an open mind. And so at the time of our work, we sometimes discussed and debated over crucial issues. In other words, we even disagreed as brothers often, not necessarily having agreed to disagree but only disagreeing based on our varying personal viewpoints.

The Death of Archdeacon Simon Anyang, 1999

Archdeacon Anyang got sick and was admitted in Hurlingham Hospital in Nairobi. His health deteriorated and, unfortunately, he died on 8 August and was buried in Langata Cemetery in Nairobi on 11 of the same month. Anyang was one of the few pastors who assisted Bishop Nathaniel Garang in the early management of the ECS Diocese of Bor. He was a good, wise Christian leader whose untimely death was deeply felt far and wide in and outside the Diocese of Bor. He was upright, forthright and a vehement protector of the Holy Bible and sound church doctrine. Anyang left his wife and children behind.

The Acquisition of My Masters Degree, 1999–2002

The importance of time: it is a universal, natural fact that man does not live twice under the sun. And in the light of this truth, it is imperative for one to do his level best to tirelessly pursue his life-goals before the sun of life goes down. One of my personal goals in life was to satisfactorily arrive at the last destination of my educational journey, irrespective of my age. How did I strategize to accomplish this noble vision? I minimized the pursuit of other important hobbies of life, divided and scheduled my precious time and used it economically.

The majority of people worldwide hold a notion that time lost can be compensated with the maximum usage of the remaining time. They are entirely subject to their own opinions. On the contrary, my opinion convinces me beyond any possible doubt that there is time for everything under the sun, time to eat, time to work, time to take a walk, time to sleep, time to talk, time to laugh, time to mourn, time to play, time to live, time to die, etc. There is no time stored away to use in compensation for the lost time. Either you lose it once and for all or you have it for useful actions in the future.

One funny thing about time, which is ignorantly overlooked by millions of people worldwide, is the fact that a person and all other living things age second by second, minute by minute, hour by hour, day by day, week by week, month by month and year by year. One of my precious times that I regrettably lost once and for all is the year 1985, which I spent in Itang, recovering from my illness. During or part of that year, I wish I had read and internalized the best English dictionary from first page to the last or just mingled with the Ethiopians and learned the Amharic language along the streets of Itang. All of us will definitely account to the giver of time of how this valuable asset has been put into use below heaven. Time is as precious as life itself.

Better use of opportune moments: another thing that I did to achieve my educational achievements was to seize any possible opportunities and utilize them fruitfully and minimize and/or turn some threats into opportunities and channel them towards the achievements of my educational goal. For instance, my presence in Nairobi was one of the best opportunities for me to use. This is simply because some possible good schools to pursue further studies are in and around this metropolitan town. Also effective and efficient communication networks are available in Nairobi. And the presence of our diocesan head office in Nairobi at the time was also another chance because Bishop Nathaniel was there to render any possible approvals whenever needed.

Fishing for scholarships: given these favourable circumstances, my educational vision pushed me forward in an earnest quest about possible avenues of funding. To get money for my scholarship at Nairobi International School of Theology (NIST), I had to write and send out more than one hundred letters to different, unknown international donor agencies. I clearly remember writing and posting forty two letters at once in various directions, and out of these, one Christian organization from Switzerland in Europe gave me a positive response by accepting only to cover my tuition fees. Until this time of writing we do not know each other physically. NIST is situated in the vicinity of Hurlingham shopping centre in Nairobi. It has now changed its name to International Leadership University. It was just a walking distance from the office of Church and Development at the time.

Unwise to kill two big birds with one small stone: as I prepared to go back to school, I decided to hand over the sceptre of the leadership of Church and Development to someone else. But, since this infant agency was still in the making, many people rendered their honest advices to and encouraged me to take the bull by the horns. That is, to concurrently continue my work with Church and Development and do my studies at the same time so as to maintain and/or increase the needed momentum within the organization.

I took their counsel despite the fact that I knew very well it was going to be a big challenge for me. Also, as a family man, to discharge both noble duties successfully was a daunting task for me. I enrolled for a Christian Ministries and Leadership course in 1999 and finished fruitfully and graduated with flying colours on 25 May 2002. I would have finished in the year before had I not postponed one semester midway in pursuit of my work in Sudan.

Although I discharged two tasks wholeheartedly and with desired results, I would not advise any ambitious person in my lifetime to try and balance the demands between a full time job and full time university studies. Yet I know I am not the first and the last person to walk the walk on this unique road of aggressive endeavours.

Memorable Events, 2000–2003

Rev. Stephen Dit's death: Stephen Dit Makok passed away in Nairobi after a long illness and was buried in Langata Cemetery in May 2000. He was a very hardworking, sociable, determined and intelligent person. He composed and sang numerous hymnal songs in the Jeng language. He spearheaded the compiling of thousands of Christian songs in Jeng and helped those of the Sudan Literature Centre publish some of them in 1999 in Nairobi.

To show his relentless zeal for his godly tasks, Dit cornered me in 1990 in Bor town and recorded all the biblical songs with which the Lord had blessed his church through me. Up to the time of his death, Dit loved to work with the church youth and Sunday school ministries. Many mourners, including myself, failed to hold their loving tears when his body was lowered into the grave. Some biblical verses were read, and some of his own songs were sung before it was covered with soil.

Paul Alier's death: my mother came from Anyuat community of the Atet clan of Makuach Payam in Bor County. Her siblings were Anyiwei, Yuol, Nyok and Akuei Jok. Nyok gave birth to Maliei and Paul Alier, among others.

Paul Alier, my uncle passed away on 27 April 2001 in his home village of Makuach after long suffering from the deadly liver cancer. He was one of the prominent officers of SPLA. He was wise, courageous, sociable and intelligent with some inborn leadership qualities. He was proactive and gifted to easily open closed doors of life. He was married to Akher Maduk and Esther and survived by some children.

According to uncle Deng Anyuat Kur, on his deathbed, Paul Alier concerned himself with only three things: firstly, the fate of his children; secondly, the continuation of the civil war, and thirdly, how SPLA/M was going to divide the national cake among the oppressed people after the war. Paul's grave is among the graves of his ancestors located in the Makuach Headquarters.

My mother's death: in year 2000, my dear mother requested me to take her home to live with her son Bech. As she was around her old age, she did not want death to catch her unaware in a foreign land and leave her bones therein. In obedience to her request, I put her on a plane and took her to Bor where her people highly and warmly received her. She decently passed away on 29 July 2001 in Werkok Boma in her son's luak in the hands of her beloved son and daughter-in-law, Mary Achol Nyiel. She received a decent burial among her people. We all loved her.

Our fourth child: we had our fourth child on 22 August 2001, nine months prior to my graduation from NIST in May 2002. On Saturday 25 of the same month, my wife and I organized and conducted a prayer meeting in our house in the Magiwa Estate in Nairobi to commemorate the death of my uncle Paul Alier and mother as well as to thank the Lord for the new person he had given us. We named him after my wife's great grandfather, Aleer-Jogaak. Bishop Nathaniel Garang blessed and baptised Jogaak on 2 September 2001 in St. Luke Church, Nairobi, and we named him John, one of Jesus's Apostles.

The death of Rev. Daniel Matiop, 2002: on Friday 22 March, Rev. Daniel Matiop Anyieth was involved in a fatal bus collusion in Nairobi, breaking his thigh. He was rushed to and admitted in Kenyatta National Hospital. I visited him there, and his injury didn't seem to be life threatening. But as time went by, his health got worse, and so he was referred to Aga Khan Hospital, one of the good private hospitals in Nairobi, where he underwent some sort of surgical operations.

Unfortunately, Matiop passed away on 6 April in the hospital, leaving behind a huge hospital bill. After the clearance of the hospital bill by the Church Missionary Society, UK, he was buried in Langata cemetery on 26 April. Much appreciation goes to Archdeacon Joseph Akol Gak who tirelessly oversaw the late Matiop from the time of his accident to his death. He looked around and mobilised funds to clear the hospital bill and other expenses. Rev. Daniel was very sociable, a wise and godly man. He left his wife and children behind.

The death of Rev. Simon Bul and Martha Anok, 2002: while Bishop Nathaniel and his diocesan administrative secretary, Archdeacon Peter Yuang were on an official visit in the United States, I heard about the untimely death of Rev. Simon Bul Manyuon and Martha Anok Bior and others upon a bus crash on their way from Uganda to Kenya. Our community members requested of the church to meet burial and other financial expenses. But it was difficult for the church body to accomplish this obligation due to a lack of money. I wrote to and told the bishop and his secretary about this unfortunate event and asked for the money. They promptly sent us some funding to meet such financial expenses. This was another tragic circumstance that faced the church and our community.

My First Visit to the USA, 2003

Our Diocese of Bor had a mutual relationship with the Episcopal Diocese of Indianapolis in Indiana State, USA at the time. Based on this mutual friendship, Bishop Nathaniel Garang received an invitation letter from Bishop Cate of the Indianapolis Diocese, asking him to visit with some key people. Archdeacon Peter Yuang went in his capacity as diocesan administrative secretary, Bartholomew Bol Deng represented our diocesan youth, and I went as representative of Church and Development. My USA visa was delayed in Nairobi, and so I followed my team members later on 3 June with a brief stopover via the United Kingdom.

My personal impression: we managed to visit several states and historical places such as Verde University while there and that gave me better exposure to the balanced development of this giant nation. I came to take pleasure in and appreciate the proper application of the rule of law – no one, yes, including the president, is above the law. I also came to treasure the value and high respect given to human life, for it is overwhelmingly in accordance with how God, the Creator of the universe upholds and sees man, the creation in his own image and likeness. Social services were up-to-date, and one of the worst national enemies that have been conquered is hunger. Cleanliness and other environmental protections are highly esteemed and kept in order. Having painted this nice picture of the USA, I am not saying that it is immune of all human's wickedness and shortcomings. But I am rather saying that in terms of some recognisable indicators of human development, it is nearer to the high standards of living and actualization.

My national contributions: being impressed by what I saw and heard, I took a bit of a mental comparison between the USA and my war-torn nation, especially Southern Sudan, and I honestly arrived at a clear conclusion that, in almost all vital aspects of human life, the gap between the two nations was very, very great in relation to its depth, height and width. Then the question came into my mind: "If my family and I were given an honouring and humane invitation to come and live in the USA on a resettlement programme, what would be my response, as the breadwinner of my family?"

And my response to this very hypothetical question was naught. Why? I have many analytical and calculated answers to this question but let me just shed some light on a few things here. It took hundreds of years, thousands of barrels of precious blood, sweat and tears of devoted ancestors, young and old, men and women, wise and fools, strong and weak to shape and mould and bring America to where it is. The same moving forces will continue to push it forward from one generation to another with one vision in mind to make it the best place under the sun for the existence of human habitations and also for God's own glory. Can Sudan also become like the USA and other developed nations of the world? If the answer is yes, who can make it happen? Why was I born in Sudan, and what national contributions does my Creator expect me to play in the development of Sudan before I exit the world? Having almost finished my educational studies, can I use the knowledge and skills that I had acquired to make some minute differences in my nation? These varied questions and answers and more challenged my human intellect and dignity, and forced me hence, to give a sincere no to that honourable and humane question.

On the question about a favourable learning environment as well as because of the divine freedom of human choice, my family's members, however, may differ with me in relation to their individual responses to this hypothetical question of such an honourable invitation should it be ever made.

It was during this eye-opening visit that God led me into the life of Brother Dave Bowman, the solid architect behind the establishment of the Memorial Christian Hospital (MCH) in Werkok in Bor County, Jonglei State. Through the connection of Bishop Nathaniel and other South Sudanese guys, Dave invited me to visit him in Grand Rapids, Michigan in August 2003. And through my invitation to him, he and other seven Americans paid a fact-finding visit to Bor in January 2004 where we received them. After their first visit to Bor, Dave formed a charitable agency called Partners in Compassionate Care (PCC) through which he mobilized the needed resources and established the MCH.

Visionaries learn more easily by seeing than hearing because vision is caught than taught. Did I catch some visions during my first visit outside Africa? Sure, I believe I caught some visions while on my first tour in the USA.

Our fifth child: on Tuesday 12 August 2003, the Lord blessed us with our lovely daughter in Nairobi while her dad was still abroad. My beloved mother demanded of us strongly before she left the world not to forget to name any daughter of ours after her whenever God blessed us with one. So we gave her the famous name of Areu and later on christened with her grandmother's name, Deborah. Archdeacon Bol Arok blessed her on Sunday 14 September 2003 in St. Luke Church in Nairobi. In the following year, she was baptised on 13 June in the same church. Reu in Jeng language means thirst, and when a girl child is born during the notable time of thirst, she is called Areu, but as for a baby boy, the name is Mareu. Thus, my mother was born in Bor during the worst period of thirst, especially in one of the dry seasons back in the days when water sources were very scarce deep in the villages far from the River Nile.

The Acquisition of My PhD, 2004–2006

Self-examination of my gifts: passing over my middle age and with some legitimate social and family issues calling my undivided attention, I decided to look urgently for some further opportunities and make the best use of my precious time to leap towards the final destination of my educational pursuit. But in which field of education was I to narrow down my studies? To turn my own eyes inwardly and examine, with a high level of sincerity, the unique attributes the Lord has bestowed upon me, I discovered that leadership is one of my prominent gifts. In fact, some friends and relatives of mine unflatteringly agreed with my findings.

Leadership problem: genuine leadership is one of the vital missing links in all socio-economic, political and religious institutions in the entire realm of mankind, and especially in Africa. There are many institutions of higher learning in and outside Africa that offer some courses and programmes in secular and biblical leadership. As a result, thousands after thousands of varying leaders stream out regularly in a dire quest about addressing different segments of leadership problems at family levels, business, political and religious sectors but with unnoticeable effects and impacts in human society.

Misconceptions of leadership: as I struggled with the essence and applications of real leadership, I came to discover that it lies centrally at the heart and the mind of societal systems of existence. But it is unfortunately misunderstood and abused to the very extent that it is merely equated to power and wealth or high levels of learning. Yes, these are good aspects of leadership, but they do not essentially constitute the core of leadership.

Let me shed some brighter light here: you see, most of the biological and other social sciences are keenly taught in particular learning environments and applied in real life situations by the learners. That is, medical experts deal with medical issues; geologists deal with some geological problems; lawyers deal with some legal issues, and so on and so forth. There is clear wisdom and a sense of direction when people struggle with particular areas of their specialties and specializations for the common good of man without being tempted and derailed selfishly to become jacks of all trades and masters of none.

Why is leadership not given to leadership specialists? It is not given to them because all human beings assume that they are leaders and have the right to lead, even when some of them cannot manage to rally behind them a few followers. In other words, since all human beings are specially created with inalienable leadership traits at varying levels to enable them to lead on different fields of leadership, beginning from family settings at the very base up to the top level of the societal ladder, people wrestle and wrangle along the ladder, irrespective of their unique leadership gifts, in a never-ending quest to find the best leadership domain. And also because leadership, especially the worldly type, mostly harnesses pride and fame plus other selfish benefits, almost all human beings believe that they are the best leaders. Because of these myopic, disillusioned and selfish thoughts, some leaders usually and fatally fall down in the process up the leadership ladder.

Using the wildlife leadership philosophy, people wrongly equate leadership to power, be it military, leadership connection, economic, religious, etc. In 'Animal Kingdom', physical strength proportionally equates to leadership; this is what I refer to as 'Wildlife leadership philosophy'. And based on this state of affairs, we always see some people, with a few minimal leadership gifts, jumping from anywhere at the lower parts to the very top of the leadership ladder, irrespective of having trodden on others in the process. Then they try to cling to the top, not by their wise adequate leadership expertise but simply because of the brutal use of their might.

In this particular generation, how many top world leaders, whether in political or other social institutions, have recognisable certificates in the field of leadership, which enabled them to enjoy the leadership atmosphere at the echelon of leadership ladder? Also how many leaders are there at the top of the ladder because of their brutal exercise of power? I am not in any way trying to turn a blind eye to the fact that there are very, very few born leaders who usually visit the realm of mankind to attend to some particular issues in the world. But leadership experiences have shown that trained leaders are far better than natural leaders because they excel and last longer in their leadership.

The more we all know leadership, the more we all misunderstand the real essence of leadership; the more we tend to lead, the more we lead wrongly, and the more we all suffer in the process of wrong leadership. You are not leading when you do not have voluntary followers (a real leader does not force people to follow him but uses sincere influence to get their true allegiance); you are leading yourself when you have no real followers; you are not leading if you are not serving your followers sacrificially; you are not leading if you are satisfying your egocentric aspirations at the very expense of your alleged followers, and the list is long.

Why the need for Christian leadership? Good leadership without a divine angle is very dangerous, ruthless and regrettable, for it lacks godly attributes to season and discharge it in line with the love of God which commands: 'Love the Lord your God with all your heart and with all your soul and with all your mind. Love your neighbour as yourself' (Matthew 22:37-38). In order to examine and apply leadership from a biblical perspective, I decided to pursue my leadership studies in Christian Leadership, as a unique field of my expertise.

The major problem that confronted me was where to find a church-related university, which offers this specific discipline of leadership, for all the schools that I had consulted failed to give me a positive response. I resorted to research online for it through internet, consulting many websites, and it was while carrying out this task with the help of Rev. Isaiah Diing Arok in the University of Michigan in the States that I stumbled upon the website of the Christian Leadership University. It is an online Christian institution of higher learning, which offers various programmes leading to certificates, bachelors, masters, doctorate degrees and doctor of philosophy. And, to my greater delight, this university offers Christian Leadership as a specific programme at different levels of studies, including PhD level.

Commencement of my studies: I immediately began my concerted studies on 2 August 2004 and continued with the same momentum with the hope of finishing on time. The presence of my own email address and regular mailbox was an added value because they enhanced the speed and the quality of my studies. I used most of the evening hours to deal with academic matters while giving my full attention to official duties during working hours. It was also easy for me to take and do such academic tasks in Sudan by making good use of my laptop, and the electricity and internet system in our head office in Bor.

Good governance from a biblical perspective: the title of my dissertation was 'Good Governance from a Biblical Perspective'. I delineated, expanded and expounded on the philosophy of good governance in God's kingdom, church, family and government (executive, legislature and judiciary) in the light of moral qualities. Moral qualities consist of moral purity (holiness, righteousness, justice), integrity (genuineness, veracity, faithfulness), and love (benevolence, grace, mercy and persistence). To build concrete, unshakable foundation of good governance, I explored the fundamental nature of good governance in the realm of the Lord and came to a logical and reasonable conclusion that God uses his moral qualities to discharge his sound governance as he deals with himself and as he deals with his entire universe. Without the application of these moral qualities, it is mere narrow-sightedness to talk of real good governance either in God's or man's kingdom. That is, without holiness, righteousness, justice, genuineness, veracity, faithfulness, benevolence, grace, mercy, and persistence as better and strong ligaments to tie, harmonize, manage and administer the leadership system, with a human face in it, the result will be bad governance. Change the man from within outwards, and he will be as perfect as his Creator.

Conclusion of my studies: I completed all my required paper work and was declared successfully graduated by the school leadership on 20 April 2006. To mark the end of my academic endeavours, my family, relatives, friends and I organized and conducted a very colourful banquet on 29 April in PARAD Office in Nairobi before I went to the USA in October of the same year to participate in our graduation ceremony. A big and colourful celebration was conducted on 17 July 2006 in my village of Werkok and attended by hundreds of people in and outside Werkok area. Seven bulls were slaughtered for the multitude of people to feast on. I sincerely love and thank all those who did participate in and made such remarkable occasions successful.

On 11 October 2006, I left Nairobi for the States via Amsterdam, Netherlands and arrived in Minneapolis the following day. Then I took an internal flight from there to Charlotte via Detroit and driven from there to Highpoint, North Carolina by Peter Ngor Anyieth and Abraham Wut. Then I moved to Jacksonville where the graduation took place on 15 October in the presence of Jacob Malak Juuk, Thon Ater Nyok, Langbeny Ruot, David Thongbor Majak, Simon Mum Nyok, Mathiang Deng,

Abraham Aluak, Riak, Panchol Machot, etc. Brother Manyok Achiek Mabiei took my graduation pictures out in the open air, put them in the internet and circulated them far and wide to my total amazement and delight.

Learn to impart and utilise knowledge: when I received my certificate, the doctor of philosophy, I looked at it squarely, just a mere decorated paper, which I could just tear into pieces and permit the wind to blow away as it likes, leaving me with just myself and heavily-laden mind. But only unless I utilize and impart the hard-acquired knowledge and skills for the common good of mankind as well as for God's own glory, no single person, apart from myself, will value my long educational pursuits and decorated papers. In the final analysis, I made two simple conclusions: firstly, I should use my educational achievements as productive tools in my hands to serve God and his people rather than to personalize them and allow them to use me as their puppet or robot. Unused educational outcomes are like precious gold buried in the depth of the earth. We should learn and practise what we acquired, or otherwise, we become like the biblical, unproductive man of one talent.

The Founding of the Mission Gardens of Christ

Dreaming some dreams: in November 2005, while I was in South Sudan, I sensed God birthing an idea into my mind. In the course of time, this dream took shape and became what is now known as The Mission Gardens of Christ (MGC). This is a kind of Christian Ministry with a global focus. At the time of my writing, it is allotted a good piece of land in Bor by both Bor County and Jonglei State authorities for its operations. It has started to operate and move towards its vision.

My Reactions to CPA, 9 January 2005

The historical signing of the Comprehensive Peace Agreement between SPLA/M and Khartoum Government on 9 January 2005 took place at Nyayo Stadium in Nairobi, Kenya, and my family and I were in the city at that time. It was a joyous moment for the worst affected Sudanese masses as well as for all the global peace lovers, for it temporarily stopped the surging bloody river of inhumanity. As for the warlords in and outside Sudan it was peace being imposed on them against their ill will because their best solution to this chronic problem lay squarely in the midst of these two options: firstly, to militarily defeat the marginalised Sudanese, most importantly the Southerners, and bring them into endless subjugation. The second option was to clear the land of its stubborn indigenous inhabitants and let those who have nowhere to lie their heads occupy it once and for all. But the Almighty God was not happy with the unnecessary death of innocent people and the enslavement of others, and so the CPA was in direct line with his will.

Instead of going to the site of the event, I decided to remain in my house and watch the entire occasion on the TV screen. As I watched and listened keenly and attentively to Dr. John Garang's historic policy statement, I was not completely pleased with the sincerity and unfortunate ignorance in which he delivered it. Of course, the Holy Scripture says "know the truth, and the truth will set you free" (John 8:32). Biblically, I was happy with his intellectual and honest speech because he said nothing but the truth. But in this world of jealousy, lies and criminality, I was not thrilled because I knew very well that jealous people in and outside Sudan were going to envy and hate him; liars in and outside Sudan were going to scorn and jeer him, and criminals in and outside Sudan were going to seek ways and means to bring physical harm to him. To back up once more my concerns with biblical truth, Jesus Christ says: "Do not give dogs what is sacred; do not throw your pearls to pigs. If you do, they may trample them under their feet, and then turn and tear you to pieces" (Matthew 7:6).

Taking my mental flight back to the late 1980s when I was fighting in Southern Blue Nile as a gallant soldier of the SPLA, Dr. John made a historical revolutionary visit outside Sudan to meet and share the vision and mission of the SPLA/M with some key nations and individuals. As with other curious revolutionaries who had wanted to touch base with what their leader was saying and how he was saying it, I keenly followed up his visit by listening regularly to the famous world radio stations, especially the BBC. Like the way he spoke at Nyayo Stadium, Dr. John did the same during his entire mission at the time, emptying unfortunately, his whole baggage of knowledge and wisdom. Knowing very well the nature of the Adamic descendants, I and others were not pleased with his genuineness. This is because we knew that some jealous people who don't want to see shining leaders where they don't expect them to be were going to turn his message of truth into a regrettable curse upon the SPLA/M in order not to make its future vision and mission successful under the direct leadership of Dr. John. Most probably, one of the best options to our worse wishers was to negatively influence some of the SPLA/M leaders and turn them against their comrades to destroy or dilute the vision and mission of the movement.

Did our worst fears come to pass? Absolutely, they did. Immediately after the return of Dr. John to the movement from his mission abroad, things began to fall apart with some senior members of the Politico-Military High Command (PMHC) withdrawing their national allegiance from the movement and turning their own guns against their own brothers and sisters. Who was to benefit from such ugly wrangling within the rank and file of the SPLA/M? Your answer is as good as mine. That specific communication mistake of Dr. John took the movement through some terrible and darkest valleys of life with the sole aim of getting rid of him from the movement. Those who don't like to see something good in our part of the world were jealous and afraid of him, and so the best option was to get rid of him. But the Lord was not with them, and so he permitted Dr. John to survive such a series of revolutionary setbacks until he appended his own signature to the CPA, marking the end of the bloody 21-year civil war in Sudan.

I had my own mixed reactions to the CPA – a reaction of happiness, of course, on the one hand but on the other hand, the unfortunate concerns about the fate of Dr. John Garang de Mabior. I shared my worry of his uncertain fate with some people such as Bishop Nathaniel Garang and others. For instance, one day I had a good conversation with Mr. Isaiah Chol Aruei in his CEAS office in Nairobi, and in the course of our friendly talks, he agreed with my concerns but pointed out that nothing was going to be done apart from just crossing our fingers and see what would unfold in the process. To show the intensity of my concerns, I expressed my naïve and desperate suggestion to Mr. Isaiah that, despite its huge benefits and prestigious title, it would be good to give the position of the first vice president of Sudan to any other capable member of the SPLA/M leadership and leave Dr. John to maintain full control of the SPLA/M in the south of the country during the six period of the CPA, 2005–2011, so as to protect him from any organised physical harm. I call my suggestion naïve and desperate because it was going to contravene with some specific clauses in the CPA as well as with human leadership aspirations. As I was not the only person with such valid concerns about the fate of Dr. John Garang, the Southerners remained with no possible options other than just to cross their fingers and put everything to God in prayer.

The Death of Mark Akuen Gak, 2005

Archdeacon Mark Akuen Gak died on 17 March 2005 in Eldoret, Kenya, after a long illness. While alive, Brother Mark served the church in various capacities such as

---

the Archdeacon of Paliau Archdeaconry, Administrative Secretary of Bor Diocese and the Principal of Malek Bible College. He was very social and intelligent. Mark was married and hence survived by his wife and grown children. Those who went under his training vividly recall his wisdom and good knowledge of the Bible and church history, especially the history of the church of Sudan.

The Death of Dr. John Garang de Mabior, 30 July 2005

I was in Nairobi, Kenya when I received various odd phone calls from our concerned and deeply bereaved people during the darkest night of the 30th of the year 2005. The people were first rumouring and later confirming the unfortunate death of our SPLA/M leader Dr. John Garang de Mabior. That particular night became long and boring with the innocent and sincere minds and hearts of Sudanese people, all global well-wishers and peace loving people filled with huge unanswerable questions, concerns and deep concerns. Through desperation, hopelessness and madness, others bombarded the Lord with innumerable questions and brought his moral qualities into disrepute. Some innocent people even took their own precious lives into their own hands to partake the journey of death with their beloved leader. Millions mourned but millions laughed and rejoiced. It was one of the bitterest pills in the history of the SPLA/M for all the concerned Sudanese people, especially Southerners, and their alliances to swallow.

Were the enemies of the marginalised and peace-loving people happy with the death of Dr. John Garang? I don't know your answer, but my perspective is that they were, especially the Khartoum Government, extremely happy because they believed that he was the formidable engine driving the movement. For those who were jealous and saw Dr. John as a real threat to their own particular personalities and wellbeing, his death was welcoming news, even if Southern Sudan was going to secede from the other part of Sudan. Prophets of doom even believed that his death was going to mark the end of the SPLA/M and bring unity of the nation instead.

Was the death of Dr. John the end of the SPLA/M and the general aspirations of the marginalised people of Sudan, most importantly Southerners? History is the best judge of that. In the life history of the movements – Anyanya One and SPLA/M – and the historical, racial and religious bondage of the black man in Sudan, people picked up a sort of mental comparison of their situation with that of the Israelites in the incarceration of slavery in Egypt. Specifically, during the life of the SPLA/M people saw Dr. John as their biblical Moses, liberating them from the bondage of slavery and leading them to the Promised Land, the New Sudan. The Bible tells us that as the Israelites were about to enter the land of Canaan, God told Moses not to cross the Jordan; so he died on Mount Nebo, across from Jericho. Then the Lord sanctioned Joshua, Moses' assistant, to succeed Moses to take the people to the Promised Land, conquer it and equally and equitably apportion the land to them.

This biblical illustration became the anchor of hope, especially for Christian Southerners, after the death of Dr. John Garang, for as they likened Moses to John, they also likened Joshua to Salvia Kiir Mayardit. It was their firm hope that Salvia Kiir was their Joshua to lead and let them enjoy the fruits of the New Sudan. As I pen this important section of my autobiography, the historic referendum which is going to allow people to cast their votes in deciding whether to secede or remain as part of the whole Sudan is just 94 days away. The Bible says you can kill the body but not the soul, so you can kill a revolutionary leader but not the vision.

Bishop Nathaniel in one of the Parishes in Bor Diocese, 1990s

The late Archdeacon Simon Anyang Mal in Bor, 1990s

Left to Right: *Elizabeth Agot, Monica Atong Mayom, Alier & Kuch Mathiang, Nairobi, 1990s*

Left to Right: John Machar & Stephen Mathiang, Bor, 1990s

Stephen Mathiang, USA, 2003

CHAPTER ELEVEN

How I Offended the Archbishop

I left Bor by plane for Nairobi on the 5 September 2008 and arrived there the same day. I found Bishop Nathaniel and his administrative secretary, Rev. John Riak Ayiei staying with my family. While there, I came to learn that Archbishop Daniel Deng Bul was also in town. He was going to receive an honouring reception ceremony the following Saturday 6 September, which was organised by some Sudanese Episcopalians.

After learning that I was back in Nairobi, Ezekiel Diing Ajang, Assistant Bishop of Bor Diocese, phoned and asked me to turn up for the reception meeting if possible. Although I came back quite exhausted from Bor due to some heavy workload, I managed to attend it. Many dignitaries, including Bishop Nathaniel Garang attended it, and the master of ceremony was Mr. Philip Aguer Panyang.

My intension was just to listen to the speakers and socialise with them and others. The ceremony went on very well with the Archbishop taking the first opportunity to address the people. He outlined his church programmes, and in his speech he mentioned, among others, that the Diocese of Bor had shown a lack of good management by ordaining unnecessarily more pastors who were hard to control and accommodate. He went on and said that, according to his church policy, one pastor should have a congregation of 200 members who would be ready to support him financially, and the rest of the pastors without churches should be encouraged to look for jobs somewhere else and/or given some vocational training to take care of themselves. After finishing his lengthy speech, some people made some comments and asked some questions. I did not make any comment or ask a question.

Do you know how I became a victim of an unorganised conflict? I saw Rev. Peter Garang Deng Adit, one of the organizers, conferring with the master of the ceremony and others. Then Garang came and asked me if I could be ready to talk on behalf of the pastors because the person, Dr. Isaiah Majok Dau, who was supposed to give a speech on behalf of the pastors was absent. As I had not prepared myself beforehand, I almost turned down the request, but knowing that my conscience was clear and clean before man and God and my personal relationship, as far as I knew, with the our Archbishop was okay, I accepted the offer. I trusted that the omniscient God was going to use my mind, heart and lips before the audience to convey his message, which is outlined below:

First and foremost, I carefully observed the needed protocol. Then I clarified that the reason why the Diocese of Bor seemed to have ordained many priests in comparison to other dioceses was the fact that during the revival of the 1980s that occurred in Bor there was mass conversion among the people of Bor in which most of the people turned to Jesus Christ as their Lord and Saviour. Due to this immense conversion and the unique scattered settlements of the people of Bor, there were urgent continuous demands on the leadership of Bor Diocese to locally train and ordain some Christians to man the rapid growing church. With the spreading of the revival within and outside the Bor area, pastors from Bor Diocese ventured out to the Nuer areas, the Mundari area, crossed the Nile River westwards to other sections of Jeng and went as far as displaced and refugee camps in and outside Sudan to minister to those in dire need.

Bor Diocese was just like a sending missionary church in that some of the pastors ordained by Bishop Nathaniel Garang were and/or are now serving outside geographic locations of the Diocese of Bor in places such as other parts of Sudan, Kenya, Uganda, Ethiopia, USA, Australia and Canada, among others. For instance, in the 1980s and early 1990s, most of the Episcopalians, especially in Bahr el Ghazal and Upper Nile regions were under the leadership of Bishop Nathaniel. But since the time such dioceses got their own leaders, some of the missionary pastors from the Diocese of Bor had returned home, and that is why they appeared to be numerous.

Because such ordinations were driven for the betterment of the entire ECS Province, I appealed to the Archbishop that the Province should help those dioceses with more pastors to find a way of accommodating them in the systems. I gave an example that SPLA/M was also struggling with how to accommodate its huge number of officers that came to be due to the war situation.

Secondly, in response to the church policy of a 200-member congregation per pastor, I appreciated it but cautioned the church leadership to see how to take care of the pastors in the meantime. I went ahead and said, given my own experience, our Sudanese congregations, particularly the Jeng congregations in the rural areas, were not yet ready and willing to shoulder such a divine obligation partly due to their low economic level and also because of their mind-set – most people believe that the church is to give to the people and not vice versa. This mind-set developed during the time of war when the church, almost the only functional institution at the time, tried to solicit external support, not only for its members but for the entire oppressed masses. To me, to change this scenario – teaching the congregations to give more rather than to receive and financially support their pastors on a monthly basis was going to take long because changing people's values and attitudes always takes a long period of time. To illustrate my viewpoint, I mentioned real cases where almost all the village pastors and their family members were in actual destitute with no decent clothing, leave alone their feeding and education of their children. Having said that, I appealed to the church leadership to find a way of taking care of those pastors materially, while the policy of the 200-member congregation per pastor was being implemented.

Thirdly, I appealed to the Archbishop in his new leadership to portray the divine ethics of good stewardship at the higher level of the ECS Province by enforcing recognisable transparency and accountability in regard to the acquisition and disposal of the church assets. I made a special mention that the church has some visible fixed assets in Juba, apart from those in Khartoum and other places, which were not managed well, in my own opinion. I went on and said that if those assets were well managed, the ECS Provincial Headquarters would have sufficient funds for its staff and other running costs.

I stated my disgust with the way in which our retired Archbishop Joseph Marona was taken care of during his sickness in 2007. For instance, after gaining an admission into one of the hospitals in Kampala, Uganda, clearing his hospital bill became a big problem to the extent that concerned church leaders in different churches, including our St. Luke Church in Nairobi, Kenya, made some announcements to mobilise some funds to clear such a humiliating bill. To me, if the church assets were managed well, money would have been available to honourably treat our Archbishop with no or little external support. "Our church is not poor, but it is poorly managed right from the top to the bottom", I concluded. Unfortunately, our retired Archbishop Marona is no longer alive as I write.

Fourthly, I explained that the leadership disturbances that had occurred in some dioceses, including the Diocese of Bor, and the reasons why some senior pastors joined the breakaway group of Bishop Gabriel Rorich was because of the ECS Province being under the leadership of Canterbury. This was simply because large dioceses such as the Diocese of Bor had outgrown their leaderships and clearly met the criteria of being divided into two or more dioceses. But whenever such legitimate concerns were brought before the leadership of the ECS Province by relevant dioceses, the responses had been negative in that Canterbury refused the creation of new dioceses due to the lack of funds and the like. With us the Sudanese, especially the people concerned, saw such loose and wide management of the church as a potential problem. For example, in the Diocese of Bor, which covered three counties of Bor plus Pibor County and other counties in Nuer area at the time, many Christians had not been confirmed, for Bishop Nathaniel was totally overstretched in the pursuance of his pastoral duties. To us, the Diocese of Bor deserved to be divided into more than three dioceses. The same applied at that particular time to other large dioceses such as Rumbek, Yirol and Wau, just to name a few. But with Canterbury, which governs the ECS Province at arm's length, it did not see from the same angle. I mentioned that such leadership frustration led to the breakdown of the ECS Province into smaller groups.

I also mentioned that the Archbishop himself, while he was still a bishop, was implicated by some people for being allegedly involved in the delaying of the Kongor Area from becoming a full diocese from the Diocese of Bor. In order to avoid such disturbances within the ECS Province, I appealed to the Archbishop to see to it that the ECS Province gets its total independence from Canterbury and maintain a kind of mutual link with it so as to enable it to deal timely and amicably with its indigenous issues.

Fifthly, based on what others and I heard, upon his ascending to his throne as Archbishop, the Province under his leadership ordered that those proposed areas which had not met the criteria (i.e. building of a concrete cathedral, bishop's salary, bishop driver's salary, bishop's car, etc.) were not going to be promoted to full dioceses. So I appealed to him to somewhat loosen such conditions because, given the economic situation of Southern Sudan in general and the church in particular at the time, it was very hard for such conditions to be met. I mentioned that even the GOSS (Government of South Sudan) was emerging from zero level and struggling to put things in order.

Sixthly, since many pastors had no proper biblical and theological training, especially in some dioceses like the one of Bor, I appealed to the Archbishop and his leadership to seek ways and means of how to find decent education for them so as to enhance the efficiency and effectiveness of their tasks.

My seventh point was directed to the general audience. As the respect bestowed upon pastors by the general public in Sudan seemed to rapidly erode due to one reason or another, I appealed to the general public to maintain their allegiance to and respect for the pastors, as God's leaders. However, I told the church leaders that respect is always not demanded but earned, depending on how the object of such respect presents himself before others. In other words, I appealed to the church leaders to carry out their tasks respectfully before man and God so as to earn other's honour and respect in return.

Archbishop's Harsh Response to My Speech

Archbishop's reaction on Saturday: in the middle of my speech, the Archbishop became uncomfortable and sent Assistant Bishop Ezekiel Diing Ajang to stop me, but I politely smiled and went ahead to the end of my talk, for I was mandated to give a word not on my own behalf but on behalf of my colleagues, the pastors. To show the magnitude of his harsh response to my speech, Archbishop Daniel Deng Bul scornfully and abusively reacted to me in public on that Saturday and the following Sunday. Since he said quite a lot in his talks, I would rather highlight some of his points in this space.

When he was given a chance to make his last response, Archbishop said that I talked as if I were not in the meeting as well as if I were not a pastor in the church. He insisted that despite the revival that took place in Bor, the ordination of more pastors in the Diocese of Bor was a clear sign of mismanagement. With regard to my appeal for proper stewardship of church assets in the ECS Province, he vehemently rebuked me about it by saying that the church must continue to collect funds from its members because it is not an organization with its own money. Although my clear point was that it must maintain unequivocal high accountability and transparency with what it already had rather than to live a kind of parasitic life of hand-to-mouth on its members.

As it was already getting dark, the occasion was brought to an end. Many people in the audience wondered about how Archbishop negatively reacted to my objective speech. Some of them even phoned and asked me whether I had any kind of historical problem with him, and my answer was an absolute no. Since I knew what I said and how I said it and why I said it, I maintained my serenity.

Archbishop's reaction on Sunday: Archbishop Daniel was given the chance to share God's word with his flock the following Sunday 7 September 2008 in St. Luke Church, Kenyatta Market. I like sitting in the first row, facing the pulpit, in this church and others so as to avoid unnecessary distraction during the church service.

With the last Saturday's memories still very fresh in my mind, I told a friend of mine that if our Archbishop was acting out of his own human nature, he would turn the divine pulpit into a launching pad to continue his merciless attack on me, but if he were in the divine garment, he would enrich and refresh our souls with God's word.

Faced with such a behavioural and spiritual dilemma on the self-character of our church leader, I told my friend that I would go to the church on time to occupy my usual seat to hear him and observe his physical expressions very well. Sitting next to me was Mr. Mach Micah. Bishop Nathaniel Garang was in attendance and Assistant Bishop Ezekiel Diing led the worship. The church was full of people as it was the first time for other worshippers to see and hear their Archbishop.

The Archbishop refused to use the pulpit to deliver his sermon; instead, he used a podium that is meant for scriptural reading and church announcements. Although some verses were read as the basis of his message, he wisely refused to use them because they were not to back up his secular message.

In his lengthy message, he began by emphasizing his points made the day before, that is, mismanagement in the Diocese of Bor and the unwavering and imperative demand of the church to collect funds from its members. He pointed out that he came to such a higher throne of leadership not because of the backing from his own people but because of others' support and God's will. So to him those who did not want him were wasting their time, for whether they liked him or not, his ten-year office tenure was guaranteed. As a former wrestler, he said he was not afraid to confront any of his opponents physically.

Amidst some jeering and applauds from some members of the congregation, the Archbishop turned his back to the congregation and said that if it were in terms of educational qualification, he had been given a doctorate degree as shown by his gown. He said that I, Mathiang did not even know how to address him, and he said, "If a person does not know how to address people, although he believes to know something, he becomes very foolish." He went ahead and said that I did not see the hat on his head; instead, I saw him just as he was still Bishop of Renk Diocese or a mere person from his own clan in the rural village of Wangelei. To express his deep anger, he said that if we were not in the church but in the government, I would have found myself in jail. With this powerful comment, Mach Micah turned and shook my hand and said, "Mathiang, the Archbishop is going to arrest you", and then I laughed and said, "Yes."

Archbishop Daniel said that there were some people who caused problems in the church, and it was his role with Bishop Nathaniel to pray to God to deal with those people, adding that "If something happen to you, it is because of our prayers." He further said that he had instructed all dioceses to compile and take all the names of pastors to his office, and whoever his name was not going to be on his list was going to find it very difficult to find a place under his system. Having just mentioned the name 'Kongor' in my speech, the Archbishop made a simple conclusion that I was siding with the advocates of the Kongor Proposed Diocese. I need not to exhaust here all the dirt and the worst bestowed upon me in front of the bewildered congregation by The Most Rt. Rev. Daniel Deng Bul if he had taken personally all the things that I have mentioned above.

In order for our church to be self-propagating, self-governing and self-financing, I thought that our church leadership would be happy to hear its junior pastors emphasising unity of the church to see how to accommodate, rather than to blame one bishop and his diocese of the huge number of pastors brought up during the revival. Furthermore, I thought that the same leadership would cherish to hear mentioning of the pastors' welfare, the ethics of transparency and accountability in the church, quick promotion of new dioceses to address some outstanding issues and to preserve the unity of the Episcopal Church of the Sudan, decent and relevant pastors' training, and pastors' self-respect and their respect by the public.

Reactions to Archbishop's Words

The most impressing thing that I have discovered in life is that there is always a very high level of serenity amidst greater turmoil when a person of controversy has very clear and clean conscience and self-recognisable innocence. This is what sustained Jesus Christ along the roughest road of unjust persecution and accusations right to the humiliating crucifixion.

As the Archbishop stood outside the church to shake hands with the members of the congregation, like a limping sheep being cruelly injured by its shepherd, I lined up lovingly with others to say hi to him. As usual, I went on socialising with and greeting other Christians. In the course of mingling with Christian friends and relatives outside the church, some of them praised me for having maintained my calmness, asked me not to react negatively towards him and leave the truth alone to take its own course. Some asked me whether I had previous grudges with him, which might have caused him to kick back on me like that, and my answer was zero. Some of the extremists went as far as saying that if they were I, being scorned and directly insulted by a seemingly holy man of God in front of a varied congregation, they would have defended themselves right in the church in any way possible. Those who were not around during these defaming incidences phoned or tried to meet me in person and expressed their feelings to me of what had occurred.

I thanked each and every one of them of their concerns about my personal integrity. I told them that as far as I knew, neither my own family nor I had had any memorable grudges towards the Archbishop and his family. I knew also very well that my words were delivered with a greater sense of maturity and responsibility, not directed to him personally but addressed to him as a church leader. If he were to call me and try to find out why I had said bad things about him in my speech at that time, I would first of all request him to enumerate the words I said, how I said them, and how he conceived them, telling me clearly what had offended him in the process. I told my sympathisers that even if I were in error, abusing my own priesthood by attacking my spiritual leader in front of our members of the congregation and other non-believers, was The Most Rt. Rev. Daniel Deng Bul right to follow my unholy footsteps by blowing his own trumpet before the jeering and applauding masses or would it have been good administratively and biblically for him to calm down his boiling nerves and follow the divine, ethnical disciplinary procedure of Matthew 18:15-17?

In conclusion, I told them that since I had and still have no ill intension towards the Archbishop, and because my words were not meant to harm anyone in particular but rather to improve the image of our church for the betterment of God's people as well as for his own glory, I had already woken up, dusted myself off and was moving on in the Lord as usual. If at all I were wrong, let God forgive me; if he were wrong, let the merciful God and I pardon him, too.

What I Am not vis-à-vis What I Am

Amoral Judgements: human beings, without being born again in Christ Jesus, are greatly corrupt morally and psychologically in their original fallen parents. And so the original fall has defamed and distorted their worldviews to the extent that they use their biased and myopic eyeglasses to view independent objects and logically arrive at some subjective and wrong judgements. Because they are blinded by their prejudices and lack of sound moral judgements, they usually examine such independent objects totally out of their real contexts to suit their own egocentrism. In view of the fact that they lack some acceptable moral judgements, they cannot do justice in the actual affairs of moral judgements, only unless they first take enough time to honestly correct their own moral defects, for the Bible says: "You hypocrite, first take the plank out of your own eye, and then you will see clearly to remove the speck from your brother's eye" (Matt.7:5).

Doing God's will: in the year 2006, after I had my school graduation on 15 October in Jacksonville, South Carolina in the USA, the church and friends in the Burlington, Vermont invited me to have a short time with them before I returned to Africa. While I was there, I put up with the young family of Akol Aguek Ngong and Thiei Machar Dengdit. At the time of my departure, that is, on 28 October the same year, young men, Daniel Akol Aguek, Mayol Thuma, Bior Kuer Bior, Awar Ayol and Achiek Ayol from Bor community came to give me a nice farewell. In the course of our brotherly and honest conversations, Akol posed a political question to me, asking about my personal opinion if our community was to request me to represent them in the political arena. I looked at them and frankly responded by giving them a positive note that I would be happy to serve them and the whole nation nicely – not the best politician and not the worst politician but just as an acceptable politician. Having said that, I told them that the Lord had not yet revealed to me to serve his people in the political field, and as a man of God, I do not rush in life to open doors of opportunities and social services unless he opens them for me. Thus, I finally told them that we should wait upon the Lord for his will to be revealed.

The vitality of self-confidence: one day a certain friend of mine and I had a good time together, and in the course of our deep conversations, he disclosed to me that some people were lobbying on my own behalf if the government of Southern Sudan (GOSS) could be willing to offer me a job, but the answer was nil. He mentioned that it was not possible because one of the senior government officials, a person whom I mistakenly held in high esteem for quite some time, was said to have lost confidence in me based on his own biased and incorrect reasons. I calmly but sadly responded by asking these questions: did I request him to have confidence in me? Who gave him the absolute right to employ or not to employ people in the government "of the people, by the people, and for the people" based on his personal discretion? Are people employed on the basis of their personal merits or on the wrong confidence placed in them by others?

If there is one thing that will let others lose confidence in me, it can be simply that I do not use my words cheaply to sacrifice my personal dignity and the dignity of others on the temporal altar of selfishness. We owe much to the government, and the government owes much to us; for the government is the collective citizenry, males and females, young and old, illiterates and literates, the weak and the strong, the poor and the rich, the religious and non-religious. People must not mistake government for personal property. If the Lord wanted me to work, serving my people in any way possible, in the government, I would get it over night. The fact of the matter is that the best confidence I want in life is to have confidence in myself and in my God.

The danger of leaders' corrupters: in the year 2004, one of my clerical colleagues met and chatted with me in my office in Nairobi. In the course of our talk, he honestly told me that some people within Bor community held a notion that I was the engine behind any malpractices done by the church leadership under Bishop Nathaniel Garang. And the reason he gave for such a belief was because of my blood relationship with the bishop himself. First of all, I thanked him for his courage and sincerity. I also thanked the Lord for having allowed him to share such damaging rumours with me. Of course, this was not my first time to hear such malicious accusations from some weak church and community members.

I left all that I was doing and took sufficient time to clarify some issues in the following manner: Although he knew, I clarified to him that my work with Church and Development was very distinct and separate from the actual administration and management of the diocesan headquarters because the work of the Church and Development was purely humanitarian and development activities that were not rendered to the church itself but to the entire beneficiaries of the Bor community. I also told him that Bishop Nathaniel, the administrative secretary and others were the ones in direct charge of key issues in the church leadership. Above all, I made it very clear to him that Bishop Nathaniel was given power and authority in the 1970s by the leadership of the ECS Province with the backing of some people from Bor to lead the church in Bor, and by that time I was pursuing my basic school studies in Juba, not even a baptised Christian until December 1977. Again I explained that when Nathaniel was promoted to the seat of bishopric in 1984, I was already in Ethiopia. Furthermore, I pointed out that between the time of my conversion to Christianity and 1983, my pastor was Kedhekia Barech Mabior in Juba, and so I had neither been leadership adviser to Bishop Nathaniel nor a member of his church for those long years. Then with my own amazement, I aired out these questions: "I do not know who was leading behind him between the midst 70s and 90s when I was not there?" "Was he too weak to rule so there was need for someone, especially a relative of his to co-govern with him?"

I went on and clarified to my honest friend that since the world is full of good leaders' corrupters, my accusers (most probably, the majority of them might be leaders' corrupters themselves) were not to blame because they ignorantly believe that all people worldwide think and act like them whenever given an opportunity to have one of their own in a leadership position.

Do you know what leaders' corrupters do to their own low self-esteemed leaders? They befriend such leaders, using flattery words and carrying out grave character assassinations of formidable and rivalling opponents and shining giants. The fact of the matter is that dictatorial leaders usually succumb to such witty leaders' corrupters, for they earnestly hunt for things to satisfy their egocentrism.

As my diocesan leader and relative, my family and I, up to the time of my writing, hosted Bishop Nathaniel in our Nairobi house during his frequent visits there. And because of the lack of a diocesan office in Nairobi since early in 2000, Church and Development used to allow him to use its office for his official work. Because of this varied proximity between the bishop and I, the leaders' corrupters saw and believed it to be a golden chance for me to befriend him and stuff him with all useless ideas of mine simply to achieve my narrow, selfish desires at the very expense of the leader himself and the rest of the followers. Good, self-assured leaders are ready to stand their leadership grounds and utter unequivocal no responses when they are flattered and tossed here and there like a hunting dog within the control of a witty hunter.

I told him that my accusers were not to blame because they wrongly believed that I behaved like them. Yet they were to blame for their naivety because the Lord has created people uniquely, and so even the so-called identical twins behave differently. They simply conferred their own viewpoints over me. But by baptising me in their name without my personal faith in them could not change me.

Thus, I am not what they thought I was. What I am is that if I host you, irrespective of your relationship to me and who you are, under my roof, I will not abuse my hospitality by dumping all nonsense on you to manipulate you to think alternatively. Some people friendly host and entertain leaders to poison them. What I consider to be acceptable leadership advice is to make sure what I give out of necessity is, first of all godly in terms of genuine love, to uphold and enhance the throne of his leadership and uplift his followers in the process. Am I a good adviser if I tell the shepherd to turn inwardly and try to harass and destroy his innocent sheep instead of taking good care of them, and he heeds my advice? What type of leader is he? What type of adviser am I? I am not an adviser of doom, but I am an adviser of joy for the general welfare of God's people as well as for his own glory.

Leadership inheritance: the same character assassins had been circulating baseless rumours that Bishop Nathaniel was building me to take over the leadership of the Diocese of Bor at the time of his retirement. But some of the best questions to pose to such narrow-minded character assassins and others are: what do the policies and principles governing the removal and appointment of church leaders, especially bishops, say in the ECS Province? If the bishopric position was openly and freely contested based on some unique criteria enshrined in the church constitution, as all of us know, what made such mere rumour mongers to spend their precious resources slandering Bishop Nathaniel and I? Am I too weak to compete openly with other colleagues of mine, and if so, then am I doing justice before man and God to look for what I cannot eventually deliver effectively and efficiently for the common good of our people as well as for God's own glory?

Until the time of my writing, there is totally no leadership inheritance in the Episcopal Church of Sudan, and even in most corners of this modern world. However, what others and I know for sure is what I called leadership distribution in Africa, especially in Sudan, whereby people enter and exit the door of leadership, not because of their leadership capabilities, but simply because of their geographic and ethnic affiliations. Based on these precarious and tribal leadership circumstances, the character assassins were doing their level best to distant me from the future leadership of the Diocese of Bor, not because of my personal inabilities, but simply because of my geographic and blood relationships with Bishop Nathaniel.

My deep faith in the Lord tells me that church leadership is a divine call, just like any other vocations, and so God forbids his people to wrestle and wrangle or use their worldly wisdom to ascend to and defile in the process the holy throne of church leadership. I am not one of those who receive the sceptre of leadership wrongly in darkness and try to shine before the deceived followers with trembling knees and heart. Above all, until the time of my writing, the Lord had not yet revealed to me to be ready for the future leadership of our diocese, and if he does, I assure you, leadership distribution will not work, for it is not practised in God's kingdom.

Seemingly forsaking my faith and the church: between the years 2000 and 2007, besides my role in the Church and Development, the church leadership gave me the below assignments: I was assigned to a newly created archdeaconry of Chuei-Kher plus a treasury task within the diocese. It was in the diocesan synod of April 2000 in Pakeu that Majer Mach Wiel and I were elected to take charge of the work of treasury for a tenure of three years. Because of my heavy workloads for the Church and Development, I tried to turn down this noble assignment, but people refused. Then I requested them to elect another capable Christian to assist me in that role, and that was how they came to elect Rev. Majer.

In the course of carrying out the assignment, he did not turn up for the work because he was very far in Boma area, discharging other noble duties both for the

SPLA and the church. Also, apart from keeping only some financial papers, the diocesan administrative secretary and his deputy in Nairobi did most of my treasury role, and that gave me a bit of breathing space.

On the other hand, I did not discharge my pastoral work in my archdeaconry to the best of my ability simply because of my competing, varied and challenging workloads. I ended up leading it at arm's length by allowing my pastors to carry out the day-to-day activities while I kept up the same momentum in Church and Development. Of course, people, particularly members of my archdeaconry, held me in very high esteem as their archdeacon. Since many rural deans and archdeacons were managing their churches at arm's length like me at the time, the church top leadership saw no problem with the manner in which I discharged my pastoral work. But was God happy with the way I was shepherding his church on his behalf? Apart from being called a shepherd, was I intimately living with and taking full care of my sheep, and if not, was I happy with that kind of distant leadership?

As I did some self-evaluations in the light of God's leadership and moral qualities, I discovered that I was letting my Lord down by letting his church down in the process of this kind of poor leadership. There is no biblical basis for part time pastoral or shepherding tasks because taking the flock to greener pastures, clean and still waters, protecting them from any physical harm, etc. demands a sacrificial lifestyle and the daily presence of a loving shepherd, the church leader.

Having clearly analysed my leadership situation within the archdeaconry of Chuei-Kher, and knowing the danger of serving two masters concurrently, the question was which of the two sceptres of leadership I should relinquish for the general welfare of our people as well as for God's own glory. As I did not intend to abandon abruptly the vision of the Church and Development, and also because there were some good leaders who were nicely governing the archdeaconry in my absence, and because of having sought God's guidance in earnest prayer, I decided to continue with my work for the Church and Development and requested the church leadership to relieve me of my tasks in the archdeaconry and see how to pass it over to someone else. So I wrote an official letter to our diocesan bishop and copied it to members of the Chuei-Kher Archdeaconry.

On 27–28 November 2005, the Diocese of Bor had another synod in Bor town. Between 2000 and 2005, no diocesan synod took place simply due to a lack of funds to bring members together from different places. I gave my report, as a treasurer, in the meeting, thanked them and requested the members to give the position to another person if possible because of my heavy workload. I said that in case some people were of the opinion of giving me another chance. So others were elected into this office.

After turning in the letter of my release from my archdeaconry to our diocesan Bishop Nathaniel Garang and Rural dean, Deng Ngueny, many people started speculating that I was going to forsake my Christian faith and the church. They derisively asked whether Church and Development was going to be my church. They wondered as to where I was going to exercise my pastoral works if pastors were to deny me some spiritual duties in their churches. These and more soul-searching questions came into their minds. Some of them were sincerely concerned with my fate as a pastor, but others questioned with a sense of their own piety and ridicule and humiliation on my part.

To clarify this unhealthy situation, Rev. John Riak Ayiei took courage and came and honestly shared with me what other church leaders were thinking about the letter of my relief. I thanked and assured him that my request for relief was sincere before man and God, and the question of my forsaking my Lord and his church was beyond the slightest dream of my life, for I personally accepted and invited him into my life as my own Lord and Saviour. In the end, I promised him that if at all there was something which I was going to forsake in future, it should be Church and Development so as to enable me pull my whole being together for his work.

I am not what they thought I was. God always helps me to do my best whenever I am given some work and wholeheartedly accepted it in return. I am not a slave of idle hands. I served the Lord; I am serving the Lord; I shall serve the Lord eternally.

Left to Right, first row: Ezekiel Diing, Nathaniel Garang, Peter Yuang;
Second row: Adau Bior, Philip Angony, Daniel Matiop, Stephen Mathiang;
Third row: Joseph Akol, ?, ?, Peter Bol
St. Luke Church, Nairobi, Kenya, 1990s

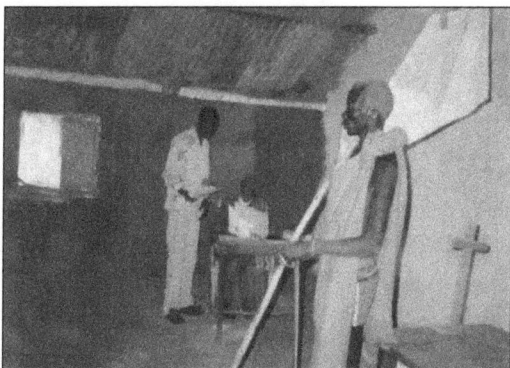

Bishop Nathaniel & Paul Kon in Church in Bor, 1980s

Bishop Nathaniel in an open air Church in Kakuma, Kenya, 1990s

Sunday's service in Zion Church, 2000, Bor

Some Glimpses and Events

A Glimpse of Bishop Nathaniel Garang

His family and early life: In line with his official documents, Bishop Nathaniel Garang was born on 1 October 1940 in his home village of Deer in Bor, Southern Sudan. His parents were subsistent farmers and herders. His biological siblings were Jangdit, Alier, Kuol, Bol, Abiei and Nyanhok. Besides the bishop, Bol is the only one alive at the time of writing.

As a great adventurer, Bishop Nathaniel left his home at an early age and went to urban centres in search of greener pastures. In the process, he landed on modern education and Christianity. Having a greater zeal to serve the Lord, Nathaniel approached the late Bishop Daniel Deng Atong in 1952 and requested of him whether he would be given a chance to train as a pastor, but his request was turned down on an administrative basis.

A member of Anyanya One: As an energetic, athletic and patriotic young man, Nathaniel joined Anyanya movement under the gallant leadership of the late William Deng Nhial in 1962. His national duty took him up to Zaire (Congo) for better military training and acquisition of armaments. Like some of his comrades, he fought the enemy and endured the jungle life.

His God's call: despite his patriotism, his faith was undeniable among his peers and others. In order for him to undergo a smooth, spiritual preparatory stage, God snatched him away from the darkest jungle of Southern Sudan, and he found himself in northern Uganda. First he worked as a worker with some companies and later as a farmer, tilling the land to take care of himself and other national and family duties while pursuing both his national and church tasks. How did he continue with his patriotic work while in Uganda? He did it through advocacy and financial support, among others.

His spirit of forgiveness: it was while in Uganda that Nathaniel found a torn page of the Bible, containing 2 Corinthians 5:17. This verse revolutionized his life spiritually. It is one of the mostly and repeatedly quoted verses in his life's story. Among many vital things that occurred to him while in Uganda, I would like to mention only two of them here. Firstly, a friend of his, living with him in the same house, stole and sold away Nathaniel's panga for a little amount of money and used the money for beer. Nathaniel seriously looked for and redeemed it with his own money without saying any bitter word to his dishonest friend. Secondly, on a separate occasion, the same person returned to the house while Nathaniel was away. He took and put some grains of maize quickly into a sack and tried to put it on his head to go to the nearby market for sale but could not do that because it was heavy. As he wrestled with it, Nathaniel returned home and surprisingly found him doing that. Without asking him why he was doing that, he helped him and put it on his head. Without any slightest sign of shame, the dishonest friend took off and sold his loot in the market and filled himself with beer. After finding that he had wronged Nathaniel several times without any negative responses from him, his dishonest friend decided, out of shame and disgrace, to part company with him. Who can assist a thief under the sun to help him get away with his stolen things if God brings him under his notice? Nathaniel is an expert in this field.

His theological training: after acquiring enough funds for his education, Nathaniel went and joined a Pentecostal Theological College in Nairobi, Kenya in 1970. The signing of the Addis Ababa Agreement between Anyanya and Khartoum Government to bring a seventeen-year civil war to an end happened while he was still pursuing his studies in Kenya. Upon the successful completion of his education, Nathaniel returned to Southern Sudan in 1973. He found that some of his guerrilla colleagues were already enjoying the dividends of peace. He turned his blind eye to those dividends and put his biblical theories into practice by carrying out pastoral and evangelistic tasks in Juba.

His priesthood and pastoral roles: as he excelled in his work, Nathaniel was ordained as a full priest in 1975 in Juba and sent to Bor Archdeaconry, Jonglei Province by the church authority in May of the same year. He was sent there to help with the expansion and spreading of God's word in the area, which was predominately covered by ATR. He did quite a lot, with the help of his few evangelists and other lay leaders and under the divine power of the Holy Ghost, to meet his goal. He strategically placed evangelist Samuel Majok Deng Mathiang in Duk-Padiet in January 1977 and evangelist Joseph Akol Gak in Duk Payuel in February of the same year to take care of God's flocks and expand the spread of the Gospel. Nathaniel remained in the church headquarters inside Bor town to do his work in and in the vicinity of the town settlement. Despite some recognisable challenges, the work progressed on very well.

Samuel Majok, Joseph Akol, Madier Ajang and John Majok Bior were ordained as deacons in February 1980 in Juba by the church leadership. In 1983, they were ordained as full priests. In the same year, John Majok Bior took over from Joseph Akol Gak who was previously posted to Pawel to take charge of the church.

His marital life: Nathaniel married Martha Atong Ajak in 1978. At the time of my writing, they have four sons, John Anyieth, Gwynne Kur, Samuel Bior and Moses Deng-Ajok. Out of the total siblings, two daughters have passed away.

His training in Anglicanism: from 1981 to 82, Nathaniel did his further theological studies, especially from the perspective of Anglicanism, in Gwynne College in Mundari, Southern Sudan. They had their son Kur-Jandit while there, and that is how he came to get the name Gwynne. Nathaniel and his family went back to Bor after his studies to continue with his work.

His bishopric roles: Nathaniel was consecrated by the Archbishop of Sudan in November 1984 in Juba as Assistant Bishop of Rumbek Diocese but based in Bor. However, the church in Bor under the leadership of Nathaniel was still not promoted to the level of a full diocese; it was just a proposed area.

Khartoum Government attempts on Nathaniel's life: Nathaniel remained inside Bor town despite the starting of the twenty-one-year civil war in Bor, for he wrongly hoped that the government troops were going to spare him, his family and other church members. But unfortunately, things turned worse in December 1984 when the church headquarters and his house were mercilessly attacked by the government soldiers by night. Despite God's protection on Nathaniel and his family and other members of the church, the attackers killed an evangelist, Jacob Akech Amol Majak.

A lost Bishop: this historical, barbaric and irreligious event led Nathaniel with his family and other Christians to abandon the town and sought refuge in the rural area under the protection of the SPLA/M. He was cut off completely from the ECS Provincial Headquarters without communication with the church top leadership both in Juba and Khartoum. He ended up labouring without his monthly salaries for many years. At the time of my writing, the church has not yet paid him back his legitimate, accrued money due to one reason or the other. Operating deeply in the rural areas amidst the civil war, Nathaniel became known by the church in Sudan and Anglican Communion as a lost bishop.

His management of spiritual revival: the revival of 1985 occurred in Bor under the leadership of Nathaniel Garang. Had it happened without his presence and spiritual guidance, it would have damaged the church because it was for the first time for the general populace, especially those who had not had prior knowledge of a biblical revival, to experience such spiritual turbulence. But based on his correct biblical and theological training, Nathaniel channelled the spread of the revival in and outside Bor area in a godly manner.

In order to take proper care of the huge influx of new Christian converts, administer wide ordination and oversee newly created churches in and outside Bor area, Assistant Bishop Nathaniel trained and ordained 12 pastors in Panyagoor in 1985. Although he was very reluctant to ordain them because, in accordance with the Anglicanism, he was not yet mandated to do so, the circumstances forced him to ordain them.

Like mushroom and wildfire, the revival engulfed the entire area of Bor, enabling the common people to see visions, dream dreams and perform miraculous signs. Even infant believers and non-Christians were amazed and totally confused by what was happening in the church. But Nathaniel kept on moving around, preaching the word of God, enlightening and evangelising the people, planting churches, training and ordaining pastors, just to mention a few. With no single means of transport, he moved on foot repeatedly to cover hundreds of miles in pursuit of his pastoral activities.

Bor becomes a full diocese: Bor was officially announced by the leadership of the ECS Province as a full diocese in 1988 under the leadership of Nathaniel. Yet he remained as Assistant Bishop because there was no legitimate authority in Bor to enthrone him as a bishop.

The spread of the revival: the revival crossed over the boundaries of Bor to the neighbouring areas, including Jeng Aliap in the western bank of the Nile. In order to rescue the situation and minimize spiritual confusion, Nathaniel crossed the Nile to Aliap area in 1988 and stayed there for some time, doing his pastoral duties. He ordered some of his pastors to go to the Nuer areas to carry out some pastoral activities.

A Missionary bishop: most of the ECS bishops in the government urban centres found it risky and difficult to venture out and oversee their flocks in rural areas, which were under the administration and management of the SPLA/M. Hence, such congregations were helpless like sheep without shepherds. These acute conditions as well as his great love for the execution of the Great Commission in and outside Sudan made Nathaniel act as a missionary bishop. For instance, he shepherded flocks and ordained pastors from different dioceses such as Diocese of Yirol, Diocese of Rumbek, Diocese of Wau, Diocese of Malakal and Diocese of Terkeka, among others. He even ordained some priests from the Nuba Mountains. He paid several visits to most of these dioceses to carry out his pastoral work, for his heart was and is still beyond the specific geographic borders of Bor Diocese.

The cofounder of the NSCC: Nathaniel and Catholic Bishop Parade Taban championed the establishment of the New Sudan Council of Churches (NSCC) in 1990 in Torit. It was established to take care of the spiritual and physical aspirations of the war-affected people, especially in Southern Sudan. He served on the board of the NSCC for many years before the signing of the CPA.

His enthronement: the Dean of ECS Province Bishop Daniel Zindo of Yambio Diocese, with a blessing from the Archbishop of Sudan, enthroned Assistant Bishop Nathaniel and Assistant Bishop Wilson Arop of Torit Diocese on 25 January 1998 in Narus. Although he was enthroned late due to the war situation, he maintained his seniority. It was a colourful occasion attended by hundreds of Christian and non-Christian believers.

His leadership challenges: with regard to his leadership challenges, Nathaniel's number one enemy was and is still Satan, the worst enemy of all Christians, because Satan does not want God's people to succeed in whatever they do in the name of the Lord. Nathaniel's other constraints, especially during the war, include but are not limited to a lack of proper basic needs, means of transport, medication, physical harm from Khartoum Government troops and their associates, a lack of properly trained church leaders to help him with the management of the church plus evangelism, discipleship and church planting. Other challenges were a lack of motivation factors for church leaders and other workers, persistent depending on the church by the war-affected masses in regard to their spiritual and physical needs, backsliding, leadership wrangling, ethnic division and jealousy and envy, among others. His children grew up in Southern Sudan until some Good Samaritans brought them to Kenya in 1993. Fortunately enough, they have reached university level. He narrowly missed death in the hands of the Khartoum Government on several occasions inside Southern Sudan.

His self-reliant efforts: in order to make his church somewhat self-propagating, self-governing and self-financing, despite the war situation, Nathaniel formed Velcro Ministries, covering various sectors of the church. Out of these church ministries, Thiech Nhialic (Beseech God) or Youth Moma came out strongly. It is currently registered as a separate church ministry under the leadership of Bishop Nathaniel. It involves groups of prayer warriors dedicated to praying for their nation, the church and other needs.

His attitude towards material wealth: in terms of wealth, Nathaniel lived and is still living like a bird of the air, depending on the Lord for his daily bread. His congregation put their charitable hands together and bought him a brand new car in 2008. Those of Wal Athieu Madol, Hakim Deng Majuch spearheaded its fundraising exercise. As a child of God, although Nathaniel is not wealthy, he and his family live a decent life. He is a man who could starve to death with food before him, unless someone volunteers to give him. His aim is not to get rich but to serve the Lord wholeheartedly.

Nathaniel's unique leadership style: some people look at the leadership of Nathaniel and wonder whether he is really a good leader in the true sense of the word. What makes them think so is the way in which he does not hold his leadership stick over his subjects as he manages and leads them. In fact, his leadership loop is quite loose in direct proportion to the level of his grace and mercy towards people. He does not like to see people, especially wrongdoers, tightly caught and strangled in the loop under his rule. Instead, he gives them sufficient space of time for the Holy Spirit to convict them of their shortcomings and to repent and turn away at their own convenient time. Although he knows clearly whenever his subjects are correct or wrong in their operations, his spirituality and godly attitude constraints him from carrying out some immediate administrative corrections on their behaviours. He does not like to point at someone and say, "You are wrong", even if such a person is actually wrong. He values the human face more than leadership attainment.

So in the process of allowing such wrongdoers under his leadership to do some kind of self-evaluations and personally correct their behavioural deviations at their own convenient times, many things go wrong, and the naïve take deliberate advantage of doing more and greater harms within the loose loop of Bishop Nathaniel's divine leadership.

I have never seen or heard Nathaniel in his leadership applying the essence of biblical rebuke and discipline. As God is slow to anger, long in patience and slow to punish so is Nathaniel as he deals with his subjects, dangling within his leadership loop. To many people, this unique type of leadership may be applicable in heaven where one day is like thousand years and vice versa. Under the sun, things demand immediate attention and correction.

Disadvantages of his leadership style: some people mistake Nathaniel for a lack of leadership and good management skills. Some evildoers and slow learners are lured to enter or remain in the loop and continue with their wrongdoings, regardless of the dread consequences. Since mistakes are not amended on time, they mushroom, causing uncomfortable circumstances among the subjects and between them and the leadership. It permits people within the system and outsiders to despise his leadership and the church system.

Advantages of his leadership style: it shows how the Lord deals patiently with his wrongdoers. It permits him to gain wider popularity with many people, especially the wrongdoers and the simple.

On a balancing scale, disadvantages of this loose leadership greatly overweigh its advantages. This is so because this type of leadership is completely irrelevant either in the modern church or any type of other business sectors, understanding fully that the current world is full of criminals and non-God fearing people. If all the people are happy within a leadership, then the leadership is not sound and happy and vice versa, for no good leadership will please all the people all the times.

Nathaniel's spirituality: relating to his spirituality, Nathaniel is a man of God. To a greater extent, he portrays the following fruit of the Spirit: love, joy, peace, patience, kindness, goodness, faithfulness, gentleness and self-control, a very humble person. In short, he loves God with all his heart, mind, soul and strength and loves others as he loves himself. His parents, brothers and sisters are not the biological ones but the saints who believe in Jesus Christ as their Lord and Saviour and do the will of the heavenly Father.

His spirituality and inborn nature terribly conflict with all types of leadership under the sun; he is more of an extreme spiritual leader rather than a secular one. Had he been a leader during peaceful times, with some gifted administrative and managerial leaders as strong pillars of his leadership, leaving him mostly to deal with spiritual issues, he would have been a very successful, admirable leader. Archdeacon Reuben Akurdid Ngong, the current diocesan Bishop of Bor Diocese, said one day that Nathaniel has not been born and would never be born again. In other words, he means that there has been no one like him, and there will be no one like him in the times to come.

A Glimpse of Prophet Paul Kon

Kon's backgrounds: Kon was born to the family of Ajith Jok Ajak sometime between the late 1950s and early 1960s in Mabior Deer. Bishop Nathaniel, Kon and I came from the same village of Werkok. Besides his stepbrothers and sisters, Kon had his own sister. Although his village was a bit farther away from mine, we grew up together in the same geographic location. Kon did not get an opportunity to go to school, and so he remained in the village, tilling the land and herding his few cattle. At his right time, he married and his wife gave birth to five children.

Kon's miraculous conversion to Christianity: in 1986, one year after the beginning of the great revival, the Holy Lord landed surprisingly on Kon. There was a minor starvation in the Bor area due to the last year's poor harvest. As Bor town was a kind of no-go-in zone because of the presence of hostile government troops therein, people in the high land resorted to seek some food items, especially maize and fish from the people living along the Nile. Kon paid a visit to his friend in that June in a place called Dhool, north of Bor town. His friend gave him some food items. Then he decided to rush back home to rescue his family members. His friend put him in a wooden canoe and took him over to the eastern bank of the Nile. He told him to hurry on in order to avoid being rained on as there were dark clouds building up in the sky.

On his way back, he was caught up by a heavy rainstorm in Berkou, a sort of No Man's Land, a marshland area between Dhool and Twonygeu. The storm became violent with thunder and lightning. As a result, he decided to squat on his food container to shelter it from the rain. Before experiencing the heavy rain, something like a big tent descended from the sky and covered him, keeping him and his food items totally out of the rain. He nervously looked up and saw that it reached up to the sky. He stayed in it while bewildering as to what was happening because he did not hear any voice. The tent was removed immediately after the rain, and he saw it no more. Thereafter, he continued on his journey back home. On the way he met some people who asked him with surprise as to why the heavy rain did not rain on him because they saw he was not wet, but he kept quiet and went on, bypassing them.

Vision to burn his idols: upon arrival at his home, Kon declined to socialise with others as usual. Instead, he took his sleeping mat and lay down in his luak, still wondering about what had befallen him on the way. In the course of that horrific and spiritual mayhem, he saw a vision with some heavenly choirs singing hymnal songs and beating drums. He also heard a clear voice, instructing him how to burn his own idols in a prescriptive manner, indicating where and how to burn them. Kon was a powerful magician who adored and worshipped some fearful idols. The worst and threatening one among them was the one given the name of Akuor.

The following morning, he shared with his family members about the vision he had had. After that he collected all the symbolic items representing the idols, put them where he was told to burn them on his compound and set them on fire. In the process of burning them, his relative priest, Michael Deng Anuol tried to help him burn them. Yet Kon refused to let him do it because Deng did not know the mannerism in which they were to be set on fire. For instance, Kon was told clearly to heap up the idols in a specific place with four entrances in line with the four geographic directions, south, north, east and west. Then he was to pull out some pieces of grass from each of his four buildings – luak, big hut (hondid), small hut (kunduk) and granary (guk) – and burn the heap, using pieces of grass from each building for each entrance. After burning them, heavy rain poured down and swept away the ashes.

Kon's baptism: Kon remained in his residence for some time, singing hymnal songs, adoring and worshiping and receiving more visions and instructions from the Lord. His innocent neighbours thought that he was insane and as such his worst, burned idol was going to kill him. What happened to him ran very fast and engulfed the entire area within no time. This news prompted Bishop Nathaniel to visit and baptise him with the historical name of Paul. Maybe, he was aware that Kon was going to do much and suffer for the sake of Jesus Christ like Paul of the Bible, and sure, he did. Nathaniel gave him a small drum and wooden cross and left him to continue with his powerful worship in his house. His stepbrother Gordon Aboi joined and took good care of him at the time by sharing God's Word with him.

The conversion of Kon's relatives to Christianity: when Paul Kon's closest relatives realised that his burned idols were powerless to kill him and his family members, and because of their fear that such idols may migrate and cause harm to them, they decided to burn theirs and go to the church, taking Jesus Christ as their Lord and Saviour. Paul did actually begin his ministry from his own Jerusalem.

Paul Kon meets Commander Kuol: according to what I heard from many people, including Bishop Nathaniel, Paul Kon's divine message was very simple and clear: to tell people to burn all their idols and turn to the living God. In order to achieve his goal, he went to Bishop Nathaniel and asked him to give him a letter to go and meet with the then Commander Kuol Manyang Juuk, the sole SPLA/M representative in the area. His sole agenda was sharing his God-given message with him. In fact, Kuol was and is still not an easy man to tamper with, although he is a Christian. Bishop Nathaniel refused to supply Kon with a letter. But he told him instead just to go to and tell his message to him.

With no shoes on, any clothing except a blanket and leather belt around his waist, his small drum, flag, a bell and wooden cross, Paul Kon left his family, trekked on a four-hour journey northwards to Kuol's headquarters in Baidit sometime in 1987. As it is always not easy to see a powerful person, especially by an unknown visitor, most importantly a common mere villager, Kon was played around, first by some guards and later by some junior and other senior officers, before getting the chance to meet face-to-face with Kuol. He brainwashed and verbally disarmed all the people he encountered with on his way to Kuol's office. The last senior officer he met and threw behind him before gaining access to his last destination was Deng Aguang Atem. Deng was another powerful and intelligent man to deal with.

After Deng ran out of his basic theological and biblical vocabularies, he ran to Kuol and told him that there was an unusual man from the realm of the spirit who wanted to see him. Like King Agrippa and the Paul of the Bible, Commander Kuol granted an audience to Kon, and, according to Kon and other reliable sources, they had a long interrogative discourse. Firstly, Kuol challenged Deng Aguang as to why he should permit such a person to reach up to his office. Kon told Kuol about his message and asked him to use force to tell people to surrender their idols to be burned. In his response, Kuol questioned the sanity of Kon and whether he had a family, but his answer was totally opposite of what he had thought about him. Kuol asked him of why God should use him instead of coming to him directly, but he told him that people were given different roles by God to do his will, and so it was his duty to see to it that all idols were to be collected and burned.

In the course of their talk, Kuol asked him the reason why should God not just come by himself and deal with such idols. Kon's response was that if God was to do that, he would kill people in the process, for evil spirits live in people. Out of frustration and defeat, Commander Kuol took the drum, the flag and the cross from Kon, raised them up and said, "God, take your things." Immediately, he asked Kon to leave. Kon finally said that he has removed the noose or the rope from his own neck and put it on Kuol's neck. This implied that since Kuol refused to give an order for the idols to be burned, he was going to shoulder any consequences. Kuol promised to meet him again in future, but Kon's reply was that Baidit was going to be in ashes at the time they were to meet.

Without returning to his family, Kon left Baidit for northern Bor, sharing his message en route with thousands of scorning and jeering people. Most of the people, particularly non-Christian believers, mistook him for being insane and homeless. But as soon as they heard his divine message and the manner in which he delivered it, they were left confused and bewildered. With no single purse or sandal, Kon continued up to some Nuer areas with his prophetic message. As a result, many people burned their idols and turned to Jesus Christ as their Lord and Saviour.

Kon came back to Bor and crossed the Nile to Aliap area in pursuit of his biblical mission. He moved from there up to Rumbek territory where he met Commander

Daniel Awet Akot and other senior SPLA officers and shared his message with them. Also he made many converts and followers for Christ in those areas, and his message reached far and wide.

Paul Kon meets Kuol on Baidit's ashes: Paul Kon decided, as being moved by the Holy Spirit, to return to Bor to revisit his footsteps and to venture into new areas with the same message. While in Bhar el Ghazel, Kon heard that the government troops made their way from the northern part around June 1987 to Baidit, chased away SPLA soldiers and burned it down together with some areas within its vicinity. This incidence took place in the absence of Commander Kuol. So he highly desired to go there and witness what the enemy had done to his headquarters. In the direct fulfilment of his recent prophecy, the Holy Spirit prompted Paul Kon to go to Baidit. Upon his arrival there, he met Kuol, two of them now meeting in the ashes of burned-down Baidit as was predicted earlier by Kon. Imagine, what came into the mind of Kuol and others who knew of Kon's prophecy and the heated debate with the SPLA Commander! As per Kon, he had no time to waste because he knew the dire consequences of people's rejection to his divine message. He proceeded on his itinerant missions, trying to persuade people to abandon their idols and turn to the living God.

Paul Kon came to write and read in Jeng language without being taught by any teacher. Most of his prophecies were of short term nature and got fulfilled at once. He could stay for many days without food or even water.

My time with Paul Kon: One Sunday in 1990, we attended the church service at Leudiet, Bor town. In the course of the service, Paul Kon entered surprisingly into the church and went straight and stood by the altar, facing the congregation. Although he was in bad shape physically and wore underwear and a blanket, I immediately recognized him. His presence in the church excited the whole congregation as was shown by a lot of murmurs in the church. The pastor in charge permitted him to greet the congregation. He began with a song, said a few, remarkable words and remained standing during the course of the whole service.

After the service, he went and stood outside the church, looking at the shining, brighter sun and drawing something on the ground without talking or greeting people. I rushed to say hi and shake his hand, but he told me to wait until he finished what he was doing. Knowing that his artistic work was going to take long, he asked me about where I was staying, and he advised me to go ahead and promised to join me later. Full of joy and expectations to have time with our prestigious prophet and blood-related brother, I went to our hut. Those with me were Joseph Maker Atot and Peter Yuang Mac, among others.

Paul Kon came and lovingly joined us in our small hut. Others followed him to hear the man of God. We embraced and greeted each other warmly in the Lord. My primary interest was to hear him talk of what had befallen him and how his abandoned family was getting along. He told me that his family was doing fine according to the report he had heard. But we could not hold our tears when he narrated what the Lord had done to him. Kon said that people, particularly non-Christian believers, had named him names. Such names are mad, deceiver, homeless, just to name but a few. To him, he did not know why the Lord had chosen him, uneducated and a mere villager, to convey his divine message to stone-hearted people instead of choosing people like Bishop Nathaniel and other famous people in and outside Bor area. To illustrate his physical and moral sufferings he had had in God's name, Kon pointed his finger towards his blind eye and told us that it occurred when he tried to disobey the Lord's commands. That is, he said the Lord pointed at his eye and said he should go and execute his orders, and in the course of that, he lost his eye. As a prophet entrusted with an urgent, divine message, Kon cut short our soul-searching and brotherly conversation and left for an unknown destination. That was my last time to see him alive.

Kon continues with his itinerant mission: Paul Kon persistently continued with his message in and outside the Bor area. He chose Pakeu, a traditional cattle camp lying between Werkok and Kapat in Makuach Payam, Bor County, to be the site where all symbolic idols were to be collected and placed. According to Kon, those idols were to remain intact for future generations to see. But they were set on fire by some church leaders after his death, for the fear that their owners might be tempted to collect them back and reinstate their loyalty and worship to them. As to why he selected that site, I do not know. He named the site Zion, and the church that was going to be built there was to bear that name. According to him, like the Jewish Zion, Pakeu was going to be where the Sudanese were going to offer their gifts to the Almighty God after its completion.

Paul's prediction of the Bor massacre: as the majority of the people in Bor refused to heed Kon's message, he predicted that God was going to deal with them harshly in the process of clearing the land of all the idols. Before the advent of the Bor massacre of 1991, Kon moved up and down inside Bor, telling people in a figurative manner to look for shoes, fishing-spears, etc. Part of the prophecy implied that they were going to be on the run and to depend on the fish from the Nile. Unfortunately, like some people in the Bible, they taunted him and disobeyed his words. At the time of the Bor massacre, God took Paul Kon, not with his family members but alone, to Bhar el Ghazel. Why he did not ask him to take his family with him to a place of safety, I do not know. During and after the massacre, people vividly recalled Kon's words, although it was too late for the Lord to avert his wrath.

Forced collection of idols: in 1992, Paul Kon returned to Bor and continued, among the civilians and SPLA remnants, with his divine message, asking people to surrender all the remaining idols to be taken to Pakeu. He said unless that was done and the Zion Church was built, the war between SPLA/M and Khartoum Government would not end.

The SPLA soldiers at the time were under the direct command of A/CDR Achiek Anot who was somewhat softer than CDR Kuol Manyang. Achiek and other senior officers such as Chol Gai Arou, Garang Ngang Abui succumbed to Kon's persistent, threatening divine message by mobilizing the remaining idols – lirpiou, bar, mangok, banydeng, etc. – and took them to Pakeu.

This shows that those whom their idols were taken by force did not whole-heartedly turn to Jesus Christ as their Lord and Saviour. This is currently the evangelistic and disciple task for the church to make sure that they are given undue freedom to make individual confessions to Christ. As northern Bor was under a different military command, their prominent idols such as mayom, aleer, etc. were not surrendered to Kon, although he was still in need of them plus others in the Nuer areas.

Envision and construction of Zion Church: Paul Kon embarked on the construction of the Zion Church in Pakeu despite the widespread and severe starvation in the area following the massacre. He designed that the church was to be in a crucifix form and large enough to accommodate thousands of worshipers. It was to have four doors, south, north, east and west, meaning that the worshipers were to use these doors in direct line with their geographic locations. In fact, by this design, Kon had the entire world and mankind in mind. He further noted that no armed forces or any other groups of people were to destroy it after its construction. He mentioned that the civil war was going to move northwards, leaving relative peace in South Sudan. He said Zion Church was going to be a beacon of hope for the people of Sudan in that, even at the time of difficulties, people would gather there to seek God's face, and automatically he would rescue them out of such problems.

With these and more healthy predictions in mind and heart, the poor remnants hewed down thousands of wooden items and hundreds of bundles of grass and palm leaves, causing a bit of environmental degradation in the area, to put the church up. The work force consisted of hundreds of people, both male and female. The place for their accommodation was just an open ground at the site of the church, and the people emulated the biblical communism: The fellowship of the believers, as quoted below:

> They devoted themselves to the apostles' teaching and to the fellowship, to the breaking of bread and to prayer. Everyone was filled with awe, and many wonders and miraculous signs were done by the apostles. All the believers were together and had everything in common. Selling their possessions and goods, they gave to anyone as he had need. Every day they continued to meet together in the temple courts. They broke bread in their homes and ate together with glad and sincere hearts, praising God and enjoying the favor of all the people. And the Lord added to their number daily those who were being saved (Acts 2:42-47, NIV).

Yes, they devoted themselves to the Scripture and Kon's prophetic message as well as to the fellowship, to the Holy Communion and to prayer. Everyone was filled with awe, and God, through Kon, did many wonders and miraculous signs. They were together and had everything in common, eating together whatever meagre thing they had with glad and sincere hearts, praising God and enjoying the favour of all people. And the Lord added to their number daily those who were being saved. In order to avoid any possible temptation, given the fact that food was very scarce, and in order to portray a high level of transparency and accountability among the people in terms of feeding, Paul Kon issued a verdict that all people should eat by day time so that each and every one was to be taken care of.

Kon's prediction of his death and his graveside: as his time to leave the world was around the corner, Paul Kon showed others the site of his proposed grave by the site of the church, at the southern part, but they failed to take note of that prophecy. In the course of the church building, he hinted to his followers that he was going to die and would be buried in three tombs. When people tried to pay much attention to his saying, he allayed their fear and told them not to be afraid as none of them was going to be affected.

News about Paul Kon and what he said and did travelled very fast in and outside Bor area. Some people even exaggerated that he should not die by a sword or any other weapon, and that he was planning to attack and capture a government garrison in Bor town with just fifty men. This rumour and other news, therefore, made government troops in Bor to become very alarmed and unhappy with him. Paul Kon celebrated a colourful Christmas occasion in the open air with his huge followers in Pakeu in 1992.

Kon's humiliating death: on 26 December 1992, government troops came out from Bor town and surprisingly headed straight for Paul Kon and his followers. Of course, some native informers led them, as it would have been hard for them to find the exact location of Pakeu. He presented himself to the brutal soldiers who immediately snatched him away from his flocks. Yet But Aduot, a disguised SPLA soldier, was immediately identified as a soldier by one of the informers, and so his life was in a bracket. They threw them in their vehicle and left Pakeu, and along the way, the soldiers inhumanely butchered Paul Kon and his colleague. They maimed Kon, fearing that if they did not do so, he would come back to life from the grave. They dumped their bodies in shallow graves by the roadside.

Then the Christians in Makuach came and exhumed Kon's dismantled body and went and buried him decently in Makuach Court Centre. After a short while, those at Zion Church got the right information, came to Makuach and exhumed Kon's body and took it back to Pakeu and buried it in his chosen place by the side of the church. This was in direct fulfilment of his prediction that he was going to be buried in three graves. Also his prophecy became very clear and true that the enemy troops did no physical harm to his flocks at the time of his capture. The only person who partook with Kon's fate along the road of death was But Aduot who voluntarily chose to offer his own life in return for his loyalty to Kon and God's word.

Completion of Zion Church: some of Paul Kon's close associates were Isaiah Malek Garang, John Kelei Chengkou, Peter Yuang Mach, Deng Anyuat Kur, Garang Ngang Abui, etc. The death of Paul Kon was not the end of his divine message because he left his devoted followers to continue with his mission through the power of the Holy Ghost. With greater zeal and burning passion, Kon's followers contin- ued with the construction of the huge church until they brought it into a successful completion in 1993. In line with Kon's word, since its construction, Zion Church has never experienced any possible attack or destruction from any hostile armed groups at the time of my writing. Also since its completion, the South Sudan began to experience some relative peace until the historic signing of the Comprehensive Peace Agreement (CPA) in 2005 in Kenya. However, it has been regularly renewed after every three years because its local building materials have been terribly eaten by termites. At the time of my writing, the natives are trying to mobilize some funds to build it with some concrete materials.

Was Paul Kon a real prophet? Was Paul Kon a real prophet and successful in his five-year mission? God, his Sender, is the One to give the correct response to this question. Yet many people within and without Bor will answer this question in the affirmative because the area was mostly cleared of idols. Kon himself turned thousands and thousands of people to Jesus Christ as their Lord and Saviour. Almost all his prophecies were fulfilled. Zion Church was built according to his own design. These few achievements can help you make your own judgement whether he was a prophet or not. As to whether the prophetic ministry is still available now in Christ's church, please turn to and read Ephesians 4:11-16.

His memoirs were recorded but got burnt in one of the huts in Pakeu after his death. However, those of his closer associates and other real witnesses, who can rewrite them from memory, are still around at the time of my writing. What is needed are the means for them to do that.

Tragic Events

Peter Yuang's death, 12 December 2009: the late Archdeacon, Peter Yuang Mach Dengariir was from Ajak-Mayo clan of Atet community of Makuach Payam. He was a member of the SPLA. On 12 August 1990, he was ordained with myself and others by Bishop Nathaniel Garang in Kapat Parish Church in Bor. He served in various capacities such as Archdeacon of Baidit Archdeaconry, diocesan secretary, etc. in the church. He did his diploma studies on theology at Berea Theological College in Kenya. Thereafter, he enrolled for his further theological studies at bachelor degree level in Mukona University in Uganda but failed to complete his studies due to some social problems.

Archdeacon Yuang was a bright young man, humorous and sociable with some in-born leadership qualities. He was a nephew of the late Achiek Dengariir. Unfortunately, death robbed us of Archdeacon Yuang at his prime age. While pursuing some revolutionary task in Pibor, Peter Yuang fell sick. He was rushed to and died in Juba Civil Hospital on 12 December 2009. His body was taken to Bor and buried by the side of the Konbek Church Parish. He was survived by his wife and children.

Mabiei Mach-Aguek's death, 3 July 2010: uncle Mabiei Mach Mayen Bior Deng-Ajok was born in the early 1910s in his village of Werkok. He was very intelligent, handsome and strong, sociable and people-centred. Uniquely, uncle Mabiei was a living traditional archive not only for the people of Deer or Juorkoch but almost for the entire community of Bor and beyond. His strong and incredible memory outlived his physical strength. I personally attributed most of my historical findings to him.

Uncle Mabiei lived a joyful and decent life to see his grandchildren and their children. He passed away during his old age of a short illness on 3 July 2010 after he became a Christian. He was survived by his wives and descendants.

First row, Left to Right: *Alier, Mathiang, Areu, Agot, Jogaak*
Last row, Left to Right: *Kuch, Kuch Bech and Ajoh, 2011, Nairobi*

PART SIX

Reflections on 2010–2011

CHAPTER TWELVE

My Perspective on the General Elections in Sudan, 2010

I first cast my electoral vote in my lifetime in the history of the Sudan General Elections on 11 April 2010 at Lualdit Voting Centre of the Makuach Constituency. But what I heard and saw with my own ears and eyes during that significant event, beginning from the time of the nominations of members, their lengthy period of campaigns and up to the days of the actual voting exercise, compelled me to find this small space in my autobiography to express my own personal reactions. But since I did not cover the whole Sudan, especially South Sudan at the time, my responses are limited to our geo-political areas. These reactions are based on electoral constituents, the impact of electoral corruption, constituents' representatives and independent candidates.

Electoral constituents: all people of a particular nation have an absolute right to be members of their own political system because they have undeniable rights to devise appropriate policies and see how to govern themselves in the best possible mannerisms in line with their collective and individual aspirations. They can do that through one political party in terms of one party-rule or through varied political parties in the case of a multiparty political system. But since all the citizenry of a nation cannot and never will be legitimate members of their own parliament or general legislative assembly simply because of their huge numbers, their only possible ways of exercising such national, political duties is for them to look inwardly, using their democratic or consensus principles, to nominate and/or elect their own representatives to act as their voice in the political bureau or any other national forums. Such representatives are not going there to represent themselves per se. Instead, they are in the parliament as the voice of the voiceless. They are not leaders but servants of their electorates. That is why the electorates have the absolute right usually to recall back any member(s) who unfortunately turn out in the process to be a lame duck.

Is there any self-elected Member of Parliament or national assembly in any nation under the sun? If the answer is nil, who then owns members of parliament? All national leaders, whether in the executive, legislature or judiciary, are in their respective positions as representatives of their general populace.

Now who is to buy who in this particular scenario of constituent – representative relationship? In an ideal situation no one is supposed to buy anyone because the two are serving one another. That is, the general voters' aspirations will be protected and met by their representative during his office tenure, and the representative will benefit out of his expected salaries. Hence, the electorates have no single right to expect hand outs from their representative because they are the ones who chose him to be their voice in the political affairs of the nation. He is there to fight and even die for their rights. Instead, the constituents are the ones to support morally and materially their representative during the electoral exercises to enable him to meet his electoral needs such as publication of materials, transport, etc.

On the other hand, the representative has no legitimate right to buy his constituent's votes if he really believes that he is going to serve wholeheartedly the members of his constituency and not his own selfish needs. Why do you buy the very people who nominate or elect you to serve them and not yourself? If they want you to buy their votes, then one may justly conclude that you are an intruder and not their real representative. Alternatively, if buying takes place in this self-explanatory situation, then the electorates and their representative may not be well versed with the political electoral rule of the game.

Did huge money exchange hands during our recent general national elections? The correct answer will come from the representatives and their members of constituencies. But to the very little thing that I know, the poor representatives were unfortunately pillaged, demoralized and disgraced by their ignorant electorates. Common statements such as "If you don't give us something, we will not vote for you", "You come to us now because it is time for election", "just take the money and choose who to vote in later because it is your money", "NCP (National Congress Party) has poured in a lot of funds to buy voters", and so on and so on were common statements during the electoral campaigns.

Why should that occur? I don't have inclusive answers to this question, although I would just like to highlight a few points here. Maybe, some of the political representatives did not genuinely fulfil their mandated obligations in their legislative organs. And because of this issue, the voters saw them as mere representatives of none other than themselves and whose big pockets must be emptied before they could go and fill them again in the parliament or so. Naïve voters also wrongly believed that political candidates were to give them money in exchange for their votes, not knowing that they are there to defend their rights at varying levels of the country. Because of high levels of poverty in the area, some voters took it as an opportunity to enrich themselves.

NCP representatives who were not making solid social and political grounds in the south of the country were certain to lose elections unless they used their financial muscles to secure votes. It is also good to mention that some political candidates who were standing on sandy grounds and happened to have huge amounts of money were left with no better option than to use their dubious deals to allure the poor voters to vote them in. But where did they obtain such a lot of money in the first place? They are the right people to tell the general public.

As tribal ligament is still stronger than national tendon in Sudan, using funds was the surer way of getting foreign voters. Above all, since most of the electorates did not properly understand why to vote, how to vote and who to vote for, and given the fact that those general national elections were in partial fulfilment of the CPA, the political candidates were tempted to use any possible means to bring elections to a complete end.

The impact of electoral corruption: the Holy Bible says the evil men and impostors will go from bad to worse, deceiving and being deceived (2Tim.3:13). Like any phenomenon under the sun, corruption usually begets corruption. There are no corrupt leaders without corrupt followers; there are no just leaders without honest followers because leaders are drawn out from the sea of the very people they lead. To stretch this analogy further, a healthy society gives birth to healthy leaders and vice versa because it is a biological truth that one is to produce its own kind.

What do you think will happen if most of the electorates are corrupt to the extent that they cannot vote for their own political representatives unless they give them some sufficient kick-backs? If they succumb and buy their votes, do you think that they will play a fair and honest representation on behalf of the ignorant, corrupt constituents? Surely, if you buy a political seat from the naïve voters, whose seat will it be? Using a simple but rational business principle, the seat belongs to the buyer. So if the seats are sold away by the ignorant voters, will it not be fair for the deceived representatives to get back their lost money in any possible ways, including malpractices if need be, during their tenure of office? Of course, the more you corrupt your way through, the more you corrupt your way out.

It is the sole responsibility of any society, most importantly the Sudanese people to learn how to make themselves clean before they expect their leaders to be clean. Otherwise, the more they sell their legitimate votes, the more they expect their representatives to be corrupt. Only corrupt people corrupt their leaders.

Unsound political competitions: given the global scene in terms of political, socio-economic and religious fields, among others, in competition there seems to be no healthy wrestling. But what matters most is the level of degree from one place to another. It is human nature for people to climb on each other's shoulders to get what they want, even if it means pushing others down in the process. The most aggressive competitor will not mind reaching the last limit and stand with his dirty feet on somebody's well combed hair. Common in such wrangling are political and character assassinations. Above all, political fields are sometimes littered with causality of which some of them may be innocent. But even if they are not innocent, does my political, temporal seat equate with the precious lives of my human brothers and sisters?

What are the obvious causes of political wrangling just at electoral level? To me, such causes are: firstly, there is always stiff competition when candidates from different parties are vying for the same seat because each party wants to maintain its legitimacy among members of that constituency. In this case the candidates are fighting on behalf of their parties. If you fail, you let down your party. Secondly, in case of serious competition between people of the same party, the obvious factors may include personal pride, greed for wealth, ethnicity affiliation, enmity, power-thirsty and other known vices.

In our recent general national elections there were numerous causalities in the political fields. Some of them will definitely become eternal victims. Due to the lack of political maturity, ignorance of the healthy rules of a political game, unrefined personal character, ethnicity connections, egocentrism, selfish ambitions, etc., some candidates unfortunately jumped on each other like competing cocks and smeared themselves with any unimaginable dirt. Of course, some people, most importantly in the game of politics, are totally immune to shame and lie. Personal relationships, sincerity, forgiveness, understanding each other, appreciating each other differences, and maintaining harmony and unity should be the cornerstones of any healthy competition, especially political rivalry. This is simply because unnecessary political wounds take longer time to heal and leave recognisable scars.

Social impact of political wrangling: one of the formidable tenets of politics is to enhance the unity of the people, beginning from the constituency stage up to the national level. Any politician is supposed to uphold and cherish the general welfare of the people, especially his own constituents, irrespective of whether they are for or not for him. But the moment the rivalling politicians localise their campaigns by turning their innocent supporters against each other, they behave and become like fighting elephants that don't care about the terrible destruction of the grass beneath them, ignoring the fact that it is the same grass on which their livelihoods depend.

Wise and healthy politicians always have the general wellbeing of their people in particular and mankind in general in the very bottom of their hearts. That is why they are always ready and willing to step down from their posts if their roles or words have or seemed to have caused misery to any members of the public. But this is not always the case with unsympathetic wrong politicians because they inhumanely believe that the utilisation of the archaic, barbaric policy of divide and rule is the best way to enable them to achieve their unhealthy political gain. These are political vampires who are usually content with some short term benefits while unmindful of their very long term bad legacy.

It is very unfortunate to note here that during our recent general national elections ethnicity politics became obvious in many areas – most importantly, between Northerners and Southerners as well as among various ethnic groups in the whole Sudan. What kind of politician do you want to be? What kind of politicians do people want to serve them? What kind of politicians does God like to lead his people?

Political roadmap: there is always a possible solution to any problem, be it political, socio-economic, religious or family, under the sun. Given the few comments that I have made above plus the vast information you know about the manner in which our political elections were and are conducted, and knowing very well that the more elections are fraudulent and corrupt, the more they negatively impact the national and individual economic statuses, societal cohesion and government functions, what best alternatives should be advanced to improve the general standards of our national elections? To me, some of the best acceptable solutions are: firstly, the South Sudan Electoral Commission should carry out a well organised and focused public sensitization, starting from boma, payam, county up to state level in all the ten states in South Sudan, informing people of what elections are all about as well as the functions of both electorates and their representatives, the political candidates. Secondly, in the event that some vital electoral policy documents are not in order, the Electoral Commission and Legislative Assembly plus other relevant national organs should develop and make them available before the next general national elections. Thirdly, the "government of the people, by the people, for the people", should bring to book the merciless politicians who like to cause mayhem among the innocent national electorates because they are not theirs but national citizens and God's people. Fourthly, both the Electoral Commission and South Sudan Anti-Corruption Commission should educate both the constituents and their representatives of the danger and the dreadful consequences of corruption during and after the political election campaigns. Fifthly, it is the national duty of the Anti-Corruption Commission to know the financial status, including the sources of funding, of each and every political candidate before the beginning of election campaigns as well as after the elections to see how much the candidate has used and for what. It is the role of the Anti-Corruption Commission to make sure that such significant elections are free of corruption, for this is one of the most important fertile grounds where corruption geminates and mushrooms before it spreads to other societal sectors. Freeing political campaigns from malpractices can save the national pride from the merciless jaws of corruption.

Thoughts on Pre-Referendum Events, 2011

The highest peak of the CPA: the highest peak of the Comprehensive Peace Agreement (CPA) was the etiquette of the South Sudan Referendum. When this significant protocol was enshrined in the CPA, NCP and SPLM were having different thoughts in minds and hearts with regards to its eventual accomplishment. The international observers were merely, on the other hand, content with the spirit and the contents of this article and hoping that it was going to occur at the articulated time. The general masses both in the north and the south of the country as well as some interested peace-loving people outside Sudan were completely pushed to the realm of illusion and imagination by the architects of deceit and rhetoric. Above all, the Almighty God took all the parties and signatures to the CPA completely by their words and knew the end right from the beginning.

What were the possible thoughts in the mind and the heart of the NCP? As I was not personally in their minds and hearts prior to and at the time of the signing of the CPA on 9 January 2005, apart from the omniscient God, the pilots of the NCP are the right people to answer this question. But based on my own intuition, the main possible thoughts were: firstly, since the path to the peak of this particular referendum for national self-determination is always full of political zigzags, and the peak is seemingly above the visible sky and has not been reached yet by the disgraced Sahrawis, the Polisario people of Western Sahara, the NCP made a calculated move and correctly believed that the deceivable people of Southern Sudan and the SPLM were going to melt into the thin air before 9 January 2011. Secondly, in view of the fact that the Addis Ababa Agreement did not withstand some political tactics from the Khartoum Government, the NCP believed that the CPA was going to fall into the same bottomless pit before reaching 9 January 2011. For me, these were the main right political calculations any human being can think of.

What were the possible thoughts in the mind and the heart of the SPLM? The right answers should come from the SPLM and the omniscient God, but these are my own opinions: firstly, because the Khartoum Government had dishonoured many agreements in the past, SPLM made whatever it could to avoid the past mistakes and drag, if need be, the NCP into the same bottomless pit which had previously swallowed the Addis Ababa Agreement. Secondly, no matter how long the journey to the realm of amicable peace was going to take, SPLM was determined to take the path of referendum as one of the best options, considering that Southerners were going to vote overwhelmingly for secession, if given the chance to vote.

Who outwits who? The worst foolish mistake made by the NCP during the CPA arrangements was in the area of military protocol, especially its consenting to the SPLM having its own separate army during the period of the CPA. On the other hand, the best wise decision made by the SPLM with regard to the CPA was in the field of the military protocol, fighting to keep its own army as a formidable vanguard during the course of the CPA implementation. Without this wise decision, CPA would have died before celebrating its first year birthday.

Fruitless attempts by the Khartoum Government to derail the CPA: the meandering path to the highest peak was littered with some undeniable causalities. It was very bad, unfortunate that the untimely death of the SPLM Leader Dr. John Garang opened the bad news of the CPA implementation. Although no one, apart from the omniscient God, knows for sure what occurred to his helicopter plane, some people, especially in South Sudan, still point fingers of unwarranted blame towards some of their brothers and sisters in North Sudan. Intentionally cheating the Government of Southern Sudan (GOSS) by the Khartoum Government over oil money continued unabated; border skirmishes between Sudan Army Forces and SPLA on one hand and the Government Militias and the SPLA on the other went on intermittently with unnecessary loss of precious lives and displacement of the innocent civilians.

Prolific supplies of armaments to some militia groups in the South Sudan from some die-hard elements within the NCP continued underneath the political blanket to turn Southerners against each other and to destabilize the infant government in Juba. While paying some remarkable lip service to the people in the south of the country and some international communities, Khartoum Government spent huge amounts of the ill-gotten oil moneys to acquire some military hardware from some foreign bodies; trained thousands of soldiers and put some of them to the South-North border in readiness for any possible military eventualities.

Some of the key elements of the CPA like the demarcation of the South-North boundaries, and the formation of the referendum commissions both for the Southern Sudan and Abyei were deliberately delayed by the Khartoum Government. NCP is also alleged to have used the might of funds by buying some weak political elements and greedy Southerners to go contrary to the general aspiration of the masses of the people in the south of the country. But what people always fail to know is that money can buy you a passport to any place under the sun but not to heaven. These are just some of the majority of the fruitless attempts employed by the NCP and its alliances to derail the smooth running of the CPA.

Was unity made attractive? Instead of making unity quite attractive, it was made very ugly. Why? Sometimes when a patient suffers with a sort of terminal illness, his doctors decline to administer proper medications to him, for they don't want to waste them. Such a patient is mostly given some painkillers not to heal him but to alleviate some pains while he journeys along the road of death.

NCP and all its alliances knew very well that Southern Sudan was going to opt for separation from the North if a truthful referendum was to take place. They fully knew that since it has been difficult to make national unity attractive from the day of the coming of the Arabs to Sudan down to the time of slavery in the south up to 2005, achieving it within just a six-year period was totally an illusions, knowing very well that some of the socio-economic, political and religious wounds inflicted by some Northerners upon Southerners are very grave and need a longer period of time to heal, although deep scares will still remain visible.

Putting yourself in the shoes of the NCP, would you timely remove serious distrusts between the Northerners and the Southerners, quickly heal such serious wounds and make unity attractive before 9 January 2011? In order to fulfil its words and as a desperate move, NCP, with the backing of the Arab League and other nations and individuals in the Arab World, hurriedly planned and came up with some vital but half-baked projects and deviously signed contracts with some parties within the Government of Southern Sudan. Although huge funds were poured in by the concerned parties, such moneys ended up in individuals' pockets, and the projects became mere 'White Elephants'. Do you believe that these costly projects were meant to make unity attractive? To me, they were just tablets of paracetamol administered by a wise physician to a hopeless dying patient.

Youths for separation: seeing that the NCP made unity ugly, patriotic youths in Southern Sudan, both in and outside Sudan, seized the opportunity, organised themselves and planned monthly meetings, campaigning for the secession of the Southern Sudan from the North. Their meetings were scheduled for every 9 of each month, leading to the day of the referendum, and their motto was to make separation attractive. They did a commendable job not only in achieving their goal but in uniting themselves as the youths of a new nation.

Southern political maturity: Southern Government under the leadership of Salva Kiir Mayardit have played some patient and mature political games since the death of Dr. John Garang de Mabior. There were times in which the NCP deliberately cornered and pushed the GOSS to the dark wall until the angered masses in the South lost their heads, blamed their government of maintaining unworthy contacts with the Khartoum Government instead of severing such relationships and declaring unilateral independence for South Sudan. Even the leadership of the GOSS became severally annoyed and severed contacts with the NCP Government when things became very dreadful.

But despite such frustrations, uncertainties and blackmailing of the Southerners by the Northerners, the GOSS, almost all the Southern political parties and the church manoeuvred the rough tide and calmly tried to take the loaded boat ashore. As they knew very well that the full implementation of the CPA was going to be in their favour, their unequivocal call to the NCP and international community was to stick to the spirit and the letter of the CPA, implementing it completely item by item.

Going back to war was not the best but the last option for the Southerners. Delay-ing the referendum due to the lack of the implementation of the South-North border demarcation and other protocols, which were supposed to come before 9 January 2011 was not considered a wise decision to spoil the only hope of the Southerners. These calm and analytical political approaches taken by the Southerners during the difficult implementation of the CPA is a sign of a little bit of political maturity in the south of the country.

The vigilance of the international community: the international participants to the CPA played some commendable roles in safeguarding the CPA by con-stantly admonishing and rendering some informed advice to both NCP and SPLM to strictly adhere to all vital terms of the CPA during its implementation. Although a few shortcomings occurred along the tiresome route of the highest peak of the CPA, things would have gone wrong totally were the international community not to keep its uncompromising watchfulness. This is an obvious indication that the current global nations are very much intertwined to the extent that when one suf-fers, all suffer and vice versa. We are what we are simply because of who you are.

Comments on the Referendum
and Post-Referendum Events

The Referendum Events

The historical journey between 9 January 2005 and 9 January 2011 was the lon-gest, longer even than the entire period of the two bloody civil wars in Sudan, for it was full of numerous uncertainties, socio-economic, political and psychological frustrations and unmerited bloodsheds. But as the Lord says all plans belong to us human beings but the end results lie with him, and also because all the bushes, marshes, battlefields and homesteads got sprinkled with the precious blood and lit-tered with the bones of martyrs and innocent people, the day for the referendum caught the NCP and other bad wishers off guard and the Southerners with deep joy and amusement.

My wife and I casted our votes in Nairobi Railways Club in Nairobi, Kenya on 9 January 2011. The whole exercise in and outside Sudan went on peacefully and smoothly. Both local and international observers commended the Referendum Com-mission for the excellent work done and called it one of the few peaceful and successful voting exercises ever held in the world. Southerners voted overwhelmingly for secession as reflected in the following stipulated results:

Region/Sate	Unity	Secession	Invalid	Black	Votes
Southern Sudan	16,129 (0.43%)	3,697,467 (99.57%)	3,791	6,807	3,724,194
Central Equatoria	4,985 (1.1%)	449,311 (98.9%)	1,523	1,620	457,439
Eastern Equatoria	246 (0.05%)	462,663 (99.95%)	70	727	463,706
Jonglei	111 (0.03%)	429,583 (99.97%)	124	238	430,056
Lakes	227 (0.08%)	298,214 (99.92%)	149	450	299,040
Northern Bahr el Ghazal	234 (0.06%)	381,141 (99.94%)	148	526	382,049
Unity	90 (0.02%)	497,477 (99.98%)	166	498	498,231
Warrap	167 (0.04%)	468,929 (99.96%)	120	432	469,648
Western Bahr el Ghazal	7,237 (4.49%)	153,839 (95.51%)	728	790	162,594
North Sudan & OCV	28,759 (23.23%)	95,051 (76.77%)	2,431	1,559	127,800
North	27,918 (42.35%)	38,003 (57.65%)	2,230	1,446	69,597
OCV	841 (1.45%)	57,048 (98.55%)	201	113	58,203

The outcomes of the referendum were respected and accepted by the whole world, including the Khartoum Government. People clearly spoke out their minds and hearts through their own secret ballots to the extent that there were no potential doubters and complainers of the results.

Why did Southerners overwhelmingly vote for secession? There are varied and numerous answers, but let me highlight some of them here.

Firstly, the long history of enslavement, exploitation, oppression, forced islamization and unmerited marginalization of the people of the South Sudan by the various merciless ruling cliques in Khartoum and their alliances forced the angered Southerners to vote for independence from North Sudan.

Secondly, Some Northerners under the leadership of the NCP Government and their alliances failed to make positive moves to redress some of the outstanding problems to make unity attractive during the CPA period.

Thirdly, the NCP Government and its alliances used the old socio-economic, religious and political styles of oppression and exploitation of the people in the south of the country during the period of CPA by continuing to recruit and arm some Southerners and turn them against their own innocent citizens in South Sudan as well as against the Juba Government. For example, unfair distribution of national resources, particularly oil money between North and South, deliberate delaying of North – South border demarcation, frequent military incursions from the North into Southern territories, especially Abyei rich areas, were some of the reasons that undoubtedly convinced people in the South that the Northerners were not interested in the unity of the nation but were greedy to cause some havoc in the South and take whatever they could lay their hands upon. So the road to secession was the best option left for the Southerners to follow.

The Post Referendum Events

The Declaration of South Sudan Independence, 9 July 2011: like any man created in the image and likeness of the universal Creator, the indigenous man of the land was the master of his own destiny. He enjoyed respect from others. He extended a hand of assistance to and received it from his neighbours. His dignity and prestige were intact. The indigenous man of the land was a man. He only paid his allegiance to his Creator.

1821–1885 marked the beginning of the darkest era of the indigenous African in the land of Sud. The foreign vampires invaded the indigenous home, overpowered the innocent man and pillaged his land. Failing to satisfy their unquenchable greed with immense natural wealth, they inhumanely turned the image and likeness of God into a mere article of trade to be sold and bought in shameful markets. So the oppressed cried to see the day of his emancipation but in vain.

1885–1898 ushered in another shameful era in the land of the Sud. The indigenous man came to bear unnecessary religious and racial brunt in the hands of his unkind half-brother. Again and again, the indigenous man became an article of trade in the hands of the itinerant trading immigrants. Despite his self-defence, the man of the land of the Sud hoped in vain to see the end of his dehumanization and humiliation.

1899–1956 marked the end of the use of the man of the land of the Sud as an article of trade in dehumanized markets, although the architects of the business shamelessly perpetuated it underground. The land of the Sud continued to suffer and suffer in the hands of the superiors. Unlike his half-brother, the indigenous man was not shown light at the end of tunnel of civilization by the invading foreigners. He continued to live in ignorance, shame and fear. So he longed and longed in vain for the day of his emancipation.

1956–1972 began the bitterest and bloody period in the history of the man of the Sud in the hands of his half-brother. The indigenous man fought and fought against his half-brother to regain his rightful place as man created in the image and the likeness of the Holy Creator but with less success. Although he obtained the smallest breathing space with exchange of his precious blood, his total emancipation was far beyond the horizon.

1972–1983 marked a tantalizing and illusory era in which the cunning half-brother administered some painkillers to the innocent indigenous man of the land of the Sud to soothe his heartache and mind-ache. Yet the man of the land of the Sud refused to be deceived and settled for nothing less than his complete independence enshrouded with his full human rights.

1983–2005 ushered in the worst period in the history of the man of the land of the Sud with the destruction and displacement of millions of human souls, beautiful and rare wildlife, remarkable vegetation, leaving thousands and thousands as disabled persons, widows and widowers, orphans, etc. The cunning and unkind half-brother shamelessly turned the indigenous man against himself, destroying a stone with a stone. This divisive policy of the half-brother left deep wounds within the innocent family of the man of the land of the Sud. Nevertheless, as a matter of life or death, and also as the last attempts for the indigenous man to attain his complete emancipation, the peace loving international arbitrators jumped in to address this chronic issue.

2005–2011 marked the last attempts by the half-brother to deceive once and for all the man of the land of the Sud. But as the wise says, "You can cheat some of the people some of the time but not all the people all the time", the indigenous man, with the help from some of his international peace-loving and just people, withstood such lies and deceit. Instead, with the help of the righteous Creator, the man of the land of the Sud turned the half-brother towards the path of justice. Sure, you can cheat people but not the omniscient Creator.

In Ecclesiastes 3:1-8), the Holy Bible declares:
There is a time for everything, and a season for every activity under heaven:
a time to be born and a time to die,
a time to plant and time to uproot,
a time to kill and time to heal,
a time to tear down and a time to build,
a time to weep and a time to laugh,
a time to mourn and a time to dance,
a time to scatter stones and a time to gather them,
a time to embrace and a time to refrain,
a time to search and a time to give up,
a time to keep and a time to throw away,
a time to tear and a time to mend,
a time to be silent and a time to speak,
a time to love and a time to hate,
a time for war and a time for peace.

On 9 July 2011, although the man of the land of the Sud had been giving birth and dying, planting and uprooting, killing and healing sometimes, tearing down and building often, weeping and laughing sometimes, morning and dancing often, scattering and gathering sometimes, embracing and refraining, searching and giving up, keeping and throwing away, tearing and mending sometimes, silencing and speaking, loving and hating and staging wars against his numerous enemies, his merciful Creator had a time for peace in store for him. Of course, his timing is not our timing.

July 9, 2011 will continue to be a significant memorial day in the hard-earned history of the Republic of South Sudan. It is a day in which the just Lord of the universe justly sealed the long awaited emancipation of the indigenous man of the land of the Sud. It was attended and witnessed by the national and political leaders of the left alone old Sudan, important international dignitaries and recognisable religious leaders. In the capital of the newly born nation, the occasion was presided over by the first President of the Republic of South Sudan, H.E. Gen. Salva Kiir Mayardit and his deputy, among others. The ten governors of the ten states of the Republic of South Sudan presided over their colourful celebrations of the long awaited and hard-earned independence.

I attended this noble Independence Celebration in my state capital of Bor. Bor is the historical and revolutionary site where the angered and humiliated Southerners under the heroic leadership of Major Kerubino Kwanyin Bol fired the first bullet on 16 May 1983 against the oppressive Khartoum Government, ushering in a bloody, protracted twenty-one year civil war. The occasion was led by our State Governor, H.E. Lt. Gen. Kuol Manyang Juuk. Kuol is a SPLA/M revolutionary veteran fighter. He has been an unswerving supporter of the SPLA/M since 1983.

What made our Independence Celebration very colourful and unique in comparison to similar events in different parts of the Republic of South Sudan was the presence of the numerous old loyal SPLA comrades, especially those who fired the first bullet on 16 May 1983 in the revolutionary town of Bor. They saw and heard the first bullet leaving the barrel of a gun at that historical moment, and God kept them safe, despite the deaths of their comrades in various battlefields, to witness and celebrate the birth of their dream. These jubilant comrades were dressed in their military uniforms. Some of them were now generals and brigadiers. All of them plus others, especially the Governor, sang revolutionary songs and danced like the energetic teenagers in their national theatre.

After singing the national anthem, the old flag of the old Sudan was slowly lowered while our new flag of the Republic of South Sudan was slowly raised at 12:30pm. Seeing the historical absence of the old flag of the old Sudan and looking at the colourful flag of the newly born Republic of South Sudan flying high in the peaceful atmosphere, made all the thousands and thousands of the jubilant participants go into the deepest commotion of joy and happiness such that I had never seen in my life. With no one guarding anyone, even the Governor, the whole congregation moved around thanking and greeting one another with tears of joy. As most of them were Christians, the celebrators praised their Creator for having seen them through their bloody history. They remembered their fallen heroes with love and thankfulness. This joyous commotion lasted for half an hour. Some participants were overwhelmed with happiness and fainted and were rushed to hospitals and their individual homes to calm down their nerves.

Why are People Happy?

Of course, you know why they are happy with their national independence. But let me just enumerate some of the causes of their happiness here:

First, witnessing the birth of any nation is not done by all its citizenry; it is a one-time occurrence; millions of Southerners, including our late hero Dr. John Garang, lived and died without seeing the national birth, although each and every generation had hoped to see the national independence in their own time. Hence, the celebrators were grateful to witness this vital day of the independence of the Republic of South Sudan.

Second, they are happy because the long bloody war between South and North Sudan was peacefully brought to an end.

Thirdly, God saw them through a series of bloody wars, and that made them happy.

Fourth, they are very grateful because their martyrs did not die in vain at last; they are happy because the widows, the orphans, the disabled, the lost natural wealth, etc. were paid for through the achievement of their national independence.

Fifth, they are happy because they regained their rightful place as human beings under the sun and no longer to be termed by any self-glorified superiors as second, third or so class citizens in their own land. Their national independence comes with their full human rights as enshrined in the UN and other internationally recognized documents.

Sixth, they are happy because their poor children and women are not going to be subjected to forced prostitution and slavery.

Seventh, they are happy because they are no longer going to give birth to children for any unnecessary racial and religious wars in Sudan, unless for the self-defence of their nation from some internal and external aggressions.

Eighth, they are happy to live in an independent nation so as to plan and manage their own livelihoods.

Ninth, they are grateful to see their independent nation have equal footings with other community of nations in and outside Africa.

Tenth, they are happy to have a free country where people are given freedom of worship, speech and congregation, irrespective of their religious beliefs and other affiliations.

CHAPTER THIRTEEN

꧁꧂

Further Wars to Fight

Is the national war really over? The answer or answers depend entirely on who people were fighting against and why they were fighting. For those who fought against their northern brothers and sisters merely to see the two parties part ranks and live as separate nations, the war is finished. But for those who fought against human beings who deliberately put them behind closed doors of socio-economic, political, religious oppression and other vices, the declaration of the independence of the Republic of South Sudan was not the end but a real onset of the protracted national wars. Without a vigorous and planned fight against such wars, ours will just remain an empty independence.

In order for the South Sudanese people to have a respectful, genuine and wholistic independence, the wars against the following national vices must continue unabated:

First, continuous war on disunity: there must be a prostrated war against disunity, tribalism, and any form of planned sectarianism. Unity in diversity must be one of the strongest tenets that cement national cohesion. "Behold, how good and how pleasant it is for brothers to dwell together in unity..." (Psalm 133:1-3). Unless our national spirit is above our tribal spirit, national unity will continue to stand on shaky ground. Unity is the strong national vanguard and the solid rock of national emancipation. No unity, no national prosperity. Together we succeed, for the Holy Scriptures further declare: "... a three-fold cord is not quickly broken..." (Ecclesiastes 4:9-12, NRSV). It is very incumbent on the entire government and other actors in the Republic of South Sudan to keenly plan for the cohesiveness of all the sons and daughters of the land and vigorously and continuously fight against any sort of divisive policies, words and actions.

Second, continuous war on corruption: there must be relentless war against all forms of corruption, for the worst poison of good governance is the embedded corruption. Corruption is totally immune to any kind of rhetoric war of words. Unless it is sternly punished by the law, it will remain as a national cancer of the bone, gnawing away the national resources for the benefit of the very few greedy individuals at the expense of the very poor majority. Let all the South Sudanese people, from the top to bottom of the national ladder, wear the gown of transparency and accountability and turn the brightest light of integrity to the shameless darkest corners of corruption. There is no healthy national sovereignty as well as national pride when it swims shamelessly in the vast ocean of widespread corruption. We and the Lord of the universe totally abhor and curse any nation of a few rich and poor majority. Either we cry together or rejoice together, for it completely makes no sense for you to be the only shining star in the midst of darkness.

Third, continuous war on hunger and poverty: there must be an on-going war against hunger and poverty. Did the South Sudanese get freedom from work or freedom to work? This pertinent war must begin at individual, family, village, boma, payam, county, state and national level. Why should the South Sudanese live in the bondage of hunger and poverty when their land is richly blessed with vast arable soils and all other natural resources? Why should they live in abject hunger and poverty when their total population is extremely minimal in comparison to their vast national territorial integrity? In fact, I have millions of other relevant, vital questions to ask in direct challenge to ourselves, but space can't allow me.

When you depend on others for your livelihoods, you lose your freedom and dignity. DEPENDENCY must be discouraged; SELF-RELIANCE must be encouraged. Apart from the weak members of the community, "...if a man will not work, he shall not eat'... (2 Thess.3:6-15). There is no perfect national independence when the public remains in the bondage of hunger and poverty.

Fourth, continuous war on illiteracy and ignorance: there must be a continuous war on illiteracy and ignorance. The prolonged and concerted oppression and marginalization of the Southerners by the successive Khartoum Governments has led to the high illiteracy rate among the sons and the daughters of the newly born Republic of South Sudan. Also this long period of oppression and marginalization kept most of the Southerners in the darkness of ignorance with no better exposure to the international civilization.

Unless the Republic of South Sudan and other actors come up with some well-planned educational programmes, declaring education for all with strict implementations as well as better and achievable strategies for long-term civic education, people will continue languishing in the pool of illiteracy and ignorance. Without raising higher the flag in this field, their national independence will not be complete. For instance, now the common man doesn't know his national and international rights as human being due to high level of illiteracy and ignorance.

Fifth, continuous war on injustice: if Southerners were staging protracted and bloody wars against the forces of INJUSTICE, will they perpetuate the same national and human wickedness among themselves in their newly born Republic of South Sudan? If so, what was their logical and genuine cause of such wars? As a newly born nation, the South Sudanese must first value and uphold human life and dignity. Let them see themselves not just as mere unworthy human beings or animals for that matter to be denied justice, oppressed, humiliated and even killed at will by the one who happened to have undeniable law in his ruthless hands or by some criminals who have no national law to tempt and control them. Instead, they must value and look at each other with love through the eyes of God as precious souls, be it young and old, rich and poor, weak and strong, etc. created in the image and likeness of God, the only Creator of the universe.

Let NO ONE be above the law; let all South Sudanese people have undeniable access to justice. Let people not take the law into their own unjust hands, but let them allow the law to take its own course for the goodness of all. Let all the South Sudanese have and enjoy equal and equitable share of the national cake. The law must be a just national umbrella, covering and protecting all its citizens, irrespective of their tribal, geographic, political, economic and religious affiliations.

In order for the people of the Republic of South Sudan to have a just and complete national freedom, they, especially the architects of law, must, "Let justice roll on like a river, righteousness like a never falling stream" (Amos 5:24). Without the diligent and honest administration of justice to all South Sudanese, the freedom is still lacking for all. Let people also defeat INJUSTICE and joyfully raise their national flag of JUSTICE FOR ALL.

Sixth, continuous war on disease: because of the long period of wars and neglect in the old Sudan, all types of known diseases have been claiming precious lives and disabling thousands and thousands of innocent people in the then south of the country. That is, death rates due to diseases and disease-related causes have been very high in the now Republic of South Sudan. Especially the mortality death rate among children and pregnant women remains to be very high in comparison to other third world countries. As we know, a healthy body is a fruitful life production, but an unhealthy body is an unhealthy ground for hunger and poverty to germinate and mushroom. When national citizens are poor in health, they become poor in mind and heart, thus, leading automatically to very poor family and national economy. For instance, millions and millions of hard-earned money in South Sudan have been pouring out and enriching the economy of other countries, with improved health situations, in desperate attempts to save the lives of sick South Sudanese. If the health condition in South Sudan is better, such huge funds can circulate within the national economy for the benefit of the whole nation. What do you think of the national masses whose very poor economic conditions can't permit them to seek external medical treatments?

Also when the citizens are unhealthy, it will definitely affect all various spectrums of the entire society, for there is no real family, community or nation without people – people are the family; people are the community, and people are the nation. Hence, unhealthy people lead to unhealthy family, unhealthy community, and unhealthy nation. National freedom without the deliberate conquest of the dreadful diseases is just an empty independence. This is a real people's worse enemy that needs a concerted fight at individual, family, boma, payam, county, state and national levels.

Seventh, continuous war on insecurity: the best and successful nation is the one that is keen on the security of each and every citizen of the nation as the first priority. A government cannot be "The government of the people, by the people, and for the people" if it fails to protect the innocent lives and possessions of its people. The single life of a national citizen is as precious as the proverbial one lost sheep of Jesus Christ, for without one, you can only have 99 but not 100. This is not the right time to lose a single South Sudanese in the merciless hands of insecurity. Let the poor person enjoy his independence of the Republic of South Sudan wherever God places him, whether in the jungle deep in the rural area or in the urban. In the realm of insecurity there is no stability, and in the absence of stability, there is continuous anarchy and underdevelopment.

How can innocent people till the arable land amidst insecurity? How can reliable investors carry on with and thrive in their businesses in the presence of insecurity? How can different ethnic communities freely socialize and learn from each other in the situation of insecurity? How can national and foreign tourists enjoy the beautiful scenery and natural life amidst the tense insecurity? How can humanitarian and community workers and other developmental agencies successfully execute their duties in the gloomy shadow of insecurity? How can even the political representatives freely move around, interact with their esteemed constituents and implement their national agendas for the common good of the people in the realm of insecurity? How can the elected government relax, think deeply and successfully pursue the collective national vision and mission for the benefit of the whole nation amidst insecurity? These are just few vital questions to paint the worst nature of insecurity anywhere in the world.

There can be no national stability and effective development without proper and inclusive national security. Security for each and every citizen, poor or rich, weak or strong, young or old, able or disabled, and his personal property is one of the strongest pillars of the national independence. We cannot be completely freed until we are collectively secured inside and along all the borders of the Republic of South Sudan.

Who South Sudanese are in God's Eyes

Jie is not just a Jie but a real brother and sister in the Lord.
Siri is not just a Siri but a real brother and sister in the Lord.
Bai is not just a Bai but a real brother and sister in the Lord.
Lou is not just a Lou but a real brother and sister in the Lord.
Pari is not just a Pari but a real brother and sister in the Lord.
Bari is not just a Bari but a real brother and sister in the Lord.
Hopi is not just a Hopi but a real brother and sister in the Lord.
Nuer is not just a Nuer but a real brother and sister in the Lord.
Ajaa is not just an Ajaa but a real brother and sister in the Lord.
Buya is not just a Buya but a real brother and sister in the Lord.
Lopit is not just a Lopit but a real brother and sister in the Lord.
Madi is not just a Madi but a real brother and sister in the Lord.
Baka is not just a Baka but a real brother and sister in the Lord.
Chod is not just a Chod but a real brother and sister in the Lord.
Gollo is not just a Gollo but a real brother and sister in the Lord.
Kuku is not just a Kuku but a real brother and sister in the Lord.
Kuma is not just a Kuma but a real brother and sister in the Lord.
Khara is not just a Khara but a real brother and sister in the Lord.
Murle is not just a Murle but a real brother and sister in the Lord.
Dinka is not just a Dinka but a real brother and sister in the Lord.
Guere is not just a Guere but a real brother and sister in the Lord.
Kresh is not just a Kresh but a real brother and sister in the Lord.
Lango is not just a Lango but a real brother and sister in the Lord.
Banda is not just a Banda but a real brother and sister in the Lord.

Endri is not just an Endri but a real brother and sister in the Lord.
Zande is not just a Zande but a real brother and sister in the Lord.
Pojulu is not just a Pojulu but a real brother and sister in the Lord.
Murus is not just a Murus but a real brother and sister in the Lord.
Benga is not just a Benga but a real brother and sister in the Lord.
Forugi is not just a Forugi but a real brother and sister in the Lord.
Bango is not just a Bango but a real brother and sister in the Lord.
Forgee is not just a Forgee but a real brother and sister in the Lord.
Kakwa is not just a Kakwa but a real brother and sister in the Lord.
Maban is not just a Maban but a real brother and sister in the Lord.
Olubo is not just an Olubo but a real brother and sister in the Lord.
Latuko is not just a Latuko but a real brother and sister in the Lord.
Otuho is not just an Otuho but a real brother and sister in the Lord.
Shilluk is not just a Shilluk but a real brother and sister in the Lord.
Toposa is not just a Toposa but a real brother and sister in the Lord.
Mundu is not just a Mundu but a real brother and sister in the Lord.
Acholi is not just an Acholi but a real brother and sister in the Lord.
Ndogo is not just an Ndogo but a real brother and sister in the Lord.
Lokoya is not just a Lokoya but a real brother and sister in the Lord.
Didinga is not just a Didinga but a real brother and sister in the Lord
Balanda is not just a Balanda but a real brother and sister in the Lord.
Anyuak is not just an Anyuak but a real brother and sister in the Lord.
Mundari is not just a Mundari but a real brother and sister in the Lord.
Kachiopo is not just a Kachiopo but a real brother and sister in the Lord.
Avukaya is not just an Avukaya but a real brother and sister in the Lord.
Makaraka is not just a Makaraka but a real brother and sister in the Lord.
Ngorgule is not just an Ngorgule but a real brother and sister in the Lord.
Nyangwara is not just a Nyangwara but a real brother and sister in the Lord.

Some Forecasts

North-South Border Disputes

As North Sudan has the inheriting tendency of robbing the South Sudan of any valuable thing, it will try by all means to accept nothing short of any unfair re-demarcation in its favour. This unfair demarcation of the borderlines may give some arable and richly blessed lands to the North Sudan. If justice is in the interest of both countries, I do not see any reason for the demarcation not to be speedily done. Abyei region will continue to be a bone of contention between the two nations, unless it is speedily and justly done.

As a new nation, the Republic of South Sudan will not be happy to see North Sudan continues to claim more territories from its territory. Without proper settlement of this vital issue, the two nations may slip into any unnecessary war like Ethiopia and Eretria. In order for the two nations to maintain a cordial neighbourhood and brotherly benefit from one another, they should try all their level best to permit justice takes its right course by accepting possible results of an independent arbitrator.

If national issues of the remaining marginalised areas, namely the Southern Blue Nile, Southern Kordofan and Southern Darfur are not quickly and justly done by the Khartoum Government, civil wars will continue in these areas between Khartoum Government and the angered people of such marginalised areas. Because of the proximity of these volatile territories with the Republic of South Sudan as well as their historical tie with the SPLA/M, such wars will fill over to the newly born nation, hence, resulting into possible war between the two nations. Therefore, it is imperative for the international community to continue putting healthy pressure on Khartoum, and it is also the national obligation of the Khartoum Government to find amicable solutions before Sudan further disintegrates into smaller autonomous nations. South Sudan, with its historical tie with Sudan, should also sincerely try to help Sudan find proper solutions to its present national problems.

Civil Wars

It is very unfortunate to mention here that the nation may experience at least one civil war as it grows and continues along the path of civilization and development. I am not a prophet of doom but a prophet of justifiable prediction. To justify this fateful forecast, I have the following primary reasons in favour of civil war(s) in the Republic of South Sudan:

First, addiction to war: because of the long period of the bloody wars between South and North Sudan, the people in South Sudan have become accustomed to the use of the gun more than the might of the tongue. So they tend to believe that personal and collective rights can only be obtained through the barrel of a gun. This reason is already quite obvious among Southerners because some people are now, at the time of my writing, waging some sort of civil wars against their own brothers and sisters. This notion will continue creating destruction in South Sudan until people come to their good senses and know that the power of speech is better than the power of a gun.

Second, tribalism: since South Sudan consists of bunches of tribes rather than a nation, any slightest mistake committed by a government system or individual is always seen from a tribal angle. At the time of the writing, the scale of tribalism predominately overweighs the scale of nationalism. For example, any person considers his own tribe as primary, while his nation takes the secondary position. Even government positions are mostly distributed on the basis of tribal and regional representation rather than on personal merits. There will come a time whereby South Sudan will evolve from the spirit of ethnicity to the spirit of nationalism. But before the young nation reaches the final destination of nationalism, the forces (especially the weak and tribal-minded elites and warlords) of tribalism will continue to allure the innocent, illiterate, poor citizens and tragically push the young nation of South Sudan into the dirty pool of civil war.

Third, political parties: as I write this last portion of the memoirs, there are already more than 20 political parties in South Sudan which acted as midwives during the birth of the Republic of South Sudan. This means that more parties were already formed before the declaration of national independence. In fact, some people in South Sudan seem to be in a kind of political hurry. Of course, this unorganized political system is one of the bad legacies of the old Sudan, which South Sudan should be prepared to address and lived with.

Now people wonder whether it is good democracy to have many political parties before a nation is born. Or alternatively it is the developing nation that gives birth to its own political parties as it moves along the path of national development? Also people wonder whether these numerous political babysitters will take good care of the newly born nation without pushing it into the deepest pool of the civil war. In other words, unless proper care is taken, this unhealthy democracy will plunge the newly born nation into unnecessary civil wars. It is quite unfortunate if some of such parties are none other than mere business companies in political uniform.

Fourth, corruption: I believe corruption means dishonesty to oneself, to God and to others in words, actions and thoughts. It is the action of doing whatever one conventionally knows to be wrong in order to meet his personal or collective desires at the expense of others. For example, all types of nepotism, bribery, lie, fraud, dishonesty, ill thoughts, giving to or demanding illicit favours from others, and all other known vices are the obvious ingredients of corruption.

At the time of my writing, there seems to be a culture of employment of government personnel in accordance to tribal lines. Government organs are mostly staffed along the line of ethnicity, depending on who have the power of recruitments in such bodies. There is also some sort of interdepartmental employment policy whereby heads of different ministries or departments lobby among themselves on behalf of their unemployed relatives to find illicit jobs for them. In order to condone their corrupt practises, jobs are mostly advertised to blindfold the public, while underground recruitments have already been done. Those who have no such leadership and family ties suffer in the process, irrespective of their high level of qualifications and expertise. As a result, it is common to find wrong people in the right places and vice versa. This un-procedural employment of civil servants is an aspect of the real corruption that is called nepotism.

Although the infant government of South Sudan has some clear policies in regard to the management of government funds, the general public still talks of some government employees who are after some unlawful gains at the expense of the poor masses. Those who are alleged to have embezzled huge amounts of government money have not yet been formally brought to book. So this raises a direct question on the strictness of the government rules and enforcements concerning the principle of transparency and accountability.

These unmerited fruits of corruption will drag the young nation into the deepest pit of civil wars. For some side-lined and unhappy citizens may regrettably opt to take the path of war, although they may have their own ulterior motives. In order to avoid this unnecessary consequence, the government must not only come up with laws and policies to fight against corruption but also see how to practically implement them, knowing that action speaks louder than words. It should catch the small fish before they become too big to catch and manage.

Fifth, illiteracy and ignorance: at the time of my writing, some educational sources alleged that the rate of illiteracy in South Sudan is seventy-six per cent (76%). This high level of illiteracy comes with a high level of ignorance too as an uneducated person does not always easily understand, analyse and interpret his internal and external environments. He mostly believes in and relies on the learned one, especially a relative, friend or closer associate. He does not know his rights and is easy to cheat, mislead and sway around by cunning, dishonest and inhumane educated guys. If he is misled, the ignorant can simply torch his own house with everything inside and terribly regret it later, blaming his own illiteracy and others.

On the other hand, an educated person among illiterate people can be their blessing or curse. For instance, a well-educated, godly person acts as the eye, ear and voice of his people. He protects and assists them to meet their aspirations. He does not mislead them to do anything against their will to achieve his own selfish gains. He cries and laughs with them and always seeks ways and means to help them get good education. This kind of learned person is a real blessing to his people.

But viewing it from a different perspective, if such an educated person is selfish, greedy, ungodly and inhumane, he will become an actual curse upon his illiterate people. That is, taking unfair advantage of the illiteracy and ignorance of his people, he will use them in any way possible, including dragging them into needless internal and external fight(s), to obtain his narrow gains at their expense. He loves to see them remain languishing in a perpetual loop of illiteracy and ignorance.

Having painted and depicted this graphic picture of the national poor education, it is very likely that some dissatisfied, uncaring, selfish and inhumane elite of literate people in South Sudan may from time to time tragically mobilize and use some of the vast illiterate, ignorant citizens against their will to achieve their own ill-benefits. Of course, others will oppose them in any way possible, and in the process of this they may unfortunately plunge their young nation into an unnecessary pool of bloodshed.

In most cases, uneducated folks behave like dry grass that easily catches fire and puts the whole forest ablaze. Hence, in order to avoid this unhealthy scenario, it is good to turn them into greener grass through proper, intentional, national, wholistic educational systems.

Foreign Influence

The last child often suffers mistreatment by its own siblings. Unless they have sound moral behaviours, its siblings can bully and take unfair advantage of its infancy by taking its belongings and beating it in the absence of its parents and other elders. For it to grow up well physically and morally, such a child always needs the constant help of kind elders, especially the parents.

Some of its sibling nations, a total of 192 in and outside Africa, act like bullying kids. These predatory nations, including North Sudan, of course, look at this newly born nation in terms of what they can simply get out of it. Even during the six-year CPA period, those who benefited a lot economically from both social services and other resources in South Sudan were from foreign nations. If proper care is not taken by the South Sudan National Government and its citizens, such greedy, unfriendly foreign nations, individuals and agencies may side and influence some weak, selfish and myopic nationals and turn them against their own nation, not for their own benefit, but for the sole gain of such external forces. Our present world is unfortunately full of inhumane, unkind, greedy vampires who can't benefit and live unless they cause disturbance worldwide.

Some unfriendly neighbouring states may even be tempted to redraw their geographic boundaries to take away pieces of land from the young nation. This is clearly evidenced by the way in which the North Sudan clings doggedly to the historically Ngok's rich land of Abyei. Even the name 'Abyei' is a Jeng name for an 'olive tree'.

I learnt of a wise girl who blatantly told her dishonest boyfriend: "You don't love me, but you love my money." Given the current level of global moral decay, I strongly believe such dishonest boyfriends are everywhere globally. So the wise girls, although they may not use the same blatant language, are to be on regular look out to safeguard their precious money.

As a last and young child in the global community of nations, which nations of the world will act as its loving parents to keenly protect and nurture it as it passes through various stages of national development? It would also be good for the Republic of South Sudan to correctly understand and know its predatory nations so as to see how to safeguard itself from them. It should have some proper and standardized criteria to honestly screen both its sincere mentoring nations as well as its covetous and selfish countries, individuals and agencies in terms of socio-economic, political, military and religious grounds. Like an innocent child, the Republic of South Sudan should not blindly embrace both its foes and friends and regret it in the end.

CHAPTER FOURTEEN

Conclusion

The Next Journey of Life

Looking behind at my life-story and seeing what the Almighty is still unfolding before me, I am convinced beyond any slightest doubt that I have a series of huge mountains to climb on and conquer for the general welfare of mankind as well as for God's own glory. I am happy that my talents, gifts, skills, knowledge and wisdom and all what I am are not rusting away but being put into meaningful utilization in line with the purpose for which I was created and born.

I am happy too for others and myself to realise that I am not a part of the global problems but rather a part of viable solutions to its serious problems. As man is born and lives once on this harsh planet, not having a second chance to undo the mistakes of his life-story, I beseech the Holy God to help me leave healthy footmarks on the globe for the next generations to hate and shun or cherish and follow.

The Names of the Months in Jeng Bor Language

For the sake of those who want to keep abreast of their Jeng cultural uniqueness, below are the names of the months in Jeng Bor language. Number 1 stands for January; number 12 represents December respectively.

1. Kol
2. Akonydit
3. Akonythiei
4. Aduong
5. Akoldit
6. Akolthiei

7. Lacwong ke nin
8. Kulthuom
9. Hor
10. Lal de diet
11. Anyiec ngol cok
12. Kon ageny

ABBREVIATIONS

ACROSS	Association of Church Resources of South Sudan
AU	African Union
BBC	British Broadcasting Corporation
CEAS	Church Ecumenical Action in Sudan
CPA	Comprehensive Peace Agreement
ECS	Episcopal Church of Sudan
EPRDF/TPLF	Ethiopian People's Revolutionary Democratic Front and Tigrayan People's Liberation Front
FEBA	Far East Broadcasting Association
GOSS	Government of South Sudan
NCP	National Congress Party
NGOs	Non-Governmental Organizations
NSCC	New Sudan Council of Churches
SPLA/M	Sudan People's Liberation Army and Sudan People's Liberation Movement
UN	United Nations
UNHCR	United Nations High Commission for Refugees
USA	United States of America

DEFINITION OF TERMS

Jeng (Dinka): A large ethnic community in South Sudan. It is a part of the Nilotic groups. Although others call them 'Dinka' they comfortably refer to themselves as 'Jeng'.

Monyjang: Moc (moch) in Jeng refers to a man; hence, 'Monyjang' means a man of Jeng. Locally, monyjang may also refer to Jeng.

Toch: A marshland which has sufficient water and grass for cattle and other animals during dry seasons. For instance, the Nile and the areas are *toch* in Jeng.

Payam: An administrative district in the Republic of South Sudan. It is right below the level of a county, and it is managed by a civil administrator.

Boma: In the Republic of South Sudan, Boma refers to a sub-district administrative locality, which is below a Payam.

Luak: It means cowshed, a shelter used for domestic animals. Men also use it to stay closer to and safeguard the animals. Luak is commonly used by Jeng and Nuer communities.

Nhialic: This is a Jeng word for God, the Creator of the entire universe and all things therein.

Tong (Tɔŋ): In Jeng language, it refers to a spear; it also refers to war or any type of conflict.

Bith: In Jeng language, it means fishing spear, a sharp iron rod for fishing.

Hot (hɣt): This is the word used by the locals for "hut" or "house" in Jeng language.